*For Cynthia, again, and the brilliant, fulfilling,
and productive life she has ahead of her.*

"*It's Not You, It's the Workplace* is full of profound insights into the reasons women around the world so often have difficulties working with other women. As a Chinese woman, Andie and Al's discussion of Asian women being stereotyped as the 'model minority' was powerful. As a woman who spends half of her time out of the United States, I believe this book will be of great value to working women everywhere."

—Yang Yang, Associate Professor, China University of Political Science and Law

"This very thought-provoking and well-researched book is a must-read for any executive who truly strives to create a culture of meritocracy."

—Stephen P. Hills, Former President, *The Washington Post*

"As one of the few female drivers racing in NASCAR, I believe it is important for women to support one another. Kramer and Harris persuasively demonstrate how women, and groups at large, can be even more effective when women work together to combat negative stereotypes and assumptions about women. This is an important book for everyone who wants to see equal representation of men and women in any field."

—Julia Landauer, NASCAR Racer, Entrepreneur, Speaker

"Andie and Al's insistence on the value of women's mutual support, advocacy, and sisterhood rang true to me. Too often we are told that women are naturally antagonistic to other women. Nonsense. This book is filled with great insights and practical tips for assuring women's workplace relationships with other women are positive and satisfying. This is a terrific book!" **—Congresswoman Jan Schakowsky**

"The belief that women inherently do not work well together is one of our most unhelpful workplace narratives. Andie and Al tackle it head-on and set the record straight with pragmatism and optimism. This book is perfect not only for women looking to achieve successful and fulfilling careers, but also for the men and organizations that benefit equally when the most talented leaders rise to the top."

—Heather Cabot, Co-Author, *Geek Girl Rising: Inside the Sisterhood Shaking Up Tech*

"As CEO of a business run almost entirely by women, creating products for women, this book provides a fascinating insight into the systemic challenges we face as a result of decades of 'gendered workplaces'. Andie and Al go beyond explaining how this impacts women's relationships with each other and offers hugely valuable advice for women looking to smash stereotypes and change the way the world works."

—**Maria Molland, CEO Thinx**

"Kudos to Kramer and Harris for debunking the long-held myth that women intentionally thwart the success of other women. With the increasing complexity of two other big jobs—caregiving for children and aging parents—there has never been a more critical time for professional women to bond together and find ways to blend work and life for personal fulfillment, career advancement and long-term financial security. This book gets rid of any perceived or real obstacles to smart women helping other smart women develop their own brands of ambition and success."

—**Kathryn Sollmann, Author,** *Ambition Redefined:*
Why the Corner Office Doesn't Work for
Every Woman & What to Do Instead

It's Not You, It's the Workplace

Women's Conflict at Work and the Bias that Built It

ANDREA S. KRAMER
ALTON B. HARRIS

NICHOLAS BREALEY
PUBLISHING

BOSTON • LONDON

First published in 2019 by Nicholas Brealey Publishing
This paperback edition published in 2021
An imprint of John Murray Press

A Hachette company

26 25 24 23 22 21   1 2 3 4 5 6 7 8 9 10

A CIP catalogue record for this title is available from the British Library

Library of Congress Control Number: 2019932111

ISBN 978-1-4736-9727-0
US eBook ISBN 978-1-4736-9729-4
UK eBook ISBN 978-1-4736-9728-7

Printed and bound in the United States of America

John Murray Press policy is to use papers that are natural, renewable, and
recyclable products and made from wood grown in sustainable forests.
The logging and manufacturing processes are expected to conform to the
environmental regulations of the country of origin.

John Murray Press Ltd   Nicholas Brealey Publishing
Carmelite House   Hachette Book Group
50 Victoria Embankment   53 State Street
London EC4Y 0DZ   Boston, MA 02109, USA
Tel: 020 3122 6000   Tel: (617) 523 3801

www.nbuspublishing.com

CONTENTS

INTRODUCTION

We write, speak, and conduct workshops across the country about the adverse effects that implicit gender bias has on women's career advancement and satisfaction. Increasingly, over the past several years as we have been talking about these issues, women have come up to us and said things like, "You're absolutely right that gender stereotypes and biases are major obstacles to women's career advancement, but you don't mention an equally serious problem for women's career success—other women. You need to talk about why women are so mean to—'hard on,' 'bitchy to,' 'hostile toward,' or 'unsupportive of'—the women they work with and what can be done about it." Anne, a middle-aged bank executive whom we coach, made a typical comment recently: "I am sick and tired of women backstabbing and spreading hurtful rumors. My male managers have all been great. But most of the women I've worked for have been selfish bitches, interested only in themselves. They did nothing to help me, and some even tried to hold me back. I never trusted any of them. The women I work with now only care about getting ahead. They have no interest in supporting me or any other woman. I'd rather work for a man than a woman any day."

We have long been aware of the extensive literature about "mean girls," "queen bees," and women's competitiveness with other women (see chapter 1), but we had always assumed that these characterizations were gross exaggerations based on little more than ad hoc anecdotes. With so many women now telling us about their personal difficulties in working with other women, we decided we needed to look more closely at their experiences and understand why they were not working harmoniously with other women. So we conducted multiple surveys, undertook extensive social science research, and interviewed hundreds of women in a variety of industries and professions across the United States. The result of our investigation is this book.

What we found confirmed our initial suspicions. First, there is no empirical evidence—none, nada, nil, zero, zilch—that women have more frequent conflicts in working with other women than men have in working with other men or than women and men have in working together. Second, there is also no empirical evidence that women are more mean-spirited, antagonistic, or untrustworthy in their dealings with other women than men are in their dealings with other men. Third, there is considerable, reliable empirical evidence that women actually spend more time supporting, counseling, and advocating for women than men do. In other words, more women than men are paying it forward to ensure the future advancement of the women (and men) who work for them (see chapter 2).

If these findings are correct—and we are confident they are—there is a major disconnect between the ways women often perceive their working relationships with other women and the reality of women's efforts to help and advocate for other women. This book is our attempt to explain the reasons for this disconnect; why, despite the clear evidence that women do support other women, so many women prefer to work for men than women; think that the women they work for are selfish, hostile, and unsupportive; and why so many women are dissatisfied with or unhappy about their workplace relationships with other women.

Women's Same-Gender Relationships

Women, far more than men, care about, value, and are affected by their same-gender workplace relationships. Women generally expect these relationships to be close, harmonious, and mutually supportive. Thus, women expect their work relationships with other women to be different from their relationships with the men with whom they work. What this often means is that when women behave toward other women in precisely the same manner as many men do—in a formal, "all business" way without any apparent concern for the other women's feelings or work/life conflicts—such women are often seen as cold, selfish, and unpleasant.

There is a fundamental asymmetry in women's views of the appropriate nature of their workplace relations with women and of those with men. Women typically think their workplace relations with other women should be supportive, marked by understanding, and involve a degree of personal engagement. This means that women who do not relate to other women in an empathic way can be seen as having serious character defects that make them disagreeable and unlikable. Women do not, however, have the same expectations of the relationships with the men with whom they work (see chapter 5).

There is a second asymmetry between the ways in which women's same-gender workplace conflicts are evaluated and how their conflicts with men and men's conflicts with other men are evaluated. When women's same-gender workplace relationships are marked by tension or conflict, other people are likely to view their difficulties as far more serious and disruptive than are men's same-gender conflicts or women's conflicts with men.[1] Men's same-gender conflicts are generally seen as part of the normal rough and tumble of high-intensity workplaces, simple disagreements about how to accomplish a job, achieve an objective, or resolve an operational impasse. By contrast, women's same-gender conflicts are often seen as personality clashes motivated by personal antagonism or petty jealousy. As a result, women's conflicts with other women are frequently viewed as catfights, with negative consequences for organizational productivity and meriting serious concern by coworkers and managers.

A third asymmetry between women's and men's same-gender workplace conflicts is that these conflicts can have far more negative consequences for the women involved than for men. Because women's same-gender workplace conflicts receive so much more attention than do men's, women are far more likely to view their conflicts as more serious than they might otherwise.[2] In addition, because women's same-gender conflicts are likely to be seen as violating prescribed gender behavioral norms—women should care about, support, and be nice to other people—women can be penalized with poor evaluations, social exclusion, and coworker animosity in ways that men never experience.[3]

It's the Workplaces, Not the Women

Women have workplace conflicts—tensions, difficulties, and hostilities—with other women for all of the same reasons men have conflicts with other men: disagreements about how best to perform specific tasks, set strategic objectives, or handle personnel problems. But women also have conflicts with other women that are quite unlike men's same-gender conflicts. These distinctive conflicts are not due to women's inherent meanness, but to interpersonal dynamics created by gendered workplaces. In workplaces led and controlled by men with strong masculine norms, values, and expectations, women and men are not dealt with, evaluated, compensated, or promoted in the same ways. Women and men may have similar educational backgrounds and may start their careers with similar ambitions, abilities, and expectations. But because women are a distinct outgroup in gendered workplaces, they experience more formidable career advancement obstacles than do men. Their opportunities for career-enhancing assignments, projects, and responsibilities are far more limited than men's, and their ability to achieve a satisfactory balance between their careers and their personal lives is far more difficult than it is for men. These obstacles intensify for women with distinctive social identities that intersect with their gender, such as race, ethnicity, age, identification as LBTQ, or parenting young children (see chapters 5 through 9).

The obstacles that make career advancement in gendered workplaces so much more difficult for women than men also make it much more difficult for women to achieve positive, supportive, conflict-free same-gender workplace relationships. In gendered workplaces, career advancement often depends on identification with the ingroup, which means that women's success can depend on distancing themselves from other women so they can be seen as different. Moreover, women often internalize the biases in their gendered workplaces, behaving toward the women with whom they work in ways that strengthen their own identification with the ingroup. In the presence of racial or ethnic bias, white women often identify with their white male coworkers, not with diverse same-gender coworkers. When mothers are criticized for not being sufficiently devoted to their careers, women without young children often join in the criticism to show that they are committed to *their* careers. Straight and LBTQ women can clash because of the different ways they perceive appropriate gender behavioral norms. And black, Asian, and Hispanic women can clash with white women and each other in their efforts to disprove the stereotypical characteristics ascribed to them.

Women's distinctive difficulties in dealing with other women, just like their difficulties in advancing in gendered workplaces, are driven by stereotypes and the biases those stereotypes foster. These difficulties are not because of women's fundamental nature, not because of the unique way they are socialized, nor because they are inherently jealous or envious of other women. Women's distinctive conflicts are about their workplaces, not their natures.

The Other Side of the Coin

It is important to keep in mind that women often have terrific working relationships with other women. These relationships might not constitute intimate friendships, but they are pleasant, supportive, and cooperative. When women have positive same-gender relationships, they are more efficient, productive, and satisfied with their careers.[4] While we have seen numerous references to a purported 2011 American Management Association survey reporting that 95 percent of working women believe they have been undermined by another woman at some point in their career, we highly doubt the validity of this statistic. Moreover, neither CBS News[5] nor we could confirm that such a survey actually exists.

Of course, some women are unpleasant and unsympathetic, while others are empathetic and inspiring; some are terrific managers, while others are ineffective; some are nasty, selfish backstabbers, while others are pleasant and supportive. Our guess—because there is no empirical evidence available—is that women fall into these categories in about the same proportions as do men.

What we do know, however, is that women worry much more about their workplace relationships with other women than men worry about their workplace relationships with other men. Indeed, most women have a profound desire to have positive workplace relationships with other women, and when those relationships are marked by tension and unpleasantness they are deeply troubled. We hope that after reading this book women will stop blaming themselves and their women colleagues when their relationships go awry and start focusing on the structural features of their workplaces that make sisterhood so difficult.

Our Audience

Most often in this book, we address our comments and advice directly to women. This makes perfect sense, for our goal is to ensure that talented, ambitious women advance as far and as fast in their careers as their ability and hard work can take them without being sidetracked, held back, or disheartened by conflicts with other women. This book, however, is also addressed to men and the organizations they tend to run. We believe men—particularly senior men with leadership roles in business, the professions, academia, and government—need to be acutely aware of the underlying situational causes of women's difficulties in maintaining harmonious same-gender workplace relationships. As we have said, the fundamental driver of women's distinctive same-gender conflicts is the gendered nature of our workplaces. The ultimate solution to conflict, therefore, is primarily in the hands of those who lead, control, and model appropriate workplace behaviors. Women can do much to avoid or overcome the conflict-inducing forces inherent in their gendered workplaces. But, if the masculine norms, values, and expectations underlying these forces are to be eliminated, it will require the active participation of everyone involved.

What Follows

Women's workplace relationships with other women can and should be positive. That does not mean that they will always be conflict-free. But it does mean that when conflicts arise, they can be resolved productively and efficiently. To that end, most of the following chapters include a section we've called "Making Things Better," which provides ideas, takeaways, tips, suggestions, and techniques that women can use to avoid, work through, and resolve same-gender conflicts. Along the way and particularly in chapter 10, we offer suggestions as to how organizations, the men who so often run them, and women can eliminate the biases that foster women's same-gender conflicts.

Throughout the book, we have included anecdotes and personal stories taken from our own experiences, the comments of the hundreds of women we've coached and interviewed, and statements made to us in the course of our research. We promised all of these women that we would keep their identities confidential, so we have changed their names and identifying characteristics.

This book is divided into four parts. Part I, "Women's Workplace Relationships with Other Women," examines the myths, stereotypes, and misconceptions about the causes of women's workplace conflicts. This is where we present the various claims that women—whether because of nature or nurture—are intrinsically mean to, competitive with, and resentful of other women. We next explain why women seek other women's support, cooperation, and advocacy—sisterhood—and why sisterhood is important for women's career advancement. We then discuss why sisterhood is so often difficult to achieve in gendered workplaces, and why same-gender conflicts often seem inevitable in such workplaces. Because women have different social identities, values, and behaviors, we also look at how these differences can interfere with the achievement of sisterhood.

In Part II, "Gender in the Workplace," we discuss the realities of gendered workplaces for ambitious women and the difficult choices such workplaces present to them. We also discuss the behavioral straitjackets into which stereotypes about gender and sexuality put women.

Part III, "Social Identity in the Workplace," examines how gendered workplaces and the stereotypes that prevail in them affect women's same-gender relationships with women who have social identities different from their own. We examine why gender isn't the whole story by looking at the stereotypes and biases that result in unique workplace experiences for Asian, Hispanic, and black women. We then discuss the stereotype-driven conflicts between women of different ages and the peculiar workplace dynamics created when women have small children. Our discussion of these issues is informed by our own surveys and interviews, as well as current peer-reviewed social science research.

Part IV, "Going Forward," presents a comprehensive perspective on how women's distinctive difficulties with other women can and should be addressed. While we've offered many suggestions in the "Making Things Better" sections of individual chapters, Part IV provides a framework for how these specific suggestions can be comprehensively implemented. We provide steps and advice as to how women can overcome their identity conflicts with other women as well as how organizations can attack workplace bias.

Part IV is followed by a glossary, in which we provide definitions of key terms and phrases we use throughout the book. The glossary is for your convenience.

About Us

A brief comment is in order about our decision to write about the career perspectives and experiences of women whose social identities are fundamentally different from our own. As two straight, white, cisgendered people, we know our writing about the feelings and workplace experiences of women with races, ethnicities, sexual orientations, and gender identities we do not share may be viewed as insensitive at best and presumptuous at worst. Indeed, we freely acknowledge that our personal experiences, privileges, status, and power are likely to be very different from many of the women we write about. Nevertheless, we are convinced that unless all of us reach out beyond our unique social identities in an attempt to understand, relate to, and expose ourselves to the scrutiny of people who are not like us, little progress will be made in improving relations between and among the great diversity of people in our gendered workplaces and in society generally.

To ensure that we approached this crucial subject with the care and insight called for, we immersed ourselves in current social science research; we extensively read the available literature on racism, ethnicity, sexual orientation, and gender identity; we conducted many in-depth interviews; and—most importantly—we obtained comments on and reactions to various drafts of this book from several dozen women of color, women who identify as LBTQ, and women with social identities different from our own. These women represent a wide range of backgrounds, professions, geographic locations, socioeconomic groups, and professional achievements. Not a single person told us that we had no business tackling these topics, all encouraged us to publish our research, and many commented that what we had written precisely captured their personal experiences. While the sole responsibility for everything in this book is ours, we have attempted to incorporate their comments, reflect their perspectives, and give voice to their concerns. The support and encouragement of so many women with social identities different from our own has led us to believe that our discussion will provide a valuable contribution to the understanding of the workplace relationships of women with women who are different from them. We certainly hope so.

PART I

Women's Workplace Relationships with Other Women

Chapter 1

Women Are Mean to Each Other—Or So We're Told

THERE IS AN ACTIVE COTTAGE industry devoted to characterizing women's workplace relationships with other women as fundamentally antagonistic. Women are said to bully other women, spread malicious rumors about them, behave in two-faced ways toward them, seek to undermine their self-confidence, and secretly plot to destroy their professional standing. Typical of such characterizations (almost always made without comprehensive empirical evidence) are the following:

- "Women are the focus of gossip and suffer humiliation, betrayal, or social exclusion at the hands of other women with surprising frequency."[1]
- "Female aggression tends to be mental and emotional like gossip and backstabbing [that is] designed to create shame, cause emotional distress and wreak havoc in a rival's life."[2]
- "Conflict among women in the workplace is out of control and has become an area of intensified research and concern."[3]

The authors of the works from which these statements are drawn all view women's same-gender workplace relationships as plagued by jealousy, envy, and competition. They think that because of evolution, socialization, or misogyny, women see other women as rivals, competitors, and

3

enemies. Behaviors such as manipulation, undermining, betrayal, back-stabbing, trash talking, and one-upsmanship are said to be the modus operandi. These authors assert that these conflicts are intensely personal and specifically intended to hurt other women's positions, reputations, and status. Because they see these conflicts as driven by internally gener-ated motivations, women are assumed to be in control of their conflicts and should be able to end them by simply understanding and ending their hurtful behaviors.

We have serious doubts that women's same-gender conflicts are the result of internally motivated envy, jealousy, or competitiveness. We also seriously doubt that these characteristics are part of women's nature. In fact, we believe this entire approach to women's relationships with other women is profoundly misguided. By assuming that there are unique, identifiable psychological differences between the sexes, these authors deflect attention from the substantial evidence that women and men are more alike than they are different. While there are differences in abilities and brain functions, the differences are very small—usually of the mag-nitude of a few percentage points across the entire population.[4]

Women and men do not have fixed feminine or masculine traits. Moreover, the workplace situations in which women and men find them-selves are far more determinative of their behavior than inherent quali-ties or characteristics. When we view women and men as having unique, distinctive, and permanent psychological predispositions, personality traits, and task aptitudes, we ignore the importance of context. Context is not just people's immediate situations, but also the totality of their lives, including the environments within which they work, love, play, and struggle. If we are ever to get to the root of women's same-gender work-place conflicts, we need to focus on the situations in which these conflicts are created, not on women's internal characteristics.

There are most certainly differences in women's and men's predis-positions, attitudes, bearings, communication techniques, language pat-terns, and so on. But we do not believe these are permanent, immutable differences. These differences are largely due to imbalances in the per-ceived power, status, and value that women and men grow up with. It is external context, not internal characteristics, that reveals the causes of women's same-gender workplace conflicts.

As we argue in the next chapter and throughout the remainder of this book, women often experience unique difficulties working positively with other women, not because of the way women are but because of the biased workplace situations women encounter. To paraphrase the title of this book, women's conflicts with other women arise not because of their personal characteristics but because of the characteristics of their workplaces.

Representative Books

The titles of some of the books published over the past decade in the "women are antagonistic to other women" genre paint a very ugly picture of women's same-gender relationships: *Tripping the Prom Queen;*[5] *Mean Girls Grown Up;*[6] *Mean Girls, Meaner Women;*[7] *Catfight;*[8] *Mean Girls at Work;*[9] *Working with Bitches;*[10] *Woman's Inhumanity to Woman;*[11] *The Bitch in the House;*[12] and *The Stiletto in Your Back.*[13] Let's take a brief look at common claims made by books in this genre before we provide our critique as to why we disagree with the fundamental claims made by these books.

Common Claims

Virtually all of these books make two common claims. First, they claim that while most women are fully aware of women's purported mutual antagonism, they are reluctant to acknowledge or discuss it. For example, in *Woman's Inhumanity to Woman*, Phyllis Chesler writes,

> When I began this work, most people, including feminist academics, were not talking about the ways in which women, like men, internalize sexist values or about the human female propensity to evil.... [As one woman said to me,] "I think you

should be writing about how men oppress women not about what oppressed people do in order to survive."[14]

In *Tripping the Prom Queen*, Susan Shapiro Barash echoes Chesler's experience:

> No matter what other topics I was asking about, I found hints of a dark secret, a problem that everyone seemed to sense but no one was willing to talk about: women's rivalry.... I emerged from my research feeling as though [female rivalry] must be a theme in *every* woman's life. *We're just not allowed to talk about it.* We'll do anything rather than face up to female envy and jealousy.... [W]e sweep all evidence of a bleak picture [of women's relationships with other women] under the rug.[15]

In the introduction to *The Twisted Sisterhood*, Kelly Valen tells us,

> It seems we've conditioned ourselves to deny, discount, and just plain swallow our intra-female hurts as something we shouldn't indulge or whine about.... Few of us are eager to acknowledge we've been burned by our "sisters." Fewer yet wish to admit that they feel unsafe with certain women or that the primary threat to their emotional security radiates not from the usual suspects like men, but from fellow females.[16]

And Michelle Villalobos confidently states in *The Stiletto in Your Back*,

> Female rivalry is something people generally avoid discussing. Personally, I dislike the notion that I am competitive with other women, and I'd be willing to bet that most of us avoid admitting—even to ourselves—when we feel insecure or when we compare ourselves to our girlfriends, colleagues or sisters and find ourselves lacking. Not to mention, perhaps we feel like

we are betraying our sex by highlighting or acknowledging that sometimes *women play dirty*.[17]

The claim that women are reluctant to talk about same-gender rivalry, competitiveness, and antagonism is puzzling. If there really is such a reluctance, why are there so many books on the topic? Why does the popular press so regularly write about women's difficulties in working with other women?[18] And why are there so many websites and blogs devoted to the subject?[19] Beyond the disconnect between the claim that women are reluctant to talk about women's rivalry and the great flood of such talk, concern about the hurtful nature of women's same-gender competitiveness has been a central theme of the modern women's movement since its very beginning. For example, the first issue of *Ms.* magazine in 1972 carried an article by Letty Cottin Pogrebin entitled "Competing with Women." In the article, Pogrebin urged women to stop seeking to raise themselves up "by standing on the crushed remains of [their] sisters."[20]

The second common claim these books make is that women's same-gender antagonism is caused by some aspect of women's own internal makeup—some fundamental characteristic of their nature, or some basic female need, desire, or deficiency. As a consequence, the authors each conclude that all it will take to improve women's relationships with other women is for women to look inside themselves, recognize why they are antagonistic to other women, and just stop being that way. For example, in *Mean Girls Grown Up*, Cheryl Dellasega writes,

It is clear that RA [relational aggression] is internally motivated [and is] a behavioral dynamic that can be changed with effort.[21]

In *Mean Girls, Meaner Women*, Erika Holiday and Joan Rosenberg advise us,

The act of self-reflection leads to awareness and awareness can lead to change.... Regardless of age, if you desire changes in your

relationships with women, you can "start wherever you are"....
If you are a woman who has treated other women in ways that
betray, exclude, demean, or devalue them, please pause and
reflect before you behave in hurtful ways in the future.[22]

Katherine Crowley and Kathy Elster, the authors of *Mean Girls at Work*,
go so far as to claim that by having read their book, you will have

gained greater knowledge and practical tools for working with
and supporting other women at work—no matter how different
they are from you. If we can acknowledge that the workplace is
naturally competitive, we can also strive to compete with one
another in fair, productive, and professional ways. Our hope
is that if you've practiced mean behavior at work in the past,
you can contain your inner "mean girl" and learn to get ahead
without resorting to covert or indirect aggression toward other
women.[23]

And Valen confesses,

Ultimately...I'm happy to leave it to the experts to figure out
what breeds our aggressions.... We can talk about the "reasons"
ad nauseam, use them as crutches to excuse or explain away
our interaction and complacency, and even feel sorry for ourselves. But at some point we really do have to look within ourselves, examine our role in it, and just "do" or stop doing certain
things.[24]

While we certainly agree that we should all strive to be nicer people,
we seriously doubt that women's individual efforts at self-improvement
will do much to end women's distinctive same-gender workplace conflicts. We believe that the only way to end these conflicts is awareness
of the biases that are found in gendered workplaces. Before developing
this argument further, let's look more closely at why so many people who

write about the difficulty women have working with other women believe this difficulty is rooted in women's fundamental natures.

Differences

While there is general agreement in the books we've discussed that women's purported same-gender antagonism—what the authors identify as women's meanness, hostility, bitchiness, competitiveness, treachery, untrustworthiness, bullying, and so forth—is due to motivations that are internally generated, there is no general agreement as to why women are supposedly programmed in this way. There are, however, three reasons that are most commonly given to explain this purported antagonism: evolution, socialization, and internalization of the dominant culture's misogyny. Although we do not believe that women's distinctive same-gender workplace conflicts are the result of the way women are, by examining each of these explanations we can begin to understand why so many people disagree with us.

Evolution

Proponents of the view that women are genetically predisposed to be antagonistic toward each other argue that natural selection operates to ensure that the genes of only the fittest individuals are passed on to the next generation. As a result, evolutionary processes have shaped women to be inherently competitive with other women in the hunt for superior mates. And, because competing for a desirable mate is directly connected to competing for the scarce resources needed to sustain their offspring, women are constantly competing with each other for everything they need or want. In other words, proponents of the evolutionary explanation of the origins of women's same-gender antagonism assert that women are inherently competitive with other women because evolution has made them that way.

Among the books that argue that women are mean to other women, the evolutionary perspective is most clearly articulated in *The Stiletto in Your Back*. Villalobos argues, "Female competition and the roots of why women 'play dirty' can be traced all the way back to our cave-dwelling, primate, pre-human and early human ancestors."[25] Women compete for the most desirable mates, primarily based on youth and beauty. And in this competition, emotions like jealousy and envy are extremely valuable. She continues, "Jealousy is 'I must protect what I have from you' and envy is 'I want what you have.'"[26] She goes on to claim that as women have become civilized and socialized, the areas of competition have significantly expanded beyond obtaining the fittest mates: "Upon entering the workforce, all of a sudden there were vastly more opportunities for self-comparison and measuring 'how we stack up' against other women."[27]

According to Villalobos, the techniques women use to express their jealousy and envy—which Villalobos identifies as "teasing, threatening, maliciously gossiping, cruelty, mind games, cliques, hierarchies, exclusion, ostracism, sarcasm, and more"—probably originated in prehistory. Today she says,

> they have now been honed, fine-tuned and sharpened to a dagger-like stiletto in the modern workplace. The capacity for envy and jealousy is passed from one generation to the next, [but] those emotions are often responses to stimuli that no longer mean what they once meant, in which case the jealous or envious behaviors—at the office, for example—can be maladaptive, rather than helpful.[28]

Villalobos' stark view is that evolution has shaped women to be inherently competitive with other women, and that conflict among women would seem to be inevitable. Her belief is so stark, in fact, that it is hard to reconcile her evolutionary perspective with her concluding advice to women: "Turn...those envious feelings into incentives for change. Once your life is better, you won't be so wrapped up in [jealousy and envy]."[29]

Villalobos is hardly alone in identifying evolution as the major cause of women's difficulties in achieving positive workplace relationships with other women. For example, Chesler clearly thinks evolution plays a major part in the "human female propensity to evil."[30] She is not, however, as certain as Villalobos that evolution is the sole factor at work in shaping women's same-gender hostilities. Instead, she hedges her bets by writing, "Girls and women may have an evolutionary predisposition towards chronic, intra-gender aggression—which patriarchal civilization may further maximize."[31] Nevertheless, she is unambiguous in claiming that "women's lifelong experience [is] of all other women as rivals and potential replacements."[32] And, she is equally unambiguous that women are highly aggressive, and that "the targets of such female aggression are not men—but other women."[33] Yet she offers no empirical support for these conclusions.

Dellasega also thinks evolution plays a major role in women's competitiveness with other women. She writes that aggression between women occurs "as a genetic protective drive to find the best circumstances to ensure the survival of children." While she notes that the need for such aggression often is no longer necessary, she claims that "this instinct to compete for resources may still motivate many women. That is, women are driven by a deeply ingrained biological need to acquire protection for their offspring."[34] According to her, this instinct is carried over to the workplace and manifested in the "drive to care for and protect your 'children,' whether they are real, potential, or metaphorical (for example, clients, projects, employees, new business)."[35]

Socialization

Other authors argue that women's antagonism toward other women is not due to evolution, but rather to how girls and women are socialized in contemporary society. According to their argument, women, unlike men, are strongly discouraged from openly expressing their negative or unpleasant feelings, such as anger and frustration. Instead, they are taught to inhibit and suppress these feelings. As a result, authors like Holiday and Rosenberg claim that women lack a healthy outlet for their negative emotions, which come out in unhealthy ways, leading women to "strike out at other [women] in covert ways such as excluding them, gossiping, or damaging reputations."[36] In other words, these authors believe that women are mean to other women because that is the only outlet they have for frustration and anger.

Holiday and Rosenberg strongly endorse this socialization paradigm:

> Even though females have made tremendous progress when it comes to leveling the playing field in a variety of academic disciplines and work arenas, enormous pressures still remain on girls and women to be sweet, kind, and nurturing, as opposed to exhibiting competitiveness or toughness. As a result, girls quickly learn to suppress feelings of anger and hostility rather than express them outwardly.[37]

In their view, women's suppression of these negative emotions comes at an enormous cost to themselves and their relationships with other women. Because women cannot openly direct their anger at the person or circumstance causing the hurt, "there is a tendency for girls and women to keep anger inside and then become self-destructive, or to turn on each other and hurt other girls or women."[38] This hostility is reinforced by women's reluctance to take their anger out on men for fear of weakening or destroying their relationships with those holding social and organizational power.

Holiday and Rosenberg argue that socialization leads to women's same-gender antagonism in another way. Despite the countless career opportunities available to women, they "continue to be socialized into rigid gender roles," and the gender roles deemed suitable for women are not considered by society to be as important, valuable, or desirable as men's gender roles. Although women are often not conscious of it, "this socialization process...acts as an oppressive force against women, and women come to accept these stereotypes as fact."[39] As a result, the authors claim, "women hurt, betray, backstab, and trash talk other women, essentially on the basis of self-hatred—a self-hatred borne out of an experience of being considered inferior from birth." In other words, women are faced from birth "with the experience of either being seen as inferior or being made to feel as if they are inferior."[40]

Barash also sees socialization as the root of women's same-gender antagonism, but she believes it operates in a different way: "Despite [women's] many gains, we're still socialized to view ourselves in relational terms."[41] This affects the way in which women compete. Men's competition is typically about task performance and external achievements; as a result, men can go out for a beer with their rivals after the contest is over. But in Barash's view, women's competition is "about [their] identities—*and*, unlike men, [women] tend to expect total union and sympathy with [their] same-sex friends. [Women] have a much harder time setting boundaries to [their] competition, which makes it all the more destructive."[42]

Like Holiday and Rosenberg, Barash believes this socialization process also forces women to conform to rigid gender norms, forbidding them from being openly angry or overly competitive. "Men tend to accept their competition as a natural, even healthy part of their lives."[43] Women, on the other hand, are far less comfortable with competition. As a result, their "ambition,…repressed desire for power, money, or success finds expression in all sorts of inappropriate places."[44]

According to Barash, as another consequence of the limited gender roles that society views as appropriate for women, women often see ambitious women as selfish, self-aggrandizing, or manipulative. In addition, she believes women are frequently uncomfortable with their own desire for career success, status, and power. Therefore, they channel such dangerous desires into resentment of other women, competing with them "at every turn, judging them not only on their work performance but also on their looks, style of dress, marital/dating status, children's success (or lack thereof), and general demeanor."[45]

Internalized Misogyny

Some authors don't claim that women's socialization has caused them to suppress their negative emotions. Instead, they argue that women's socialization has caused them to internalize the dominant culture's misogynist ideology: women are fundamentally inferior to men. According to this claim, when women internalize this sexist view, they depreciate their own self-worth as well as the worth of all other women. As a result, Chesler notes that "women become hostile towards [other] women and do not like, trust, respect, or find their statements to be credible."[46] In other words, women are antagonistic toward other women because they don't like who *they* are, themselves, much less who other women are.

For example, Holiday and Rosenberg argue that women as a group are oppressed and that like members of all oppressed groups, women internalize aspects of their subjugation and "come to believe in their imposed inferiority. Though women frequently have a hard time admitting they experience themselves as being inferior to men, largely this appears to be true."[47]

According to Tanenbaum, the author of *Catfight*, the most dangerous outcome of such a sense of inferiority "is self-hatred: girls and women disparage themselves and disassociate from other females."[48] When women hate themselves, they become angry and frustrated. Because there is no constructive outlet for these feelings, women either turn them inward (where they are corrosive of their self-confidence, sense of self-worth, and ambition) or they express them through indirect, hurtful attacks on other women. As Holiday and Rosenberg say, "Meanness thus becomes the strategy for increasing self-importance, popularity, or to achieve the desired goal."[49]

Tanenbaum argues that although women have made so much progress in so many areas, they are still "expected to conform, more or less, to a narrow role."[50] This restrictive gender role means that women are forced to compete with each other if they are ever going to succeed. And, when women are forced to compete exclusively against other women, they "tend to be more underhanded and personal in [their] attacks than men are."[51] According to Tanenbaum, because women feel powerless, they lash out at others who are in the same powerless position: other women. She explains that when a woman "belittles other women, she can prove her superiority among women—and is one step closer to the inner circle of men."[52]

Critique

We believe the fundamental fallacy underlying all of these books is the assumption that women are inherently different from men. Researchers have concluded that "basic patterns of male and female brain asymmetry seem to be more similar than they are different."[53] Consistent with the arguments we advance in this book, researchers have found that the behaviors that are so often linked to unique gender characteristics depend more on people's actual situations—what they are doing, the conditions under which they are doing it, and the expectations of how they will perform while doing it—than on their gender.[54] For example, in a study of the personality traits of single fathers, single mothers, and married parents, researchers found that the traits of single men with childcare responsibilities were more like those of mothers (single or married) than like those of married fathers.[55]

Of course, there is extensive literature arguing that women's and men's moral sensitivities and relational patterns are fundamentally different. Some authors, including feminist psychoanalysts Nancy Chodorou and Jean Baker Miller[56] and psychologist Carol Gilligan[57] claim that male gender identity is defined by separation, while female gender identity is defined by intimacy. They assert that these two styles of identity demonstrate that women's and men's natures are different, enduring, and unchangeable.[58] Nevertheless, as Carol Tavris points out in *Mismeasure of Woman*, "research in recent years casts considerable doubt on the notion that men and women differ appreciably in their moral reasoning, or that women have a permanently different voice."[59] With respect to the evolutionary explanation of women's antagonisms toward other women, researchers have found no evidence that women have a greater desire for or concern with a secure, committed, sexually exclusive relationship than do men. Indeed, most men and women equally value these features of intimacy.[60]

It's Not Nature, It's the Workplace

Perhaps most significantly, research confirms that the characteristics ascribed to women's nature, which supposedly set them apart from men, are characteristics that women and men both have when they lack power in their careers and interpersonal relationships. In other words, women's employment characteristics—not their unique gender characteristics— determine how they approach their jobs. Thus, researchers have found that *both* women and men in dead-end, unstimulating jobs tend to focus on the same pleasurable aspects of their jobs: their relationships with others. According to Rosabeth Moss Kanter, the author of *Men and Women of the Corporation*,

> [Men] *with low opportunity look more like the stereotype of women in their orientations toward work*...they limit their aspi-rations, seek satisfaction in activities outside of work, dream of escape, interrupt their careers, emphasize leisure and consump-tion, and create sociable peer groups in which interpersonal rela-tionships take precedence over other aspects of work.[61]

But as Tavris argues, it is hard to kill the idea that women are funda-mentally oriented to interpersonal relationships and are best suited for work with people, while men are fundamentally oriented to independent task performance and are best suited to work with money. In any form, however, the claims that women have a "caring nature," a "feminine love of gossip," or a "different voice" is a view that continues to justify keeping things the way they are. Tavris explains,

> Thinking in opposites [that is, women are this way, men are that way] may be a comfortable habit, but the results are often haz-ardous to our relationships, social policies, and private lives. For one thing, it twists our way of thinking about the differ-ences that do exist between men and women into stable perma-nent qualities...People develop, learn, have adventures and new

experiences; and as they do, their notions of masculinity and femininity change too. Thinking in opposites frames the possibility for change in [far too] limited ways.[62]

We do not mean to suggest that all of the books we have been discussing are without valuable insights. Quite the contrary, the authors' discussions of the counterproductive characteristics of women's same-gender competition, the hurtful nature of women's envy and jealousy of other women, and the self-destructive nature of internalized misogyny provide highly valuable information about women's same-gender workplace conflicts. Our objections to these books stem from their tendency to blame the women for their workplace difficulties, rather than to blame the situations that gendered workplaces put women into.

MAKING THINGS BETTER

- There is no evidence to support the view that same-gender tension, conflict, and obstructionist behavior are uniquely female problems. There is solid evidence, however, that similar workplace conflict is viewed more negatively when it involves two women than when it involves two men or a woman and a man.[63]
- Don't get sucked into believing the narrative that same-gender conflict is a problem for women but not for men. These views can become a self-fulfilling prophecy, playing directly into prevailing gender stereotypes that men are cut out for leadership but women are not—blaming the source of gender inequality on women's own behavior, rather than on systemic gender bias.

Chapter 2

Sisterhood

THE BOOKS WE DISCUSSED IN chapter 1 focus so strongly on women's supposed mutual antagonism that they ignore women's desires to relate to other women in supportive, noncompetitive ways. Yet women's efforts to achieve such positive same-gender relationships are far more common and pervasive than are instances of internally motivated hostility toward the women with whom they work. Indeed, the aspiration for a close, powerful, and focused alliance of women—a sisterhood—has been a centerpiece of the modern women's movement since its very beginning. Robin Morgan's 1970 collection of essays, *Sisterhood Is Powerful: An Anthology of Writings from the Women's Liberation Movement*, is emblematic of this aspiration.[1] The essays in the book are all premised on the conviction that by working together, women will be able to effectively combat gender discrimination and sexual exploitation and, most importantly, to achieve their individual life goals.

The public proclamation of the reality of sisterhood and the certainty of its power were at their peak in the decade following the publication of Morgan's book. In 1970, women across America celebrated the 50th anniversary of the adoption of the Nineteenth Amendment to the US Constitution, granting women the right to vote. One women's group draped a banner on the Statue of Liberty that read, "WOMEN OF THE WORLD UNITE."[2] And, after 50,000 women marched down Fifth Avenue in New York City, Betty Friedan declared women finally understood "the power of our sisterhood" and that "the politics of this nation will never be the same."[3]

The United Nations declared 1975 International Women's Year and designated the years 1975 to 1985 as the Decade of Women. President Gerald Ford appointed a National Commission on the Observance of International Women's Year, and in 1977 this commission convened the National Women's Conference (NWC) in Houston, Texas, which was attended by 20,000 people.[4] Addressing the NWC, Coretta Scott King declared, "There is a new force, a new understanding, a new sisterhood against all injustice that has been born here. We [women] will not be divided and defeated again."[5]

Of course, the notion of sisterhood goes back much further than the early days of the modern women's movement. In Charlotte Perkins Gilman's 1915 utopian novel *Herland*, for example, the author creates a country of three million girls and women and no boys or men. When three scientists discover this country, they find a highly advanced civilization with beautiful architecture, orderliness, cleanliness, and a pervasive sense of home. Instead of competition, they found an "extremely high sense of solidarity" and a "limitless feeling of sisterhood."[6]

A somewhat later but real world demonstration of sisterhood was reported about the Women Aviators 1929 National Air Derby (popularly dubbed the "Powder Puff Derby"), an airplane race from Santa Monica, California, to Cleveland, Ohio. When Amelia Earhart's propeller was bent upon landing in the desert 175 miles east of San Diego, she asked the other competitors to delay the start of the next leg of the race for three hours so she could get a new propeller for her plane. And the other competitors agreed to the delay.[7]

> Waiting there for Earhart seemed like the sporting thing to do, and the women were nothing if not good sports. In the air, when passing each other they waggled their wings in greeting, even though doing so made them lose valuable seconds. Earhart was flying in a cabin, not an open cockpit, so she carried some of the women's luggage, even though the extra weight could clip her speed.[8]

The high hopes of the 1970s for political and societal transformation through the power of sisterhood are now mostly forgotten. Indeed, the very notion of an all-embracing alliance of women that would end sexism and gender bias is generally recognized to have been a pipe dream. Moreover, American women are more ideologically divided today than ever before, and the key goal of the NWC—passage of the Equal Rights Amendment to the US Constitution—is a conspicuous casualty of that division (see chapter 3).

Nevertheless, the desire for sisterhood of some sort is still very much alive. While it may now be conceived in far more modest terms than it was in the 1970s, sisterhood is frequently invoked in efforts to gain support for female political candidates, in the formation of women's affinity groups at many major US organizations, and in former secretary of state Madeleine Albright's often repeated condemnation to "a special place in hell" of those women "who don't help each other."[9] Perhaps the current conception of sisterhood was best expressed by journalist and author Sophia A. Nelson:

> We learn early as girls that other girls (who will grow up to be other women) are both our competition and our co-conspirators. Therein lies our conflict. Yet, deep inside we all know that we are at our best when we have our "sisters" (biological or not) at our side cheering us on and watching our backs.[10]

Contemporary Sisterhood

There are many prominent instances of this more modest vision of sisterhood. Popular power duos like Tina Fey and Amy Poehler as well as Taylor Swift and Karlie Kloss make clear that a woman's strong relationship with another woman can make them both better.

Less visible to followers of popular culture, but equally exemplary of the pursuit of sisterhood, are Geneva Robertson-Dworet's efforts to break men's dominant control of the film industry. Robertson-Dworet is a screenwriter best known for films such as *Captain Marvel* and the 2018 remake of *Tomb Raider*. She is outspoken about sharing that all of her big breaks have come from female executives, and she insists that if other women are to get similar career breaks, more women need to get involved behind the scenes in Hollywood. Specifically, she says,

> I think there's, thank God, a greater awareness in the industry that we need more female voices, not just on the creative side, but also on the producer and executive side. People out in the world who don't work in this industry assume that you just get a female director, and then everything is great.... [But] you need female decision-makers on the executive side as well, because they're the ones vetoing what the female director or female writer might be saying.[11]

Robertson-Dworet doesn't just talk the talk; she walks the walk. When she found out that she and her friend Lindsey Beer were the final candidates to write the script for *Dungeons & Dragons* (scheduled for release in 2021), she persuaded the studio to let the two of them team up and write the screenplay together.[12]

The importance of women's collaboration in Hollywood is all the more vital given how difficult it is to present female characters who don't fit traditional gender stereotypes. Beer is often told that her female characters need to be more "likable," implying that otherwise they will come across as bitchy.[13] Robertson-Dworet points out the "depressing" tendency of male directors to request a "normal girl," as if there was a one-size-fits-all option. As Beer commented, "Female characters also need to have motivations that aren't just a man or children. I know a male screenwriter who said he could think of 300 motivations for his male character, but all he could think about for his female character was that she had kids to go save. It's just a subconscious bias."[14]

Why Sisterhood Is Important

The gender stereotypes that constrict Hollywood's creative process—women are "nice" or "bitchy," "normal" or "not normal," and "really interested" only in a man and children—are the same stereotypes that limit women's advancement in all traditionally male careers. Thus, as we discuss at greater length in chapter 4, women are stereotypically seen as interested in interpersonal relationships, not the single-minded pursuit of career objectives. They are thought to be communal—friendly, unselfish caretakers—and, lacking in the quintessentially masculine characteristics of business and professional leaders: decisiveness, strength, and independence.[15] Leaders are stereotypically seen as interested in achievement, not interpersonal relationships.[16] Yet, when women behave in stereotypically masculine ways, they might be viewed as competent, but they are also likely to be regarded as cold, selfish, and far less likable than men who behave in exactly the same way.[17]

It is not just gender stereotypes of these sorts that are obstacles to women's career advancement. Senior male leaders, like many people, prefer to work with, support, and promote people who are like them—in the case of senior male leaders, other men. Such affinity or ingroup bias works in tandem with gender stereotypes to create a self-reinforcing dynamic that perpetuates men's dominance over organizational leadership, "powerfully if unwittingly communicat[ing] that women are ill-suited for leadership roles."[18]

Much can be done to counter the discriminatory treatment of women in the workplace. As we discuss in our book *Breaking Through Bias*, women can use communication techniques to manage their impressions to avoid or overcome gender bias.[19] Managers can be educated about why it is so much harder for women to advance in their careers than it is for men to advance. Organizations can adopt policies and practices that interrupt the operation of affinity and gender bias when people—women as well as men—make career-affecting decisions. And a sufficient number of female managers can be hired to create the critical mass needed for women leaders to begin to dismantle their organizations' masculine norms, values, and expectations.[20] But beyond these steps, an important key to countering the discriminatory treatment of women in the pursuit of career success is sisterhood—women supporting, mentoring, and advocating for other women.

Sisterhood Is Not the Same Thing as Friendship

Sisterhood does not depend on women having close, personal relationships with other women. Sisterhood does not necessarily involve confidences, disclosure of disappointments and successes, and revelation of fears and aspirations. Sisterhood involves nothing more than the recognition that when women work together, rather than competitively, they are a stronger, more effective force for their mutual advancement. Sisterhood is about mutual support, not intimacy; cooperation, not confidences; shared purpose, not shared feelings. Sisterhood is an ethical, political, social, and economic relationship. It does not need to be a personal one.

We are all in favor of women's same-gender workplace friendships. Indeed, such friendships are enormously positive and can make life both at and away from work more satisfying. Our point, however, is that just because friendships may not be present in the workplace does not mean that women should give up on sisterhood. Quite the contrary: women don't need to be friends to be sisters, they simply need to respect one another, be committed to common objectives, be allies not antagonists, and be advocates not critics.

In an interview, Carol, a midlevel executive at a major chemical company, told us that her last promotion had almost come out of the blue because a senior woman she barely knew treated her like a sister. She said to us, "I was in this project development meeting discussing a very tough environmental problem our company was facing. After discussing the issue for some time, I spoke up and suggested an entirely new approach to the problem. This senior

(Continued)

woman, the only other woman in the meeting, immediately spoke up and said, 'I think that is the first really sensible thing that has been said. I think you should be put in charge of this project.' I don't know whether the men agreed or were just too surprised to object, but the next thing I knew I was heading the project and had a promotion."

Building Sisterhood

While sisterhood can be spontaneous and ad hoc, an effective and sustained workplace sisterhood depends on some sort of purposeful association, network, or community of women. This can be structured formally or informally, and it might or might not include men. There are advantages and disadvantages to both informal and formal networks, just as there are to both single-gender and mixed-gender networks. The important point, however, is that a powerful, continuing, and satisfying workplace sisterhood depends on a commitment of time and space within which women can interact with one another for reasons *other than* their workplace responsibilities. In other words, there need to be opportunities and locations where problems and ideas can be discussed, connections made, and advice obtained.

Professional Networks

When women participate in effective networks, they typically find support, gain confidence, and become more strongly motivated to succeed.[21] Women's lack of participation in such networks is one of the main reasons they drop out of or fall back in their careers.[22] Indeed, a recent Accenture study found that women's participation in a women's network is strongly correlated with women's advancement. Accenture also found, however, that the vast majority of women work for organizations without such a network.[23]

Nevertheless, even in organizations without formal women's networks, by forming informal networks—lunch gatherings, occasional programs, mentoring arrangements, support groups, and peer counseling—women can build strong, mutually supportive relationships.

The extraordinary benefit women can obtain from active participation in an informal network was recently convincingly demonstrated by a study of 728 graduates of a top-rated MBA program.[24] Based on a review of 4.55 million anonymized emails sent among the students in the 2006 and 2007 classes, researchers found that the extent of women's social networks strongly predicted the leadership positions they obtained on graduation. The importance of women's social networks was all the more important because women's examination scores, grade point averages, work experiences, and social abilities had no significant statistical correlation with their leadership job placement. To have real payoff in terms of leadership placement, women's social networks need to have three characteristics: high connection with other well-connected people across the school-wide social network ("high centrality"); an "inner circle" of predominantly female contacts; and a degree of randomness so that their network contacts do not overlap with third-party contacts. Indeed, researchers found that women whose networks had centrality in the top quartile and a female-dominated inner circle had an expected job placement level that was 2.5 times greater than women with low centrality and a male-dominated inner circle. Even women who had networks that resemble those of high-placing men—high centrality—"are low-placing, despite having leadership qualifications comparable to high-placing women." Thus, 77 percent of high-placing women had "an inner circle of strong ties to two or three women who communicate[d] intensely with one another."[25] By contrast, low-placing women had a male-dominated network and relatively weak ties with women in their networks.

High network centrality, a same-gender inner circle, and a degree of randomness appear to allow women to address the dual concerns of women pursuing career advancement: broad access to public information and "gender-specific private information and support." Women who had social networks with these characteristics were able to obtain not only a great deal of information about job availability and requirements but also nonpublic information about how companies treat women, how women leaders are regarded, whether there was a hostile work environment, and the sincerity of a commitment to gender diversity. As Nitesh V. Chawla, one of the co-authors of the study, stated, they found "that the circles benefit from each other, suggesting that women gain gender-specific private information and support from their inner circle, while nonoverlapping connections provide other job market details." [26]

Although, this study looked at the value of informal networks for women's search for high leadership positions, its findings can certainly be used by women already in their careers to structures their own informal networks to help them advance. Take, for example, an informal network that Andie is a part of.

Andie has been involved for many years with a group of women lawyers called the Dancing Queens. The women live in different cities across North America, work in different legal organizations, and have different areas of legal specialty. They meet several times a year to catch up and to discuss current career difficulties or opportunities. They look to each other for advice on how to handle office politics, difficult clients, gender bias, and family matters. They keep in touch throughout the year, referring clients and projects to each other, introducing each other to contacts, and helping each other obtain speaking engagements, podcasts, and webcasts. They view each other as sisters.[27]

There are advantages to formal, employer-sponsored employee resource groups (ERGs). For example, ERGs typically offer the advantages of organization, continuity, resources, regularity, and facilities. Despite Accenture's finding about the lack of women's networks at most businesses, approximately 90 percent of Fortune 500 companies have women's ERGs.[28] Typically, these formal networks are designed to build relationships and provide leadership training, professional development, and education.[29] Such ERGs, referred to as output ERGs, offer services to individual members that purportedly will help them advance in their careers. At their best, output ERGs provide an organized way for women to connect with other women, build relationships with senior women leaders, and share strategies and ideas for career advancement.

There is another type of ERG—an outcome ERG—that seeks to remove career disparities, eliminate bias, raise awareness, and change the attitudes of senior management. Outcome ERGs seek to spur collective action for change. Unfortunately, true outcome ERGs are few and far between.[30]

Unfortunately, women's ERGs are too often more promise than reality. When they exist in organizations with gendered workplaces, they are often viewed with benign neglect at best and suspicion at worst. Senior women are often reluctant to participate in them, junior women can avoid them for fear of being stigmatized by their made colleagues, and ERG leadership is frequently left to junior women who lack in-depth knowledge of their organizations' political and cultural norms.

Despite the problems with both formal and informal networks, many women find such networks valuable simply because they provide them with the opportunity to drop the pretense of 'we are just like men,' candidly exchange experiences and ideas, learn from role models, and strengthen social connections.

Jill, a midlevel manager, told us that getting together with a group of her women colleagues "always renews me, gives me strength, and allows me to see the bright side of things. I wish we could get together more often."

The opportunity to strengthen social connections may be the most important benefit of a women's network. Strong social connections are a powerful predictor of career success.[31] In a culture that continues to depict women as either pleasant assistants who lack leadership potential or as competitive, catfighting bitches, women's networks can provide safe spaces within which women can find the support base and discussion forums that are essential for the connections at the heart of sisterhood.

Commercial Networks

Because so many women lack access to strong women's networks, there has been an explosion of commercial ventures designed to facilitate women's networking. Part cheerleading groups, part career-coaching venues, and part social clubs,[32] these female empowerment businesses vary in their approaches, from simply providing listservs to being full-service resource centers. All of them, however, seek to attract women who are willing to pay for female support, companionship, and advice.

These commercial communities can create real value when they provide women with safe spaces to experience strong interpersonal connections with similarly situated women. As Shawn Achor wrote in the *Harvard Business Review*, "The greatest predictor of success and happiness is social connection....If people feel like they are...fighting inequality alone, or striving for success alone, they burn out....But there is a powerful, viable alternative to individually pursuing success and happiness: doing it together."[33]

Resistance to Sisterhood

Approximately 85 percent of corporate executives and corporate board members are white men, a percentage that has remained basically unchanged for many years.[34] We have argued that women actively supporting the advancement of other women is an effective way of countering the severe negative consequences for women's career advancement that typically result from such a concentration of male power at the top of major American organizations.[35]

Unfortunately, however, when women actively promote other women, they often face career penalties. For example, in a study published in the *Academy of Management Journal* [36] and summarized in the *Harvard Business Review*,[37] researchers found that women who openly helped other women advance often receive negative workplace evaluations precisely because of their support. In one study, the researchers surveyed 350 executives about their diversity-valuing behaviors—behaviors that promoted demographic balance within their organizations. They found that no executive, female or male, received a higher competence or performance rating when they engaged in such diversity-valuing behaviors. Thus, despite all of the vigorous back-patting by our major organizations about their commitment to diversity, not even white male executives received any career-related advantage for actually working to create diversity. But more discouraging, women executives who reported they frequently engaged in diversity-valuing behaviors actually received *much worse* competence and performance ratings from their managers than women who did not actively promote gender diversity.[38]

In a second study, researchers asked 307 working adults to evaluate a fictitious manager after the manager had decided to hire either a woman or a man. The researchers found that both female and male participants rated the fictitious female manager as *less effective* when she hired a female job applicant than when she hired a male applicant. As in the first study, the effectiveness rating of the fictitious male manager was not affected by whom he chose to hire. In other words, white male managers can hire people who look like them without penalty, but women managers are judged harshly if they do the same thing. Men hiring men is seen as normal; women hiring women is seen as favoritism.[39]

These two studies have serious implications for the realistic possibility of building effective sisterhoods in gendered workplaces. But if author Sophia Nelson is right, as we believe, women are at their best when they have their sisters at their side cheering them on and watching their backs, then ways must be found for women to advocate for each other's advancement without fear of career penalties.

Countering the Resistance

The most obvious way to eliminate negative career consequences for women advocating for the advancement of other women is to get a sufficient number of women into senior management. Women's same-gender advocacy would no longer be seen as favoritism. But there is an obvious chicken-or-egg problem here. It seems unlikely that senior male leaders are going to advance a significant number of women out of the goodness of their hearts, yet if senior women push for more women to join their ranks, they risk suffering adverse career consequences. So what are the realistic possibilities?

Heroic Measures

Anne Welsh McNulty, a former managing director at Goldman Sachs and a senior executive at Goldman Sachs Hedge Fund Strategies Group, proposes a bold strategy for getting a critical mass of women into senior leadership. She writes, "The antidote to being penalized for sponsoring women may just be to do it more—and to do it vocally, loudly, and proudly—until we're able to change perceptions. There are massive benefits for the individual and the organization when women support each other."[40] McNulty's recommendation strikes us as heroic but highly risky for women in middle management. Doubling down on advocating for the advancement of other women may be a viable strategy for senior women leaders secure in their positions with the support of the C-suite, but it is likely to have very little upside potential—and a good deal of downside risk—for other women.

Collective Action

A less courageous but far safer strategy is for women to channel their support and advocacy for other women through their organizations' ERGs or their own informal networks. When women can come together as a group, they quickly realize that their career difficulties are not unique to themselves but are actually collective obstacles to women's careers generally. Realizing they are not alone can provide women with positive benefits, increasing their self-confidence, and helping them concentrate their energies on concrete steps forward. Alexandra's story is a good example of how this can work.

We met Alexandra after she invited us to speak at the women's network at her company, a large multinational construction firm. Alexandra started an informal women's network in her office a few years ago. In a short time, the informal network has grown to include six different offices. Three of the networks are in large offices that can easily support meetings and events to connect women and build professional relationships. The other three offices do not have a critical mass of professional women. Alexandra has arranged for each of the three large offices to "adopt" one of the smaller offices. The cross-office synergy has been very empowering for what has become a large group of women. Important workplace connections have been successfully developed. By collectively advocating for women's advancement, Alexandra believes the networks have been highly effective without negative career consequences for individual women.

Channeling efforts to boost women's careers through ERGs or informal networks may also provide women leaders with the cover (protection) they might be looking for to help other women. Indeed, anything that can be done to reduce the tendency of senior-level women to distance themselves from junior-level women is a highly positive step.

Enlisting Male Allies

Another way to avoid the penalty women often pay for actively trying to lift each other up is to enlist senior male leaders in the effort. This can often be difficult for at least three reasons. First, many men are genuinely convinced that their organizations are true meritocracies in which women and men are treated in precisely the same ways. Moreover, they are likely to believe women are already well represented in leadership positions. For example, a recent study found that at companies where only 10 percent of leaders were women, nearly 50 percent of the men in those companies felt that women were "well represented" in leadership.[41]

Moreover, a recent Boston Consulting Group study found that men age 45 and older, that is, those commonly with decision-making authority in corporate environments, significantly underrepresent the obstacles that women face in hiring, retention, and advancement. Indeed, only 25 percent of older heterosexual white men see obstacles for women in the workplace.[42] The most common approach to dealing with men's lack of appreciation for the seriousness of the bias-driven workplace obstacles women face is formal antibias training. While antibias training can be useful, it needs to be done carefully so as not to create a backlash. When seeking allies for specific women's initiatives, the most effective technique is frank one-on-one conversations. When a male leader is approached by a woman colleague who asks for his support to create greater gender diversity, it can be difficult for him just to say "no." He is likely to listen to her reasons for why gender diversity is important and why his support is critical. Once such a dialogue gets started, the chances are good that the man can be enlisted as an ally. Further, the more senior the man, the easier it will be to gain additional male allies. If people at the top of an organization support diversity, the men below will likely follow that lead.

Second, while some men incorrectly believe that women are already well represented in their senior leadership ranks, other men have been scared off because of the #MeToo movement. It has become difficult to enlist men in efforts to advance women because of backlash to #MeToo. In a 2018 survey, Leanin.Org found that almost half of male managers are uncomfortable participating in common work activities with women such as mentoring, working alone, traveling, and socializing together.[43] Men's reluctance to engage with women at work has severe negative consequences for women, putting them at a disadvantage to men. With so many more male than female managers, when men avoid, ignore, or exclude women from interpersonal exchanges, women lose access to leaders, mentorship and sponsor opportunities, and learning experiences on the same terms as men. This backlash is affecting women at all stages of their careers, as the story from Kristine illustrates.

"As a graduate student, I was lucky to have been able to reach out and connect with many mentors, both male and female. One of my male mentors would give me career advice and life advice, such as how to balance my studies with my personal relationships. His advice was always helpful. He is a genuinely nice and thoughtful person who truly wants to see me succeed in my career.

"I have now started my career, and one of the last times I met with him, he said we needed to meet in a public location, rather than his office. At first I thought he just wanted a change of scenery. But after our meeting at a local, overcrowded coffee shop I realized he was concerned about talking with me behind the closed door of his office. I have known this man for five years, and I know he would never even think of hurting or harassing me. But because of #MeToo, he is now concerned about appearances and worried about his reputation."

There is no escaping the fact that many men don't want to expose themselves to even the possibility that they will be suspected of an inappropriate workplace relationship.[44] So efforts need to be made to overcome this concern. One way is for women leaders to have candid one-on-one conversations with cautious men about the importance of interacting with and supporting individual women. Another way is to structure activities so that several people are present. Along those lines, mentorship can be required by an organization's formal program. Organizations should establish formal mentorship programs so it is known that *this* man is expected to be working with *this* woman on her career development. And yet another way is to establish ground rules for business travel and out of the office meetings; for example, all one-on-one mixed-gender meetings must be conducted in conference rooms or a public venue, not hotel rooms. One way or another, when men are confident that their mixed-gender activities will be appreciated, not questioned, they often can be enlisted as allies.

The third reason men are reluctant to mentor and sponsor women is that they often claim they are too busy. This excuse, however, is commonly a cover for their basic discomfort with involvement in women's advancement initiatives. The same men are unlikely to say they are too busy to mentor or sponsor other men. Once again, the best approach is a one-on-one conversation, with a woman colleague making the case for the importance of more women in leadership positions and suggesting why *this* man's support would be effective and valuable.

Enlisting senior men in the effort to advance women into leadership positions is an important step toward changing the discriminatory nature of the dominant culture in gendered workplaces. When men stick up for women at meetings, ask women to elaborate on the points they make, praise women for their contributions, and make sure that the women on their teams are seen as valued participants, it can be more effective than when women do the same things on their own. And when men call out incivility, gender snubs, and microaggressions against women, they are less likely than women to be accused of being too sensitive or not being able to take a joke.

Men also can be powerful allies simply by being willing to listen and objectively examine situations that women view as problematic. When women know there are senior men to whom they can go to express their concerns and ask their questions, they feel more valued and are likely to perform better than when such male support is absent. Women may be at their best when they know other women "are at their sides and have their backs," but active male support is a very effective way to break through gender bias.[45]

Sisterhood Is Already Being Built

Despite the very real career penalties women can pay for advocating for the advancement of other women, many women clearly want to do precisely this. A 2015 survey by KPMG of more than 3,000 professional and college women, found:

- 86 percent of women reported that seeing women in leadership roles encouraged them to believe they could attain leadership themselves;
- 83 percent recognized that the steps they take in their careers will set the stage for the careers of future generations of women;
- 76 percent said they plan to personally take active steps to help other women advance in their careers;
- 67 percent said they believe they have learned the most important lessons about leadership from other women;
- 91 percent said it was important for them to be positive role models for other women in the workplace;
- 91 percent of younger women (ages 25 to 39) have had a positive role model, most often a woman; and
- 40 percent of older women (ages 40 to 64) said they have acted as positive role models for other women and helped them advance in their careers.[46]

In a 2012 study, "Leaders Pay It Forward," Catalyst found that 65 percent of high-potential women who received career development support are now supporting talented junior women, and 73 percent of such women—compared to only 30 percent of men—are working at developing other women. As Ilene H. Long, president and CEO of Catalyst, stated, the study "shows that women are in fact actively helping each other succeed."[47]

The KPMG and Catalyst studies are both good news, but to date, women's efforts to help other women—just as all other diversity and inclusion initiatives—have not significantly moved the needle measuring women's participation in senior leadership. We are convinced, however, that the needle can be moved through a series of active and committed individual and organizational activities. This will require more, not less, attention to the importance of sisterhood—a sisterhood with an increasing number of sincere, dedicated male allies. With women working together and men supporting their efforts, we believe it will be possible to make the organizational changes needed to end the discriminatory consequences of affinity and gender bias. We return to this effort in chapters 10 and 11.

To conclude this chapter, here are some ideas and suggestions to overcome or avoid women's same-gender conflict and to support a workplace sisterhood.

MAKING THINGS BETTER

- Women should not expect their same-gender workplace relationships with other women to have the same personal intimacies as their relationships away from work. Colleagues can have friendly, courteous interactions without the personal connections they seek in their private lives.
- Don't buy into the stereotypes that women don't help other women. Women are more likely than men to mentor junior employees, and it is women, not men, who primarily mentor other women.
- Keep in mind these interesting findings from the Families and Work Institute: Women executives who report that a woman was the most helpful person in their careers are more likely than other women to have reached senior leadership reporting levels. This means while support and mentoring by women and men are essential for leadership development, "women mentoring women is of special importance in women's careers."[48]
- The most effective ERGs are those that focus on outcomes, rather than outputs. Outcome ERGs seek to remove career disparities by making systematic changes to organizations. If you have the opportunity to build your organization's ERG, focus its mission on measurable changes in women's leadership achievements. If your organization already has an output ERG, see what you can

do to expand its mission to support collective actions that eliminate bias and benefit and advance the women in your workplace.

- Be sure that women have a voice—not just a seat—at the table. Desegregate your organization's ERG to ensure that it doesn't simply have a white women's agenda. Include, and more importantly—listen to—women with different social identities and intersectionalities to be certain that their concerns are actually being addressed.

- Don't limit your networking efforts to women in your own organization. Use your trade associations, supplier networks, customer contacts, civic activities, and charitable activities to connect, learn from, and bond with other women.

- Get a mentor or two. Don't wait for your organization to pair you up with someone. Take the initiative and seek out women—and men—colleagues who you believe can be helpful. Mentors are most likely to be someone with whom you work closely, without regard to whether that is a woman or man. Identify people who are likely to believe that collaborating with you is in their personal self-interest. Cast a wide net for prospective candidates. Don't ask, "Will you be my mentor?" Instead, go to them to learn about their successes and their failures. Ask how they got to where they are. Ask what they would recommend you do to advance in your career.

- Carefully assess how you can most effectively advocate for other women in your workplace. You might decide to do this actively and openly, or quietly without fanfare. It is important that you make it known to the women you work with that you support them, are behind them, and want to help them get to where they want to go in their careers.

- Stand up for other women. If a woman is interrupted or ignored in a meeting, don't let it pass. If women are not getting assigned to important career-enhancing projects, ask why that isn't happening. You can build your sisterhood one woman at a time.

- Keep an eye on the senior women in your organization. They are the key to building a truly powerful workplace sisterhood. Build personal relationships with them. Don't be put off by agentic (stereotypically masculine) management styles. Don't ask for special favors but do seek their advice, counsel, and wisdom. Sincere compliments work with women just as they do with men. Don't be reluctant to tell them you respect their achievements.

Chapter 3

Not My Sisterhood

I N CHAPTER 2, WE ARGUED that an active workplace sisterhood is an essential part of a comprehensive attack on the biases holding women back. We also identified certain institutional dynamics that work against the development and effective functioning of a successful sisterhood. But it is not only the penalties that gendered workplaces may impose on women who actively support the advancement of other women that work against sisterhood. In subsequent chapters, we discuss the interpersonal dynamics resulting from women's differing social identities that often make sisterhood difficult, dynamics created by their differing races, ethnicities, sexual orientations, gender identities, ages, and family situations. In this chapter, we focus on three additional dynamics that often work against sisterhood: the differing strengths of women's gender identification, their differing career aspirations, and differences in ideology.

Gender Identification

The strength with which women consider their gender as important to their personal identity varies significantly. Strength of gender identification is measured in a variety of ways. For example, women might be asked to respond to a set of statements about their feelings when they are at work.[1] Such statements might be something like: "At work, being a woman is important to me," "I feel connected to other women at work," "At work I feel part of the group of women," and "I identify with other women at work." Another approach might be to ask women about their feelings as a member of a specific group, in this case women. Such statements might be something like: "I identify with this group," "I have strong ties to this group," "This group is important to my self-image," and "Being a member of this group is an important part of how I see myself."

Women are typically asked to respond to such statements based on a graduated five- or seven-point scale, with 1 indicating "completely disagree," and 5 or 7 representing "completely agree." After tabulating their responses, women are then classified as having low, medium, or high gender identification.

The strength of women's gender identification could also be determined simply by asking them for a self-description. In 2017, for example, the Pew Research Center asked women how womanly or feminine they were. Thirty-two percent said they are very feminine, 54 percent said they are somewhat feminine, and 14 percent said they are not too feminine or not at all feminine.[2]

High and Low Gender Identification

We doubt that high or low gender identification has a significant bearing on women's same-gender workplace conflicts. There is no reason to suppose that high and low gender identifiers are likely to have *more* conflicts in dealing with one another than any other random groups of women.

Such high and low gender identification, however, has been shown to be significant in predicting how women will respond when they are aware that women as a group are being treated in a biased or discriminatory manner. Research has shown that women with low gender identification are likely to respond to discriminating situations by seeking to differentiate themselves from other women, while women with high gender identification are likely to respond by seeking to improve the situation for women in general.

A 2011 study of senior policewomen found that women with low gender identification were likely to respond to their organization's gender bias by characterizing themselves in decidedly agentic (masculine) terms, emphasizing their differences from other female officers, and downplaying or denying the presence of gender bias ("women and men receive equal career support"). Such senior officers were also likely to withhold career support from their female subordinates.[3] In other words, women with low gender identification are likely to respond to gender bias in highly self-protective ways.

Female police officers with high gender identification were found to respond to identical biased conditions in very different ways. They were likely to display concern for women generally rather than for their own personal situations. They were also likely to seek to increase women's opportunities for career advancement, develop networks of mutual support, and actively cooperate with other women in their efforts to move up.

The researchers concluded that their findings "suggest that work environments shape women's behavior by stimulating women with low gender identification to dissociate with other women and to display queen-bee responses as a way to achieve individual mobility."[4] Thus, the researchers conclude that queen-bee behavior—masculine self-descriptions, distancing from other women, and denial of gender bias—is "an outcome of gender discrimination in the workplace." Organizations with pervasive gender bias devalue women by threatening their personal identity.

> Women can cope with such threats by trying to improve the standing of their group...or by improving their individual careers....When women come to perceive their gender as a liability, this may induce them to advance their career through queen-bee behavior. Although queen-bee behavior may benefit individual women, because it leads women to distance themselves from other women, it also reduces the likelihood of improving opportunities for other women and increases the

tensions, conflicts, and incivilities between the queen bees and other women subordinates.[5]

This study strongly suggests that queen-bee behavior is a likely response of low-gender identifying women to gender discrimination, and eliminating such behaviors depends on "organizations...actively reducing experiences of gender bias and initiating steps to improve the position of women. Only when women at work no longer see their gender as a liability...will the queen-bee phenomenon become extinct."[6]

Career Aspiration

As the study of senior policewomen makes clear, the strength of an individual woman's gender identification can yield valuable information about her same-gender workplace dynamics. Other recent studies have shown that differences in a woman's career aspirations can be explained by looking at her identification with two distinct and largely independent variables: women and feminism.[7] What the researchers found was that the strength of a woman's identification as a woman generally reflects her attitudes toward what it means to be a woman in terms of characteristics, interests, and values. On the other hand, the strength of a woman's identification as a feminist generally reflects her attitudes toward what it means to be a woman in terms of the advantages and status of women in comparison to those of men.

These two dimensions of self-identification were found to be independent and largely nonoverlapping. Thus, women can have different combinations of high or low identification with women, and they can have high or low identification with feminism, resulting in four categories. Women can strongly identify (1) with neither women nor feminism, (2) with women but less so with feminism, (3) with both women and feminism, or (4) with feminism but less so with women.

Each of these four different ways in which women can think of themselves predicted their attitudes with respect to gender issues and career aspirations.

- Women who highly identify with women place a great deal of importance on the traits and characteristics considered to be gender-typical or that conform to gender stereotypes.
- Women who highly identify with feminism see higher levels of sexism in society, feel greater discontent with the current power distribution, are more involved in collective action, and express greater disapproval of the disadvantaged social position of women as a group.
- Women who identify strongly with women but not with feminism are likely to highly value traditional female gender roles and to disavow feminist concerns about the social position of women.[8] And if they have a low identification with feminism, they are likely to have low workplace aspirations.
- Women who highly identify with feminism, whether they strongly identify with women or not, are likely to be committed to improving women's social status.[9]
- Women who identify strongly with both women and feminism are likely to have high workplace aspirations. [10]

In other words, a woman's high identification with women does not motivate her to pursue greater women's empowerment *unless* she also has a high identification with feminism. Women who do not have a high identification with feminism or exposure to powerful counter-stereotypical women typically have internalized traditional gender stereotypes and developed a psychological barrier to aspiring to leadership.[11] Workplace conflicts are common between women aspiring to leadership positions (resisting gender stereotypes) and women not seeking such positions (having internalized gender stereotypes). Such aspirational differences are exacerbated by the ready acceptance and perpetuation of gender stereotypes in gendered workplaces. The important point, however, is that women on different sides of this aspirational divide are highly unlikely to see each other as potential sisters.

Gender Ideology

In chapter 2, we briefly mentioned that American women are more ideologically divided today than ever before. To understand the roots of this division and how it fosters women's same-gender conflicts, a brief recounting of the history of the modern women's movement, as well as more recent events, is useful.

Until 1977, there appeared to be a broad consensus at the national level about the need to secure women's rights (other than abortion rights), encourage an expansion of women's societal roles, and secure women's equal economic opportunities. Since the 1940s, both major US political parties had supported the Equal Rights Amendment (ERA) to the US Constitution. In 1971, the US House of Representatives passed the ERA by a vote of 354 to 24, and in 1972 the US Senate did the same by a vote of 84 to 8. Congressional support came from across the political spectrum, with strong support from liberals such as Ted Kennedy and conservatives such as Strom Thurmond. Indeed, Thurmond declared that the ERA "represents the just desire of many women...to be allowed a full and free participation in the American way of life, without hindrance, just because they are women."[12]

One Step Forward, Three Steps Back

In 1977, the National Women's Conference (NWC) was convened in Houston, with delegates from every state and territory.[13] Inside the convention center, delegates thought they were living in a halcyon time of near-universal support for assuring that women's legal, social, and economic status was equal to that of men's. This illusion of ideological consensus, however, was being shattered at precisely the same time as the NWC was proclaiming universal sisterhood. On the same weekend as the NWC, a pro-life, pro-family rally convened in Houston just a few miles away. The rally's purpose was to denounce the ERA, the need for expanded rights for women, and the very legitimacy of the NWC. On that weekend, Houston and the country witnessed the first public display of the profound division among American women over the gender values they held dear and the structure of the society they desired.

The legal and societal changes sought by the NWC were set out in a National Plan of Action, which included the following statement:

> We speak in varied accents and languages but we share the common language and experience of American women who throughout our Nation's life have been denied the opportunities, rights, privileges and responsibilities accorded to men . . . . Man-made barriers, laws, social customs and prejudices continue to keep a majority of women in an inferior position without full control of our lives and bodies . . . . Too often we find our individuality, our capabilities, our earning powers diminished by discriminatory practices and outmoded ideas of what a women is, what a woman can do, and what a woman must be . . . . We demand immediate and continuing action on our National Plan . . . so that by 1985, the end of the International Decade for Women proclaimed by the United Nations, everything possible under the law will have been done to provide American women with full equality. [14]

In direct contrast to the goals of the NWC, the rally did not seek to secure women's equality with men. The rally sought rather to reinforce women's caregiving and domestic roles and to sharply distinguish women's and men's appropriate societal occupations. Phyllis Schlafly, a conservative social and political activist, was the principal force behind the rally. She spoke for many previously silent women when she denounced the NWC as an effort to "drive the homemaker out of the home" and "forbid [women] to identify [with] their traditional roles as wives and mothers." At the rally, Schlafly declared that "American women do not want ERA, abortion, lesbian rights, and they do not want childcare in the hands of government."[15]

After 1977, strong bipartisan support for the ERA evaporated. Moderate Republican women who had been in the NWC's leadership were attacked by their own political party, and proclamations of universal sisterhood were silenced. As Tanya Melich, a Republican cofounder of the National Women's Political Caucus, later wrote, women at the NWC, like many people across the United States, had been living in a "cocoon,"[16] unaware of the fierce opposition to everything the NWC had hoped to accomplish.

Both sides of this ideological divide had strong, articulate leaders. On the antiabortion pro-homemaker side, Schlafly made clear, "We want a society in which the average man earns more than the average woman, so that his earning can fulfill his provider role in providing a home and support for his wife, who is nurturing and mothering their children." [17] On the ERA side, Gloria Steinem took precisely the opposite position, declaring, "We are talking about a society in which there will be no roles other than those chosen or earned. We are really talking about humanism."[18]

Since 1977, the political division over these different gender ideologies has only sharpened. In 1980, the Republican Party dropped its support of the ERA, and since then, its presidential platforms have consistently reflected an antiabortion and traditional-family agenda. The Democratic Party, in contrast, has continued to support the ERA and the NWC Plan's key recommendations.

Ideological Divisions in the Trump Era

The ideological divide over gender was on full display in the 2016 presidential campaign. Former secretary of state Hillary Clinton was a vigorous advocate for women's rights, access to family planning, and the availability of quality, affordable childcare.[19] Donald Trump, on the other hand, was openly opposed to these objectives,[20] and his misogynistic comments were widely reported.[21]

American women were deeply divided in their support for the

candidates. While 54 percent of all women voted for Clinton, only 45 percent of white women did.[22] Given Clinton's strong women's-rights stance and Trump's perceived hostility to women's issues (and women themselves), why didn't more white women vote for Clinton? Many explanations have been offered: the fact that white women have historically supported Republican presidential candidates; Clinton's involvement in Benghazi; her emails; her Wall Street speeches; her negative comments about Monica Lewinsky; her personality; women's dislike and distrust of powerful, successful women; and white women's strong alliance with white men (63 percent of whom voted for Trump). Undoubtedly, all of these explanations have some validity, but we believe at least one other factor played a major role in how women voted in 2016: strong differences in gender ideology.

Clinton's and Trump's positions on women's issues mirrored those of the NWC and the rally. It is hardly surprising, therefore, that Steinem vigorously advocated for Clinton, and Schlafly was an early Trump endorser.[23] Moreover, researchers have found that the message and vision about gender rights, roles, and relations that appeal to Democratic voters are precisely the opposite of the message and vision that appeal to Republican voters.[24]

This ideological divide among American women over women's appropriate rights, status, and responsibilities spills into the workplace, where it becomes a source of tension, controversy, and conflict. In our surveys and workshops, we often find that women experience open antagonism at work from women with a gender ideology different from their own. Here is an example.

Ann and Jane were colleagues doing a joint presentation on an important project when Ann happened to mention she had voted for Trump. Jane said that "of course" she had voted for Clinton and that she couldn't believe a senior executive like Ann could have possibly voted for Trump. Jane said, "Trump is a sexist who demeans

(Continued)

women." Ann replied, "Trump is upholding traditional American values and will keep the country safe." By the time they put on their joint presentation, their personal hostility was obvious to everyone attending. They have not worked together since.

Politics in the Workplace

Our personal observations about women's workplace antagonism because of differing gender ideologies have been confirmed by two polls surrounding the 2016 election. The American Psychological Association (APA) found that during the 2016 campaign, 27 percent of American workers felt they were negatively affected by political talk at work, including feelings of isolation from their colleagues, negative views of their coworkers, and an increase in workplace hostility. This APA survey found that 54 percent of workers avoided discussing politics with colleagues, and 20 percent avoided contact with some coworkers because of their political views.[25]

In a spring 2017 follow-up poll, the APA found that the negative effects of political discussions at work had increased. Workers felt more cynical and negative at work because of political talk, and 40 percent reported at least one negative outcome from workplace political conversations, including a more negative view of their coworkers and increased workplace hostility. In addition, 24 percent reported avoiding some coworkers because of their political views; 16 percent had a more negative view of their coworkers; and 17 percent said team cohesiveness had suffered. The percentage of women reporting negative effects from workplace political discussions increased from 9 percent before the election in 2016 to 20 percent in 2017.[26]

While the APA polls do not specifically identify the subject matter of toxic workplace political conversations, undoubtedly a principal topic is gender rights, roles, and responsibilities. In 2017, the Pew Research Center found that Democratic and Republican voters were sharply divided with respect to women's rights. Democrats tend to be closely aligned to the NWC plan, while Republicans tend to support the views expressed at the rally. Pew found that Democrats are more than twice as likely as Republicans to believe the United States hasn't gone far enough when it comes to giving women equal rights (69 percent versus 26 percent). While 18 percent of Republicans think the United States has gone too far in giving women equal rights, only 4 percent of Democrats agree. Digging deeper, Pew found that 58 percent of Democrats see recent changes in gender roles as allowing women to lead more satisfying lives, while only 26 percent of Republicans agree. Further, 48 percent of Democrats—as opposed to 32 percent of Republicans—believe these gender role changes have made it easier for parents to raise their children.[27]

More than 40 years after the NWC and the rally, Americans remain sharply divided on the question of whether women have full equality with men. Almost 70 percent of Democrats believe this has not been achieved, while only about 25 percent of Republicans think the same.

Women on opposite sides of the ideological divide over gender issues are unlikely to be interested in building a sisterhood with each other. Indeed, this ideological divide cuts to the very heart of the notion of sisterhood. With such a deep ideological division, hostility, suspicion, and dislike are more likely to be the order of the day than mutual respect and support.

Fortunately, there are ways to overcome or avoid these conflicts, and we provide some ideas and suggestions next.

MAKING THINGS BETTER

- Recognize that women you work with may have different ideological perspectives than yours. This is the first step in avoiding conflict with them, and this knowledge allows you to focus on career-related objectives and avoid political ones.
- Keep personal views about appropriate gender roles for women out of the workplace. Different ideological perspectives are not likely to have a direct effect on most workplace projects and should be separated from actually getting the job done.

- The highly masculine nature of gendered workplaces and the aspirational, ideological, and gender identification of women provide a useful model for understanding many same-gender workplace conflicts. But they do not provide a complete picture of all organizations, women, or workplace same-gender relationships. Many successful women *do* foster the development and advancement of other women; some organizations (though not as many as we wish) sincerely and effectively encourage women to join senior management; and many women work day in, day out with other women harmoniously and productively.

- Sisterhood needs to be built with other women who are prepared to join in displays of mutual support. When women are uninterested or hostile to this very effort, whether because of low gender identification, low career aspiration, or a fundamentally different gender ideology, treat these women with understanding and respect but move on. There are bound to be women who think like you do. Find them and move forward with them.

PART II

Gender in the Workplace

Chapter 4

Our Gendered Workplaces

FOR MOST OF THE LAST century, there was a sharp division of labor between women and men. Among urban married couples in middle and upper socioeconomic groups, men worked outside of the home, while women worked in the home tending to family and hearth. As recently as 1950, only 26 percent of married women worked outside of the home.[1] In the 1960s, however, women began entering the workforce in record numbers. By 2005, more than 60 percent of married women were in the workforce.[2] In 2016 almost 57 percent of *all* women 16 years of age and older were working—up from 33 percent in 1950.[3] With their increased workforce participation, women now make up almost 46 percent of the total US workforce[4] and 46 percent of the total workforce in the European Union.[5]

When women started moving into traditionally male career fields, it was expected, at least by prominent advocates for women's rights, that women would rise in their careers until they held senior leadership positions in numbers equal to men. Despite the enormous progress women made during this period, that did not happen.

While women have made truly impressive educational gains,[6] they still lag far behind men in virtually all major leadership roles. For example, women are only 17 percent of equity partners in major law firms, only 13 percent of law firm managing partners,[7] only 16 percent of medical school deans,[8] and only 18 percent of governors.[9] Women now hold

36 percent of firstlevel or midlevel manager positions in S&P 500 companies, but they are only 25 percent of executive and senior officials and managers, 9.5 percent of top earners, 18 percent of corporate board members, and 6 percent of S&P 500 CEOs.[10] Indeed, since 1972 only 62 women have led Fortune 500 companies.[11] This snapshot of women's leadership achievements is even bleaker than it might otherwise appear when we realize that almost all of their progress was made between 1960 and 1990.

"You've Come a Long Way, Baby" was perhaps the best-known advertising slogan in the 1970s and 1980s,[12] and it aptly characterized women's career progress during that period. But shortly after the slogan stopped running in 1990, women's advancement came to a screeching halt. The question is why.

Stalled Careers

Many explanations have been offered for women's failure during the past 30 years to increase their representation in the senior leadership ranks of business, the professions, academia, and government. Frequently offered reasons include: women prefer to be with their children than in the workplace; they don't ask (or don't want) to move up; and they lack the ambition, confidence, and core competencies needed for leadership success. But study after study proves these claims to be false. For example, a 2017 study by the Boston Consulting Group found, "On average, women entered the workforce with the same—or higher—levels of ambition as men, in terms of their desire to hold leadership positions or be promoted.... It is also unequivocal: having children does not affect women's desire to lead. The ambition levels of women with children and women without children track each other almost exactly over time."[13] As a 2011 report by Catalyst makes clear, even when women do everything they are told they need to do to get ahead, they still fail to advance as far and as fast as men.[14] In other words, women with high ambition, terrific abilities, a can-do attitude, and desired behavioral characteristics are still judged to have less leadership potential than their male counterparts. As Ilene H.

Lang, president and CEO of Catalyst, commented, "This study busts the myth that 'Women don't ask.' In fact, they do! But it doesn't get them very far. Men, by contrast, don't have to ask. What's wrong with this picture?"[15]

What's wrong is that (consciously or unconsciously) women are not being evaluated for purposes of advancement in fair, nondiscriminatory ways. There are several reasons for this, but all of them have their roots in the gendered nature of our workplaces—workplaces that are dominated by men and operated in accordance with masculine norms, values, and expectations.

In gendered workplaces, women's capabilities, accomplishments, and potential are depreciated in three distinct but mutually reinforcing ways: through affinity bias, gender bias, and sexual dominance. We briefly touched on affinity and gender biases in chapter 2, but they deserve more comprehensive consideration. Sexual dominance is not frequently mentioned as a cause of women's poor prospects for career advancement, but it needs to be given far greater attention than it has received to date.

Affinity Bias

People tend to be drawn to, want to associate with, and seek to provide support for people who are like them. In other words, people tend to favor other people with whom they have an affinity. This bias toward people who share our distinctive characteristics is ubiquitous and shapes many aspects of our lives, including our workplace teams, social circles, residence locations, occupational choices, and personal affiliations.

Within all gendered workplaces, affinity bias operates to divide participants into an ingroup and one or more outgroups. The ingroup consists of the members of the management team and those who are like them, which means the ingroup is often white, male, able-bodied, and heterosexual. Because women are a distinct outgroup in these organizations, they are often selected for career-enhancing assignments only after their male counterparts have been considered, asked to join important teams far less frequently than men, and excluded from the men's informal networks and social activities.

Excluding women from men's informal networks has more far-reaching negative consequences than is often realized. Without access to such networks, women miss out on a process that author Sue Madsen notes "is foundational for successful long-term leadership,"[16] depriving them of opportunities to obtain the mentors[17] and influential sponsors available to men.[18]

Affinity bias does not mean that male managers *consciously* think that women cannot do particular jobs, are not as competent as men, or lack men's leadership potential. Affinity bias does not depend on evil intent. It operates simply by virtue of the fact that most men prefer to work with, hang out with, coach, mentor, and sponsor other men. They find doing so with men to be easy, conflict free, and efficient. As a result, without even being aware of their favoritism, male managers often simply don't invite women to join teams, work on high-visibility projects, or participate in informal social activities. Moreover, as members of a conspicuous outgroup, women are not as likely as men to be listened to in meetings, have their views solicited on important issues, or be given credit for their accomplishments. Here is an example.

Abby, a senior marketing executive, told us that even though she has made it on to her organization's senior leadership team, her views are often ignored at meetings where important management decisions are being made. As the only woman in most strategy meetings, Abby often finds it difficult to be taken seriously. She recently went to the president of her company, who leads many of these meetings, and told him of her concerns. They had a wide-ranging conversation, and Abby thinks he was shocked by what she had to say. At any rate, since then, she believes he has become a much more effective meeting leader. He will call on her, try to stop others from interrupting her, and make sure her ideas are given proper attention. She told us that she sees some real progress when the president is running the meetings—but often not otherwise. So, she is working hard to speak up and persist.

Affinity bias also leads to an expectation that the career paths of future leaders will conform to the career paths of the current (frequently male) leaders.[19] Thus, gendered workplaces typically reward workers who are "willing to put work above all other considerations"[20] and who have had continuous, linear careers. Again, not surprisingly, senior (frequently male) managers prefer to work with people who are pursuing careers in the same ways that they did. As a result, career paths that are typical for men, but not for women, are likely to be rewarded.[21]

Gender Bias

As we will discuss more fully in chapter 5, people frequently ascribe characteristics to men, women, leaders, home, and family on the basis of common (generally unconscious) stereotypes. Thus, women are assumed to be—and thought they should be—communal: pleasant, caring, and modest; and men are assumed to be—and thought they should be—agentic: decisive, competitive, and forceful. And, of course, common stereotypes suggest that leaders are decisive, competitive, and forceful. Therefore, common, pervasive societal stereotypes operate to identify men as natural leaders and women as their assistants and helpmates.

Unfortunately, people frequently think in these stereotypical terms, so that the fairness of their evaluation processes is often undermined. If senior managers (unconsciously) think men are better than women at difficult or challenging projects, prolonged negotiations, or key profit and loss responsibilities, then women will not be given the career-advancing opportunities that men receive. Moreover, women will be judged more critically, held to higher standards, and paid less for similar work than comparably situated men.

Gender bias is likely to be particularly strong in gendered workplaces where it works in tandem with affinity bias to deliver a one-two punch to women's career advancement prospects. Women are seen both as different from members of the ingroup and as less competent, ambitious, and competitive than ingroup members.

Gendered Workplaces Create a Double Bind

Societal stereotypes create a variety of double binds—lose/lose choices—for women in their pursuit of career success. Being seen as too soft or too hard—the Goldilocks Dilemma was discussed at length in our book *Breaking Through Bias*—being an "angry black woman" or a "mammy" (see chapter 7), and being a "Dragon Lady" or a "Lotus Flower/China Doll" (see chapter 6) are only a few of these double binds.

In gendered workplaces, women's desire for sisterhood and individual career success creates another such double bind, what we call the "Sisterhood or Career Success Dilemma." If women actively work for gender equality, they will undoubtedly bond with other women and may even achieve a measure of success in reducing discriminatory workplace practices. By doing so, however, as we saw in chapter 2, their competence and performance ratings are likely to suffer, reducing their chances for individual career advancement. On the other hand, if women attempt to maximize their chances for career advancement by conforming their behavior, management style, and relationship patterns to the male norms of their organization, they are likely to be seen by other women as selfish, cold, and unlikable. This double bind is often particularly painful because most women sincerely want both to help other women advance and advance themselves (chapter 2).

The Sisterhood or Career Success Dilemma exists because gendered workplaces—which is where most high-status, highly compensated career opportunities are found—are structured, managed, and promoted so as to remain gendered workplaces. Too many women in senior leadership threatens men's dominant workplace status.[22] The practices, procedures, values, and expectations in gendered workplaces, therefore, operate (whether or not unconsciously) to limit women's ability to reach the senior leadership ranks.[23] Thus, in gendered workplaces, although women may want to help and advocate for other women, the only apparent path to career success steers them sharply away from doing so.

In gendered workplaces, women often treat other women with a lack of civility not because of some inherent same-gender hostility, but because they find themselves on different horns of the Sisterhood or Career Success Dilemma. Women working to advance the goals of sisterhood can be viewed by other women as "losers" who are looking for special treatment, while women who choose single-minded pursuit of their careers are seen by other women as selfish, cold, and unlikable. There is no shortage of suspicion and wariness on both sides.

Of course, same-gender incivility is not inevitable even in strongly gendered workplaces. *Breaking Through Bias* is our effort to provide ambitious women with the tools and techniques to advance in gendered workplaces with their positive same-gender relationships intact. But there is no denying that gendered workplaces create powerful dynamics that frequently force women into conflicts with other women. If those conflicts are to be avoided, everyone—women, men, and the organizations themselves—must recognize that the problem is the nature of the workplaces, not the nature of the women working in them.

Sexual Dominance

Power in an organization can be defined as the ability to affect performance, function, or workplace characteristics. Obviously, hierarchical status and formal position and authority are the primary sources of workplace power. But unwelcome and inappropriate language and conduct with a decidedly sexual edge are also sources of such power.

Because of the #MeToo movement, the great bulk of public attention has been directed toward sexual harassment and assault. Such behaviors are a much larger societal issue than many employers make them out to be.[24] Very often, however, offensive sexually related conduct does not rise to the level of actionable harassment even though it can still have highly negative consequences for women's work performance, professional advancement, and mental health. For example, locker room talk, dirty jokes, sexualized comments, obvious assessment of women's physical appearance, excessive attention, and unwelcome casual touching or contact are all instances of men asserting their power over women. Indeed, the US Equal Employment Opportunity Commission (EEOC) found that almost 60 percent of working women had experienced unwelcome sexual attention; sexual coercion; or sexist, crude, or sexually offensive behavior[25]—the most common behavior was sexually hostile behaviors designed to insult or put women down rather than to pull them into a sexual relationship.[26] And, whether women labeled their unwelcome sexually related experiences as harassment or not, they experienced similar negative psychological, professional, and health consequences.[27]

Not surprisingly, the EEOC found that inappropriate sexual conduct of all sorts is more likely to occur where there is a lack of gender diversity.[28] Other risk factors for such behavior identified by the EEOC include women's nonconformity with workplace norms (such as women challenging their organization's gender expectations by being highly agentic), the presence of high-value employees (typically men who are viewed as too valuable to lose), and significant power disparities between the male ingroup and the female outgroup.

Beyond these risk factors, as we argue in an article in the *Harvard Business Review*, sexual harassment—whether legally actionable or not—is one kind of conduct on a continuum of interconnected inappropriate behaviors stretching from gender bias to incivility to unwelcome sexual language or behavior to harassment to assault.[29] In other words, when women experience disparities in their career opportunities, incivility from their colleagues or supervisors, or unwelcome sexual language or conduct, it is far more likely that they will also experience actionable sexual harassment.

As the EEOC also found, inappropriate or unwelcome sexual behaviors are far more likely to be used by men to silence, intimidate, and frighten women than to entice them into sexual relationships. For example, in a 1991 *New York Times* article, "Sexual Harassment: It's about Power, Not Lust," Daniel Goleman recounted the following story:

> Consider the case of a male supervisor who, in the midst of a conversation with a female employee about an assignment, asked her out of the blue, "Are you wearing panties?" and then blithely

continued the conversation seemingly pleased that he had left her rattled.

Goleman went on to quote psychologist Lonna Fitzgerald, who told him,

Professional men don't go around putting used condoms in your desk, as can happen in a blue-collar setting. It's more likely to be something like what happened to a woman lawyer I know at a large international firm. As she was sitting at a conference table with other executives, all men, she said, "I have two points," and one of the men interrupted, "Yes you do, and they look wonderful." She felt humiliated that the men were laughing at her as a way to avoid taking her seriously.[30]

It may well be that such blatant sexist comments are less likely to be made in workplaces today than they were in 1991, but the apparent blasé acceptance by a substantial portion of the US population of President's Trump's outrageous sexist comments—Arianna Huffington is "angry," Hillary Clinton couldn't "satisfy" her husband, Megyn Kelly is a "bimbo" whose blood "you could see...coming out of her wherever," a former Miss Universe is "Miss Piggy," and saying he frequently grabbed women "by the pussy"—suggests that there has not been much progress in this regard over the past almost 40 years. Moreover, the EEOC reports that workplace sexual harassment is on the increase, not the decrease.[31]

Whatever the form of the inappropriate sexual behavior, it is less about sex than it is about keeping women in their place, devaluing their role in the workplace, and making them vulnerable. Thus, the more masculine the values and traditions of the workplace, the more likely it will be that women will experience such behavior. For example, women surgeons and investment bankers rank among those most likely to suffer sexual harassment.[32]

Inappropriate sexual behavior mixed with affinity bias and gender bias very often creates a highly toxic cocktail for women in gendered workplaces.

Women's Responses

Gendered workplaces can be frustrating, confidence breaking, and ambition killing for many women. As we saw earlier, this is a large part of the reason for women's stalled progress into senior leadership ranks. Women in such workplaces have four basic choices: leave, accept second-class status, try to get ahead by becoming one of the boys, or pursue advancement by attempting to overcome or avoid bias and harassment on their own or by building sisterhood and seeking systemic changes. This section explores each of these options more closely.

Leaving

Because of their exclusion from important networking opportunities, frequent lack of recognition, overly critical evaluations, disparities in compensation, and concern about harassment, women leave their careers earlier and in far greater numbers than men.[33] Representative of available information about this greater attrition of women from promising careers, a 2017 report by *Forbes* found that women leave the tech field at a rate that is 45 percent higher than men.[34]

There is a widely accepted view that women leave the workplace because they would rather do other things—raise children, have more time for themselves, provide community service—than continue to pursue demanding careers. Perhaps the best-known expression of this view is the 2003 article "The Opt-Out Revolution," which appeared in the *New York Times Magazine*.[35] After recounting familiar statistics about women's low representation in the leadership of traditionally male career fields, the author, Lisa Belkin, writes, "Measured against the way things once were [in the 1960s], this is certainly progress. But measured against the way things were expected to be, this is a revolution stalled." In her view, many highly educated and talented women are opting out of their careers because they are rejecting the workplace, choosing home over potentially promising careers. But is this actually true?

We know that there has been no recent uptick in the rate at which women leave the workplace. Indeed, the percentage of women opting out has actually changed "surprisingly little over the past 30 years."[36] But even though we are not in the middle of an opt-out revolution, why do women leave their careers in far greater numbers than men?

We know that women enter the workforce with optimism and ambition. Women's desire to achieve personal career success is made clear by PricewaterhouseCoopers' 2018 survey of 3,627 professional women ages 28 to 40 from around the world. This survey concluded that women today are more confident and ambitious than ever before.[37]

- 82 percent of women are confident in their ability to fulfill their career aspirations;
- 77 percent are confident of their ability to lead;
- 73 percent are actively seeking career advancement opportunities; and
- 75 percent reported it was important to them to reach the top of their chosen careers.

But women's confidence and ambition change in gendered workplaces. A survey by a global management consulting firm, Bain & Company, found that during the first two years of their careers, more women than men aspire to senior leadership positions (43 percent versus 34 percent), and women's and men's confidence that they can reach senior leadership is about the same (27 percent versus 28 percent). But things change dramatically after two years. Women's aspirations for top management positions drop 60 percent (to 16 percent), and their confidence in their ability to reach top management drops 51 percent (to 13 percent). By contrast, men's ambition remains the same, and their confidence in reaching top management drops by only 11 percent (to 25 percent).[38]

This sharp decrease in women's ambition and confidence is in large part the result of women's experiences of their gendered workplaces as hostile, unfair, and arbitrary. As one recent study found, the greatest contributors to women's waning ambition are the lack of opportunity for advancement, lack of support from managers, and a scarcity of female role models.[39] Women leave the workforce for the same reason that their ambition wanes: they just don't see a promising, satisfying career ahead of them. Here is Gwen's story.

Gwen told us the following about her experiences in a national engineering firm. "For what seemed like my whole life, I wanted to be an engineer like my dad. When I started my first job, it was as if I had a contagious disease. No one talked with me. The new male engineers got all of the interesting projects, and I got the after-thought projects. I would ask to be put on important projects but was always told, 'Next time.' But nothing ever came my way. After about four years I moved to another engineering firm, and found my skills were not where they should have been for a fourth-year engineer. I could never catch up and I finally left engineering."

A study by the Harvard Business School of its graduates found that the majority of its women MBAs who had left their jobs—that is, who opted out—did so only as a last resort after finding themselves stuck in unfulfilling roles with few opportunities for career advancement. In fact, the researchers found that very few of HBS's women graduates left the workplace solely to take care of their families.[40] As one of the women Belkin profiled in her *New York Times Magazine* article commented, "Among women I know quitting is driven as much from the job-dissatisfaction side as from the pull-to-motherhood side."

Accepting Second-Class Status

Many women who might otherwise leave their careers in gendered work-places choose instead to accept second-class status and to "grin and bear it." Women make this choice for a variety of reasons, including econom-ics, security, insurance coverage, retirement benefits, and the lack of alternative work opportunities. Whatever their reasons, women who do stay in unsatisfying job situations will identify with Bethany, a friend of ours whom we introduced in *Breaking Through Bias*. Bethany, an ambitious and talented corporate attorney, sent the following email to us:

In all of the major corporations where I have worked, younger, not as talented men have been promoted over me. Men in power pick younger men who remind them of themselves. It takes a special man to recognize that diversity of thinking in business and the C-suite is beneficial. But men who would like to help women are often afraid that doing so will make them look weak. It is easier for them to just keep finding "mini-me's" to promote so they don't have to deal with the fallout from their male colleagues.

My current boss recently told me he was considering promoting a new hotshot male lawyer, two years out of law school with no law license (he has never taken the bar exam) to be assistant general counsel because he has "the right characteristics." I expressed my concern that this young man was not nearly ready and didn't have the experience (or law license) for such a position. My boss got very angry and said to me, "I have every confidence in my ability to pick the right people to hire and promote." And of course, he had the power to do whatever he wants.

I could go on for hours, days, weeks, and years. I am just angry, bitter, and disappointed. Despite how frequently I tell myself "just do your time in Folsom Prison," I can't shut off my ambition and strong desire to succeed. But, when success doesn't come, I just get more angry and bitter. As I have gotten older, I have gotten better at just "doing my time," but when I do this, I feel I am letting down the other professional women in the organization. I just don't seem to be able to win.[41]

Bethany's story is hardly unique. A recent poll of more than 5,000 employees from a variety of organizations in many different business areas found that only 27 percent of senior level women are satisfied with their access to opportunities and resources.[42] Thus, while workplace unfairness causes many women to leave their careers, many others, like Bethany, resign themselves to "doing their time in Folsom Prison."

Becoming One of the Boys

In gendered workplaces, the processes and procedures used to evaluate talent, potential, and accomplishment are likely to be based on stereotypically masculine (agentic) characteristics: assertiveness, competitiveness, decisiveness, and nonemotional rationality. In other words, career advancement is often highly dependent on the extent to which a person meets expectations of behaving in highly masculine ways. It is entirely rational, therefore, for some women in such organizations to seek to get ahead by downplaying their femininity and emphasizing a masculine leadership style.[43] In other words, these women see career advancement as dependent on their being more like the senior men whose ranks they want to join than like the women they want to supervise.[44] Joining the men's ingroup, however, depends on women doing more than adopting agentic leadership styles. Women choosing this route for career advancement also need to become one of the boys: developing or feigning an interest in all things sports, joining men's social and networking activities, avoiding association with women's groups or initiatives, and making it known they are different from other women.

The techniques women use to project a masculine, agentic leadership style are nicely captured by Ridhi Tariyal, CEO of a Silicon Valley start-up.

I have strategically deployed a variety of traditional masculine tropes to convey I am competitive, competent and intent on empire building.... Women like me exist in professional and personal ecosystems that devalue not only femaleness, but also any perceived "otherness".... There are a few seats made available to women at tables of power and influence. We morph, mask and transform so we are perceived as belonging in them.[45]

By seeking to conform to the cultural norms of their gendered workplaces, ambitious women are simply following a well-documented pattern of outgroup members attempting to gain admission to ingroups.[46] Conforming to their organizations' dominant masculine norms, values, and expectations may not be sufficient to get women into the ingroup, but women often see it as a necessary first step.

Once women achieve a degree of leadership responsibility, they often feel even more intense pressure to maintain, promote, and conform to the dominant masculine culture. Because of their conspicuous minority status, women often feel under constant scrutiny as to their behavior, appearance, associations, management style, and work routine. They often feel a need to play a part to assure the men that they value the same things the men do.

> Brian, a senior manager in a major accounting firm, told us about the time the one female partner in his practice group went into labor to deliver her third child. She was applauded by the rest of her partners (all male) because she remained on a conference call to restructure a client's business transaction until minutes before her child was actually born.

The few women leaders in gendered workplaces seldom feel sufficiently accepted by the dominant culture to allow them to let down their guard. Here is another story.

> Charlotte, a good friend of ours, is an executive vice president at a major manufacturer. We often compare notes with her on gender issues. In a recent conversation, Al asked Charlotte whether she felt as if she was fully accepted by the rest of her senior management team, all but one of whom are men. Charlotte laughed and quickly said, "Are you kidding? In half of the meetings I attend, I am the
>
> *(Continued)*

only woman, and everyone is just waiting for me to say something stupid or that I cannot support with data. I am constantly asked to justify my recommendations—even though the men are not—and junior men have no compunction in challenging me. When there is another woman in a meeting or on a team, the men seem skeptical if I encourage or support her ideas. I am sure they assume that when I do so it is just an instance of girls supporting girls. I keep trying to build my male peers' trust, but it is a very, very slow and painful process."

A Fourth Way

We recognize that we have been painting a pretty grim picture of women's situations in most of our country's major organizations. However, the statistics on women's lack of progress in breaking into senior leadership in numbers commensurate with their educational attainment and initial career ambition confirm this picture. Fortunately, opting out, accepting second-class citizenship, and becoming one of the boys are not the only options available to talented, ambitious women. It is, indeed, possible for women to take control of their own careers and work with others to seek changes to the discriminatory patterns of gendered workplaces.

We know a lot of highly successful women in gendered workplaces who actively support other women and want nothing to do with a boys' club. These women have all had to overcome the discriminatory effects of affinity and gender bias. We wrote *Breaking Through Bias*[47] in large part because of those women and because of our desire to help other women replicate their success. A central theme of that book is the importance for women to learn to manage the impressions other people have of them to avoid or overcome gender bias. And the principal techniques for doing this involve women using *both* communal and agentic behavioral characteristics in different amounts, depending on the objectives they want to accomplish and the context and nature of the situations they are in.

In one study, for example, researchers tracked 132 female and male

MBA graduates over an eight-year period.[48] Women who were comfortable using both agentic and communal communication techniques received 1.5 times as many promotions as agentic men; 1.5 times as many promotions as communal women; twice as many promotions as communal men; and three times as many promotions as agentic women.[49]

Women can use impression management techniques—which we define as conscious efforts people make to shape or change others' impressions of them—to advance in their individual careers. They can also join together with other like-minded women and men to take collective action to seek structural changes to gendered workplaces. We've discussed some of the ways women can go about such collective action in chapter 2. Women can pursue collective action simultaneously with their efforts to achieve individual career advancement.

We are firm believers that women in gendered workplaces do, in fact, have a fourth way available to them in their quest for career success. It must be recognized, however, that such workplaces place enormous pressure on women to leave, accept second-class citizenship, or attempt to join the boys' club. To avoid the undesirable consequences of such pressure, women, as we discuss in *Breaking Through Bias*,[50] need grit, a positive perspective, a coping sense of humor, and a confident self-image. Gendered workplaces are often difficult to navigate even for very talented, ambitious, and hardworking women. While women can deal with the career-destroying pressures created by gendered workplaces and avoid their hurtful consequences, this is possible only if they are aware of the causes and nature of these pressures. Once women have this understanding, we believe career success is possible even in gendered workplaces.

In addition to what we say in chapters 10 and 11, we discuss some steps to make things better here.

MAKING THINGS BETTER

- Stalled careers are often the result of gender bias and sexual domination in gendered workplaces. Understanding the dynamics of these situations can allow you to communicate in ways to over-come or avoid their discriminatory consequences.

- We identified four basic choices for women who find their gen-dered workplace frustrating, demeaning, confidence breaking, and ambition killing: leaving, accepting second-class status, becoming one of the boys, or individually or collectively over-coming biases and harassment. All workplaces have unique characteristics. Because of those characteristics, other responses may be entirely possible. For example, your organization might implement unique training programs or leadership development programs, senior male leaders might be encouraged to under-take unique projects that are precisely tailored to your talents and interests. The point we're making is that you need to carefully assess your workplace before deciding how best to proceed.

- Every woman has her own reasons for deciding to stay in her organization or to seek a new position. In considering your deci-sion, make a detailed list of all of the reasons to stay and all of the reasons to leave. Just seeing the pros and cons in writing can become an important first step in your analysis. You can revisit and fine-tune your list as you consider your next steps.

- If you consider stepping away from your career for any period of time, keep in mind there are often unintended consequences. In particular, career reentry can be very difficult.

- Sometimes women find that things can change for the better. Ear-lier in this chapter we mentioned Bethany, our friend who was constantly overlooked by her male boss who promoted younger talented men instead of her. Bethany's example showed some of what happens when a woman resigns herself to a workplace of frustration, anger, and disappointment. In the time since Beth-any originally sent us that email, her company has undergone a management restructuring. Bethany's boss was replaced by a tal-ented woman general counsel who appreciates talent and is not concerned about surrounding herself with people who qualify as "mini me's." Here is a recent email from Bethany:

I got a great review now that my former boss was demoted and is now my peer! I got a bonus for handling an important trial in another state, and it was the highest amount the CEO can sign off on without going to our parent company. I also got the highest ranking of "outperforming." Life is good in my career for a change. I am trying to bask in it.

- In gendered workplaces, because of the Goldilocks Dilemma—women tend to be seen as too hard or too soft but rarely just right—women need to present themselves as competent and forceful while packaging those qualities in a style that is pleasant, shows a concern for others, and is respectful of others' ideas. Women can dial up (or down) their communal or agentic behaviors to overcome or avoid gender bias. The mix of these characteristics varies, depending on the nature and context of the situation—more decisive, aggressive behavior in times of crisis or great challenge; more inclusive, listening behavior when brainstorming or planning. Joining the boys' club is not the only way to advance in gendered workplaces.

- Women in positions of power can help other women advance, support their successes, mentor them, sponsor them, and push for organizational change.

- Organizations need to increase the number of women in the pipeline, in its middle levels, and at the top. Women need to see that there is a future for their careers. A key step toward doing this is for organizations to take bias out of career decisions—hiring, assignments, promotions, and leadership positions. We discuss this in chapter 10. In addition, both women and men need to be rewarded for their diversity and inclusion success.

- Senior leaders—both women and men—should be encouraged and rewarded for mentoring and sponsoring women working their way up. They have the responsibility to work toward increasing the percentage of women in senior leadership positions.

- If you experience inappropriate sexual language or conduct at work, recognize that it is often about power, not sex. In most situations, inappropriate language should be challenged immediately. A response back that you can't take a joke, or any other "gaslighting comment" should be immediately refuted. If you say something like, "I love good jokes BUT that was not a joke. I expect you won't do that again," you might be able to put a stop to such inappropriate comments. For inappropriate sexual conduct or actionable sexual harassment, you should follow company procedures and EEOC guidelines.
- If you're having trouble advancing in a gendered workplace, we recommend reading *Breaking Through Bias*[51] as the first step in developing your plan of action for moving forward.

Chapter 5

Stereotype Straitjackets

STEREOTYPES ARE EMPIRICALLY UNSUPPORTED GENERALIZATIONS about the characteristics of members of a particular, distinctive group of people. They foster attitudes and behaviors that are generally unjustified and biased. The bulk of scholarly attention and the focus of our book *Breaking Through Bias* is on how stereotypes negatively influence career-affecting decisions and how these discriminatory consequences can be avoided. But stereotypes also function as prescriptive and proscriptive norms governing the behaviors that are appropriate and inappropriate for members of the stereotyped group. Thus, for example, gender stereotypes prescribe how women and men *should* behave—women in feminine ways, men in masculine ways—and proscribe how women and men *should not* behave—women in masculine ways, men in feminine ways. Of course, such prescriptive and proscriptive stereotypes are not legitimate standards of appropriate behavior, but ideological blinders that unjustifiably limit the range of praiseworthy conduct engaged in by members of the stereotyped group. As a consequence, such prescriptive and proscriptive norms put people into what we call stereotype straitjackets.

Gender Norms

People generally think women *should be* communal—that is, unselfish, friendly, modest, deferential, empathetic, cooperative, and concerned with others. By contrast, people generally think men *should be* agentic—that is, independent, assertive, forceful, unemotional, decisive, competitive, and risk-taking. Because communal and agentic characteristics are often (incorrectly) believed to be nonoverlapping, contrasting qualities, people generally think women *should not* be agentic and men *should not* be communal. The behavioral norms laid down by gender stereotypes are enforced through people's (including members of the stereotyped group) praise and reward of prescribed behaviors and through criticism and punishment of proscribed behaviors.

Violation of Behavioral Norms

The way in which gender norms are enforced and resisted is a major source of women's same-gender conflicts. Some women want these gender norms upheld, and they disapprove of women who violate them. Other women believe these norms are outdated limitations on their career opportunities and resist conforming to them. Women on different sides of this divide over the legitimacy of appropriate gender behavior can easily find themselves in conflict with one another, which is often manifested through incivility.

Incivility can be experienced in a variety of ways: being ignored or excluded, treated rudely or disrespectfully, criticized brusquely or dealt with sarcastically, or interrupted or talked over. Incivility is a relatively mild form of "counterproductive workplace behavior."[1] More severe forms of such behavior include interpersonal aggression, bullying, and deliberate social and professional undermining. These more severe hostile behaviors are typically engaged in with the unambiguous intent to harm another person. Workplace incivility, by contrast, is not necessarily designed to harm someone else so much as it is to express disapproval, displeasure, or distaste at another person's conduct, appearance, or intentions.

It might be thought that in gendered workplaces, women would face more incivility from men than from women. This view could be based on an assumption that men resent women for encroaching on their turf, threatening to undermine their masculine culture, or it might be based on an assumption that men do not believe women are able to pull their own weight.

It turns out, however, that in gendered workplaces, women report significantly more incivility from other women than they do from men.[2] Such female-instigated incivility against other women is most often the direct result of efforts to enforce or resist conformity with gender behavioral norms.[3]

Agentic Women

As we noted in chapter 4, women often believe that their career success in gendered workplaces depends on conforming to their organizations' dominant masculine culture. Because senior male leaders are, by and large, agentic, women believe they also need to be agentic to succeed. The problem is that when women behave agentically—forcefully expressing their opinions, taking charge, giving orders, and making assignments— they violate prescribed gender norms and thus they become targets for other women's incivility.[4]

Studies show that employees who behave in disruptive or provocative ways are much more likely to be subjected to incivility than employees who don't rock the boat.[5] Agentic women are often seen by other women as disruptive and provocative, casting agentic women in an unfavorable light by behaving in a conspicuously norm-violating and unflattering manner. In an effort to display their displeasure, women who (consciously or unconsciously) believe women should conform to the prescriptive gender norms will often react by distancing themselves from agentic women.[6] This phenomenon, often called the "black sheep effect,"[7] allows women to both express their displeasure at the black sheep and make it clear that they are not like those women who violate stereotypical gender norms.

While both women and men generally endorse conformity with prescriptive gender stereotypes, women are more likely than men to see other agentic women as a threat to their social identity. As a result, women resist and derogate agentic women far more than do men.[8] In other words, agentic women are seen as black sheep because they fail to conform to the behavioral norms that dictate what they should be like as women.[9]

Women Managers

Women are particularly likely to impose stereotype straitjackets on their women managers. In a recent study of women's expectations of their managers, women initially reported that they expected the same things from their female and male managers: mutual respect, honesty, approachability, willingness to listen, sufficient trust to allow them initiative, and consistency. When the researchers probed deeper, however, they found that women have quite different expectations. Women expect their female managers, in comparison to their male managers, to display a higher degree of emotional understanding of and support for them. They also expect their female managers to see them as equals, take a holistic view of them as people, understand the complexities of their lives, and provide them with the flexibility to accommodate those complexities.[10] In other words, women expect female managers to conform to prescriptive gender stereotypes by being "more understanding, more nurturing, more giving and more forgiving than men."[11] As one study participant stated, "You expect women to understand you more, and to be wired psychologically more similar, therefore you expect more empathy and compassion."[12]

The rub is that women managers in gendered workplaces are unlikely to want to be seen by *their* managers as treating female subordinates less critically than they do male subordinates, or any differently from the way male managers treat their subordinates. Thus, wholly apart from whether female managers actually exhibit strongly agentic behavior, they are likely to fail to meet the stereotypical expectations of female subordinates.

Meg told us she would often ask her boss, Sue, for extra time to complete projects and to "cut her some slack" because of her family responsibilities. Meg was hurt when Sue recently told her, "Enough is enough." Sue pointed out that Meg never asked the men she worked for to give her special treatment, and Sue reminded Meg that all of the accommodations Meg asked for fell on Sue's shoulders and disrupted Sue's projects. Meg realized Sue was right. She would never have dreamed of asking her male supervisors to understand her scheduling issues and cut her the same slack. She realized she had expected Sue to be a different kind of boss just because she was a woman. Meg came to see her expectations of Sue as unfair and inappropriate.

Many women never realize that they hold their women managers to different, often higher standards than their men managers. Instead, they view women managers who act just like men as cold, selfish, and unlikable—prime targets for incivility.

Hierarchical Relationships

In their book *In the Company of Women*, Pat Heim and Susan Murphy argue that positive relationships between women depend on both women perceiving that the distribution of self-esteem and power between them is equal. They refer to this as the "power dead-even rule." While we seriously doubt that their power dead-even rule is, as they claim, the "hitherto invisible natural law" controlling women's same-gender relationships,[13] there is no denying that a key aspect of women's prescribed behavioral norms is to be empathetic to and supportive of others—particularly other women.[14]

Conformity with such behavioral norms can be difficult if there is a wide divergence in women's respective status and power. When women are unable to see their same-gender workplace relationships in terms of mutuality, let alone equality of power and status, they can become resentful, hostile, and critical. This can be particularly true when women are promoted over other women with whom they previously enjoyed an essentially egalitarian relationship. Because their relationship is no longer marked by interdependence and mutuality,[15] newly promoted women managers often find it difficult to meet their former female colleagues' expectation that their personal relationships will continue unchanged. When such relationships don't remain the same, the female subordinate will often resort to incivility to convey her displeasure with their changed relationship.

Of course, women's relationships with their male managers are most certainly not marked by an equal distribution of power or status. These relationships, however, are seldom problematic for women in the same ways that their relationships with their female managers can be. Women simply do not expect power to be "dead-even" in their relationships with men. The fact that women's expectations for how their women managers *should* relate to them are often disappointed is one of the principal reasons women so often report they would rather work for a man than a woman.[16] It also helps explain why women managers grow more disliked the higher they climb the leadership ladder while men become more liked as they grow more powerful.[17]

Successful Women

As we discussed earlier, when women violate prescriptive gender norms by behaving agentically, they are "sanctioned and disliked."[18] Surprisingly, however, researchers have found that in gendered workplaces, women who are highly successful can experience these same interpersonal penalties even if they do not behave agentically.[19] For example, in one study, women were given information about a woman who had been highly successful as a manager in a traditionally male field. Nothing in the information suggested that she behaved agentically in any way. Yet, when female participants were asked to evaluate the woman manager, they *inferred* that she was agentic and lacked communal qualities.[20]

Without any confirming information, women characterized the female manager as selfish, insensitive, cold, and manipulative.[21]

Why would women assume that an unambiguously successful woman in a traditionally male job is interpersonally unpleasant and disagreeable? Indeed, why would women disparage a successful woman rather than take pride in their shared gender? Here is an example.

When Andie joined a large law firm as a partner, she hired an assistant from outside the firm. During Jill's orientation, she came into Andie's office clearly upset. Jill told Andie that when she had introduced herself to the training coordinator, the trainer responded, "Oh, so you're working for the Dragon Lady." Andie had never met the coordinator and did not—to her knowledge—behave like a Dragon Lady. It quickly became apparent that in the trainer's mind because Andie was a partner and a woman, the coordinator assumed she must be nasty and difficult to work with.

In a series of studies designed to answer why women assume highly successful women are unpleasant, researchers found that women often view career success in traditionally male roles as very difficult to achieve. Thus, when a woman has succeeded in such a role, other women are forced to assess themselves in terms of *her* achievement, and when they do, they often come up short. In other words, a woman who is successful in a traditionally male career field sets such a high bar for other aspiring women that being forced to compare themselves with her can be ego bruising.[22]

Given the often painful nature of this same-gender comparison process, researchers found that characterizing a highly successful woman as interpersonally hostile and unlikable allows other women to "reduce the ego-deflating consequences of an upward social comparison."[23] Thus, to avoid the possibility of a negative self-evaluation, women will often seek to characterize a successful woman as sufficiently dissimilar from them—"she is an unlikable bitch; we are nice people"—so that she can be excluded from interpersonal comparisons. When a successful woman is regarded as violating prescriptive gender behavioral norms, she becomes irrelevant to the comparison process that underlies other women's self-evaluations.

Women and Meritocracy

Gendered workplaces continually pat themselves on their backs for being meritocracies.[24] A true meritocracy would be a workplace in which everyone was evaluated and rewarded without regard to their gender, race, ethnicity, or other social identity in a transparent, just, and fair manner. It would be a workplace in which opportunities, status, power, position, and compensation were based on merit, not favoritism, friendship, family, or any other tie to or identification with existing leaders. And a meritocracy would be a workplace in which quality, quantity, and consistency of work rather than familiarity, affiliation, or cultural identity determined recognition and economic reward. If anyone believes they are pursuing a career in a workplace that is a true meritocracy, we have a bridge we would like to sell them. Nevertheless, gendered workplaces loudly proclaim that they are, in fact, meritocracies, and they proudly point to the (few) women in their managerial ranks as "evidence that sex discrimination is no longer an obstacle to women's success in the workplace."[25]

When companies proclaim they are meritocracies, they are actually more likely to *increase* rather than *decrease* the discriminatory consequences of gender bias. In a 2010 study, researchers found that "managers making decisions about employees on behalf of an organization will be more likely to discriminate against women when that organization explicitly promotes itself as meritocratic."[26] While the researchers are not absolutely sure why this happens, the result makes sense. When managers explicitly endorse this belief in a meritocracy, it serves as an implicit assurance that they are unbiased and fair. Therefore, the managers don't need to worry that their decisions are discriminatory—thereby making future biased decisions more likely.[27] When managers feel "their motivations are not in question," they can "feel less constrained by social norms and be more likely to allow stereotypes to influence their decisions."[28]

The perpetuation of the myth of meritocracy hurts women's same-gender relationships in two distinct ways. First, when women do not advance as far and as fast as their male counterparts, they can blame themselves, concluding that they are not getting ahead because *they* lack some essential career characteristic, and if they were just more talented, committed, or hardworking, they would be recognized and promoted.[29] Women are less likely to realize that they are failing to advance because of the discriminatory consequences of affinity and gender bias and that they should join forces with other women to push for equal treatment. As a result, women are likely to either scale back their ambitions or double down on their efforts to display that they are worthy of the desired reward. Either way, the gendered workplace wins and sisterhood loses.

Second, those few women who do rise to (near) the top in gendered workplaces often come to think of themselves not as lucky tokens but as extraordinary examples of talent, ambition, and hard work. They can see themselves as proof that gender discrimination does not hold deserving women back. If other women are struggling with career advancement, it is because those other women don't have the right stuff. Again, when women feel this way, they pull away from other women and ignore the need for organizational reforms to ensure the advancement of women generally.

Whether women respond to the proclamation of meritocracy by judging themselves as inadequate or as proof that their organizations are meritocracies, they allow gender stereotypes to put them in metaphorical straitjackets. These stereotypes define their success in terms of masculine characteristics and behaviors. As a result, women who do not succeed conclude that they are not sufficiently like men, and those who do make it conclude that they are not like other women. Neither is necessarily true, of course, but the stereotypes and the straitjackets they create severely limit women's perspectives, moving them toward same-gender incivility and away from sisterhood.

The Boys' Club

In chapter 4, we discussed the pressure women can feel in gendered workplaces to distance themselves from other women. Indeed, two 2011 studies found that a common strategy for women seeking to advance in gendered workplaces is to stereotype, withdraw from, and criticize other women.[30] Joan Williams, founding director of the Center for Work Life Law at the University of California Hastings College of Law, calls this the "why would I hang out with losers?" strategy.[31] Marissa Mayer's frequently quoted comment "I'm not a girl at Google, I'm a geek at Google" is a good example of this strategy.[32] And Sherry Lansing, former CEO of Paramount Pictures, was "famously chummy with the men working in Hollywood but standoffish with the women. She has vigorously denied ever facing discrimination or prejudice."[33]

In gendered workplaces, ambitious women can quickly internalize positive qualities associated with masculinity and negative qualities associated with femininity. If women have absorbed this ideology, they *must* also believe that they are different from other women if they are to continue to believe they can get ahead. Therefore, it is only natural for them to hang out with the men; display no interest in supporting, advocating for, or involving themselves with efforts to advance other women; exhibit no sympathy for other women's work and life tensions; and disparage as unneeded any workplace initiatives designed to increase gender diversity.

Of course, when women act in this way, the women from whom they are purposefully distancing themselves feel put down, devalued, and disparaged. In response, the women who are feeling put down are likely to treat the distancing women with a decided lack of civility, creating a perfect occasion for a tit-for-tat response. Thus, the highly masculine cultural norms prevailing in gendered workplaces can force a separation of women into "distancing" and "distanced" camps, with little civility between them and less chance for sisterhood.

Sex Norms

Women also seek to impose—and resist the imposition of—stereotype straitjackets created by pervasive societal attitudes about sexual orientation, gender identity, and gender expression. Women identifying as LBTQ—lesbian, bisexual, transgender, and questioning or queer—are a diverse group. We are in a period of extraordinary change with respect to the rights and recognition of individuals who identify as LGBTQ. (The G is for gay, when men are included in the category.) As one example, California and Oregon now allow their residents to identify as "non-binary" instead of "female" or "male" on their driver's licenses and state identification cards.[34] And the US Equal Employment Opportunity Commission (EEOC) is seeking (or at least it was before the Trump administration came to power) to have Title VII of the Civil Rights Act interpreted to provide protection for LGBTQ people in the workplace.[35]

LGBTQ Identifying Individuals and Careers

The most definitive estimate we have of the size of the LGBTQ population is 4.5 percent of all US adults,[36] but there are many reasons to believe that this estimate is far too low.[37] A more reasonable estimate appears to be somewhere between 8.2 percent, which is the proportion of millennials who identify as LGBTQ,[38] and 10 percent, which is the estimate often given by LGBTQ advocates.[39] If either of these estimates is correct, a larger percentage of the US population is LGBTQ than is Asian (5.8 percent).[40] However, we have far less information about the workplace experiences of individuals identifying as LGBTQ than we do about Asians. One thing we do know is that adults identifying as LGBTQ face considerable workplace discrimination. A 2017 report from the US Commission on Civil Rights reviewed a large number of studies and compiled the following statistics about the extent of discrimination experienced by LGBTQ adults because of their sexual orientation or gender identification:

- Anywhere from 21 to 47 percent of LGBTQ adults have faced employment discrimination.
- 7 to 41 percent of LGBTQ adults have experienced verbal or physical abuse in the workplace.
- 10 to 28 percent of LGBTQ adults received negative performance evaluations or were passed over for promotion.
- 38 percent of LGBTQ employees who were out of work had experienced discrimination or bias.
- Job applicants who could be identified as LGBTQ received 30 percent fewer callbacks.
- 57 percent of LGBTQ employees experienced at least one form of employment discrimination at some point in their lives.[41]

Beyond these statistics, we do not have qualitative information about the specific difficulties LBTQ women face advancing in their careers. While we know the percentage of openly LGBTQ lawyers as reported to the National Association for Law Placement—2.64 percent[42]—we don't have comparable information for corporate managers, doctors, and engineers. We also don't have comparable information on how many LBTQ women are senior executives at Fortune 500 companies or how many earn graduate degrees. While we know that 92 percent of Fortune 500 companies have policies prohibiting discrimination based on sexual orientation,[43] such a corporate policy, in and of itself, tells us nothing about the actual career advancement experiences of LGBTQ employees. Without quantitative information about the extent and nature of LGBTQ participation in professional and corporate leadership, it is difficult to say with certainty how and why women's career advancement is hurt by their identification as LBTQ.

Workplace Conflicts

Women who identify as LBTQ come into conflict with each other as well as with non-LBTQ women because of stereotypes about what they are like, what they should be like (heterosexism), and why they shouldn't be the way they are (moral disapproval). We discuss these in this section.

Lesbian Stereotypes

Common stereotypes about lesbians are that they are masculine, butch, and angry. Based on these stereotypes, lesbians are often thought to be highly agentic, and, as a result, they can be subject to the same sorts of uncivil behaviors from other women that agentic women generally experience. Moreover, because lesbians' sexual orientation and/or gender identity and expression can be seen as violating gender behavioral norms, lesbian women are often subjected to incivility from other women regardless of whether they express themselves in agentic ways.

Conflict among lesbians and other women can also result from microaggressions. For example, straight women might speak of lesbians in what can often be seen as disparaging ways (dyke, queer, or butch), telling heterosexist jokes in their presence, and excluding lesbians' partners and children from workplace family events.[44] Here is an example.

> Sarah, a lesbian friend, told us the following story. "At work, I am defined and evaluated primarily by my sexual orientation, and not by my professional capabilities and accomplishments. I had been hesitant to 'come out' and now I am sorry I did. The women I work with appear uncomfortable around me, frequently fail to include me in their social outings, and generally act like I am an undesirable member of their gender. As far as I know, there are no other lesbians in my department, and I feel very isolated. I am seriously thinking about moving to a new company where my sexual orientation would be unknown, and I would be able to build some work relations with other women without my sexual orientation getting in the way.

While it is clear that incivility can occur between straight women and lesbians,[45] there is no statistically significant correlation between women's identification as LBTQ and their rating as effective, likable, or desirable bosses.[46] Thus, although stereotypes about lesbians certainly exist, we do not know whether these stereotypes trigger their evaluation as being less effective leaders than their straight counterparts.[47]

In addition to workplace conflicts between straight women and lesbians, there are workplace conflicts between cisgender (or "cis") lesbians (lesbians that identify with their biological sex) and transgender (or "trans") women.[48] These conflicts "can go far beyond [cisgender lesbians] simply excluding trans women from their events and organizations, and actively harass, mock, and out trans women."[49] Cisgender lesbians

who aren't intentionally transphobic can still harbor fears and stereotypes based on their lack of familiarity with trans women (the same goes for trans women, who can be suspicious and fearful of cis lesbians). One persistent stereotype in the cis lesbian community is of trans women presenting a narrow, old-fashioned sort of femininity of the type that many lesbians have dedicated themselves to dismantling politically and socially.[50]

Thus, between cisgender lesbians and transgender women (many of whom can be lesbian or bisexual themselves), "misunderstanding and mutual ignorance [are] particularly likely to lead to conflicts, hurt feelings, or exclusion.... The constant need for trans women to explain, educate, and advocate for themselves in the very spaces that are supposed to be safe and friendly can be highly alienating."[51]

Heterosexism

There is pervasive social bias that heterosexuality is the only normal sexual orientation, and, therefore, that any other sexual orientation is abnormal and undesirable.[52] The assumption that heterosexuality is normative imposes a particularly uncomfortable stereotype straitjacket on lesbians. When they remain in the closet, lesbians are often "subjected to heterosexual comments or jokes in the workplace because of the physical invisibility of their sexual orientation and assumptions by others that they are heterosexual."[53] By remaining in the closet, lesbians are therefore "exposed to a hurtful psychological dynamic" because other people might assume that they are heterosexual.[54] Despite their discomfort with such situations, lesbians often fear that if they come out, they will face real discrimination, and so often "hide their sexual orientations—to be invisible—to avoid the risk of losing their jobs or of being harassed or rejected by fellow workers."[55] Here's Avery's story.

Avery, a lesbian who is not out at work, describes her workplace isolation as painful. She is afraid to come out for fear she will be even more isolated than she is now. She even fears losing her job or being denied the next promotion. She is afraid that she will be called sinful by her religious colleagues and treated uncivilly by her colleagues with anti-LBTQ feelings. Because of these fears, Avery plans to continue to keep her sexual orientation invisible.

Moral Disapproval

As Avery mentions when she cites her reasons for staying in the closet, lesbians often experience intense hostility from traditionally religious women who see lesbians' sexual orientation as morally wrong.

There is, in fact, a strong correlation between a person's religiosity and her or his negative attitudes toward homosexuality.[56] As a result, LGBTQ individuals who work with others who have a high level of religious dedication and belief report experiencing high levels of homophobia.[57] This was illustrated by Ilona's situation.

Ilona is a lesbian who presents and carries herself in a very stereo-typically feminine way. She does not fit the traditional agentic stereotypes about lesbians. Ilona was on the fast track at her company, working in its Atlanta office, when she was promoted and moved to another office in the Midwest. Active in Atlanta's LGBTQ community and her company's LGBTQ employee affinity group, Ilona

(Continued)

looked forward to starting an LGBTQ group in her new city. Ilona was settling in comfortably until she spoke with her immediate supervisor and her supervisor's boss (both women) about starting such an affinity group. Their response was quick and forceful. They told Ilona that this would never happen in "our God-fearing city." They told her that she would go to Hell if she did not repent. Ilona reached out several times to her company's human resources department, but nothing was ever done to intervene or help her with the hostile situation. For the first time in her career, Ilona's work was criticized as "below expectations," and she was put on a performance review plan. Things went from bad to worse, and Ilona eventually left that company and returned to Atlanta to look for a new position.

This moral disapproval can be particularly strong and hurtful when transgender women are involved. Here is Kipp's story.

Kipp, a transgender woman, was born biologically male but identifies and presents as a woman. She uses the pronoun—she—and dresses as a woman. At Kipp's current job, she was told "no matter what gender she identifies with, she must use the men's washroom. Kipp cannot bring herself to do that. Two women colleagues found Kipp leaving the women's washroom and reported her to senior management. Kipp then started to use the guest washroom in her company's reception area because the door has a lock. Soon after, however, Kipp was told that the guest washroom is only available to guests, not employees. So Kipp began waiting until her lunch break to use the public women's washroom in the building's lobby.

A few weeks later, the two women who had first reported her to management saw her coming out of the women's washroom in the lobby and again reported her.

(Continued)

Kipp's trips to the human resources department were useless. She has been told that there is nothing they can do to help her. The state in which Kipp lives and works—along with the majority of other states—does not explicitly prohibit discrimination based on gender identity or sexual orientation.[58]

Kipp knows there is no future for her at her present employer and is planning a move to a state with legal protections for sexual orientation and gender identity.

Positive Relationships

Many straight women and LBTQ women have strong, supportive, and satisfying relationships. Straight women typically don't inquire about the nature of other straight women's sexual activities, practices, or preferences. In fact, there is no reason that they should care about the sexual practices of women who identify as LBTQ. Like so many other same-gender conflicts, the secret to eliminating them is to find ways to counter the hurtful consequences of negative stereotypes. Lesbians are no more—and no less—agentic than other women; there is no right or superior sexual orientation, and there is no justification—biblical or otherwise—for the moral condemnation of LBTQ women. As the US Supreme Court said in declaring unconstitutional state bans on marriage between same sex couples, "The Constitution promises liberty to all within its reach, a liberty that includes certain specific rights that allow persons, within a lawful realm, to define and express their identity."[59] The elimination of conflict between straight women and LBTQ women similarly requires everyone to acknowledge that all women have the right to define and express their identity.

To avoid conflicts between women over gender differences, sexual orientation, and gender identity and expression, we provide some ideas and suggestions in chapters 10 and 11 as well as here.

MAKING THINGS BETTER

- Get to know the pervasive gender stereotypes that are frequently applied to women and consider the straitjackets that these stereotypes impose on the women you work with as well as on yourself. By understanding gender stereotypes and the biases that flow from them, you can anticipate workplace situations that are likely to bring you into conflict with other women. This knowledge can help you respond constructively to those situations.

- Stereotypes should always be considered in light of the context of the situation. In many circumstances, to say that a man is assertive is to ascribe to him a positive characteristic, while to label a woman as assertive is usually to impute to her a negative characteristic. But if a woman lawyer who is cross-examining a witness is described as assertive, this might be viewed as desirable. Likewise, toughness is a quality we tend to admire in men but view as undesirable in women. Yet, when a woman facing unfair criticism stands her ground and calmly refutes the accusations, we might very well admiringly say, "She's tough, she can really hold her own." Similarly the word "dominant" is typically seen as a very positive quality in a man but unattractive in a woman. Yet, to describe a woman tennis player or negotiator as dominant can be a high compliment.

- Women can reduce the consequences of gender stereotypes by adopting a strategy known as *gender blindness*. By focusing on the similarities with the men with whom you work, as opposed to differences, you can overcome the stereotype threat in gendered workplaces.[60] Of course, gender blindness does not mean being completely blind to gender, which would be an impossible task. Rather, gender blindness is a way of deemphasizing your focus on differences between your attributes as a woman and those of your male counterparts. By downplaying differences and focusing on similarities, you can increase your perceived fit and confidence at work.

- Recognize that some women might fear LBTQ women because they themselves have questioned their own sexual orientation, gender identity, or gender expression. Working with LBTQ women can force others to think about themselves in ways that might make them uncomfortable.
- Some straight women might be hostile to LBTQ women because they are afraid the LBTQ women are interested in them as romantic partners, and they want to avoid a sexual comment or pass. Even if this turns out to be true, this is something that can be addressed the same way other unwanted romantic overtures are handled.
- Derald Wing Sue, a psychology professor at Columbia University, provides suggestions as to how individuals can reduce their heterosexism in his book, *Microaggressions in Everyday Life: Race, Gender, and Sexual Orientation.* Sue wrote, "Cultural changes… [required to overcome heterosexism] are massive. However, there are things that can be done if we personally become committed to individual change." He suggests taking the following steps:
  - Become free of heterosexual assumptions, and become aware of ethnocentric heterosexist language and vocabulary in everyday use. Using inclusive language can go a long way to altering your own worldview.
  - Educate yourself: develop partnerships and relationships; make a strong effort to understand LGBTQ hopes, fears, and concerns; and attend LGBTQ events.
  - Become an ally of the LGBTQ community.
  - Help educate others that homosexuality is not a mental disorder (it was declassified as a mental disorder in 1973) and challenge assumptions that sexual orientation is pathological.[61]
- Give everyone you work with a fair chance and evaluate them on their merits, not their sexual orientation, gender identification, or gender expression.
- Everyone—particularly people in leadership positions—should keep an open mind and heart about other people and learn how to be an active ally to LBTQ women in the workplace.

PART III

Social Identity in the Workplace

Chapter 6

Gender Isn't the Whole Story

WOMEN HAVE MANY DISTINCT IDENTITIES that intersect with their gender to create what are now called *intersectionalities*.[1] Women with differing intersectionalities can face significantly different stereotype-driven obstacles to their career advancement in gendered workplaces. As a result, women with different intersecting identities are likely to have very different workplace experiences, which can negatively affect their same-gender workplace relationships. Before discussing why women with differing intersectionalities can find it difficult to forge close, supportive, and conflict-free relationships, let's look at a relationship between two women with no intersectional differences.

Sheryl Sandberg, the author of *Lean In: Women, Work, and the Will to Lead*, recounted the following story in an opinion piece in the *New York Times*.

The top two female cross-country skiers competing at the 2014 Winter Olympic Games were Marit Bjørgen and Theresa Johaug. The older skier, Bjørgen, had been the reigning cross-country champion for more than a decade when Johaug, a wunderkind eight years her junior, burst on the scene threatening to dethrone her. Rather than resent the younger woman, Bjørgen took Johaug

(Continued)

under her wing, mentored her, trained with her, and became her close friend. As Johaug commented, "[Because of Bjørgen,] I have become the cross-country skier I am"—and she said this after Bjørgen had beaten her by less than three seconds to win the gold medal. These women were intense competitors *and* supportive friends.[2]

According to Sandberg, Bjørgen and Johaug are "an extreme example of something that happens every day: women helping one another, professionally and personally."

Bjørgen and Johaug's mutually supportive relationship is a valuable reminder that conflict is by no means inevitable between women competing for career success. Even so, let's look more closely at Bjørgen's and Johaug's identities. They are both Norwegian, white, and middle-class; they have similar educations, career objectives, and sexual orientations. They have the same routines, diets, abilities, and health. While their ages are different, they are from the same generation. In other words, Bjørgen and Johaug are remarkably similar, so much so that it is quite natural for them to be close friends, even sisters.

In today's workplaces, of course, women frequently work with other women who do not share all of their distinctive social identities. As a result, women in gendered workplaces work with other women subject to different stereotypes, socialized in different ways, and exposed to different workplace dynamics. As a consequence, they are likely to be working with other women who have different perspectives on their strengths, vulnerabilities, career options, and life opportunities. For example, women of color are likely to see the workplace through a lens colored more strongly by, for example, their race or ethnicity than their gender. In considering women's same-gender relationships, it is essential to recognize that gender isn't the whole story.

In this chapter we focus on the same-gender workplace relationships of two large minority groups in the United States: Asian women and Hispanic/Latina women. In chapter 5, we discussed workplace relationships involving LBTQ women, and we discuss workplace relationships involving black women in chapter 7, younger and older women in chapter 8, and mothers and others in chapter 9.

Immigrants

We refer to women who were born in (or whose ancestors are from) a country in Asia as "Asian women." We refer to women who were born in (or whose ancestors are from) Latin America, the Caribbean, Central America, and South America as "Hispanic women." We understand that these broad categories mask the wide diversity in cultural norms and values among both Asian women and Hispanic women. We use these broad, comprehensive categories, however, because most of the studies and surveys do not separate Asian or Hispanic women by their countries of birth or ancestry. In addition, despite whatever differences they may have, most women in these broad groups are subjected to similar stereotypes and have had similar workplace experiences. Although we discuss only Asian and Hispanic women in this chapter, we believe people of different races and ethnicities face similar issues. We hope this discussion will ring true to women with other social identities and intersectionalities not directly addressed here.

In 1960, there were 9.7 million immigrants (people born outside the United States) living in the US, making up 5.4 percent of the US population. By 2016, there were 43.7 million immigrants living in the United States, making up 13.5 percent of the total US population.[3] Forty-two percent of immigrants in the United States are five years of age and older, and of all US immigrants, 43 percent speak Spanish at home.[4]

Looking at immigrants arriving in the United States since 2004 (which we call "new arrivals"), the number of new Hispanic arrivals has declined steadily, while the number of new Asian arrivals has increased steadily.[5] As a result, as of April 1, 2016, Hispanic and Asian immigrants each made up close to 30 percent of new arrivals, and together they made up well over half of all of the new US immigrant population.[6] Among the total immigrant population, Asians make up 26.9 percent and Hispanics make up 51 percent.[7]

Looking more broadly at the racial and ethnic breakdown of the female portion of the US population, 61.7 percent are white, 17.1 percent are Hispanic, 12.7 percent are black, and 5.8 percent are Asian.[8]

Asian Women

Although Asians are often lumped together for demographic purposes, Asians are not a unitary group. Asian women come from such different countries as Japan, China, Korea, India, the Philippines, Vietnam, and Pakistan. They differ among themselves in terms of their cultural practices, educational background, length of time in the United States, and how well they speak English. Nevertheless, many Asian women are subject to similar stereotypes, and as a consequence their relationships with other women are likely to reflect similar patterns.

Model Minority

Asian Americans are frequently referred to as a "model minority," and it is easy to understand the reason for the phrase. While Asian women make up only 5.8 percent of the total US female population, they comprise 12 percent of the professional workforce.[9] Forty-nine percent of Asians over 25 years of age have attained a bachelor's degree or higher, but only 31 percent of whites, 18 percent of blacks, and 13 percent of Hispanics have comparable educational achievements.[10]

There is a similar pattern with respect to household income. In 2010, Asians' median household income was $66,000, while that of whites was $54,000, Hispanics was $40,000, and blacks was $33,300. By 2017, the Asian American median household income was more than $70,000,[11] while the median household income for the entire US population was $61,372.[12]

Forgotten Minority

Given these statistics, Asians do, in fact, look like a model minority. They are the highest-earning, best-educated, and fastest-growing minority group in the United States today.[13] Because of their accomplishments, Asians in general—and Asian women in particular—are given little or no attention in most diversity programs.[14] As Buck Gee and Denise Peck recently wrote in the *Harvard Business Review*, "Asian Americans are the forgotten minority in the glass ceiling conversation."[15] And once we look beyond all of the positive statistics, we can see a clear pattern of discrimination in Asian women's career advancement.

In the science, technology, engineering, and math (STEM) fields, for example—areas in which Asians are thought to excel—Asian women are not advancing as far or as fast as men or any other group of women.[16] Twenty-one percent of Asian women with PhDs in science or engineering employed by universities and four-year colleges are tenured, compared to 40 percent of similarly credentialed white women, 32 percent of black women, and 30 percent of Hispanic women. Of tenured women, only 9 percent of Asian women are full professors, compared to 22 percent of white women, 15 percent of black women, and 17 percent of Hispanic women. The same pattern holds true for women scientists and engineers employed by government[17] and private industry.[18]

The low representation of Asian women in STEM managerial ranks is confirmed by a 2017 report from the Ascend Foundation on Asians' career experiences in Silicon Valley.[19] While Asians are the largest racial cohort (47 percent) of "professionals" (entry-level nonmanagerial employees with a college degree or higher), white women and men are twice as likely as Asians to become "executives" (managers within two reporting levels of the CEO). In fact, Asians are the least likely of *any minority group* to become Silicon Valley executives.[20] In other words, among all minority groups, only Asians have a *negative* gap between their representation in Silicon Valley's talent pipeline and their representation in senior leadership. At the same time, there is a *positive* gap for whites between their proportion of the pipeline and their proportion in senior leadership.[21]

The Ascend Study makes clear that this is not likely to change for the better as more millennials move into the managerial ranks. Between 2007 and 2015, there was no meaningful increase in Asians in the ranks of midlevel managers, much less among senior executives.

Looking specifically at gender, Asian women lag in leadership representation behind not only Asian men but also white, black, and Hispanic women and men.[22] While racial bias results in pervasive discrimination against Asian women, gender bias also holds them back. Thus, Asian men are 85 percent more likely to be executives than are Asian women.[23] Peck, co-author of the Ascend report, commented that "minority women continue to bump against the double-paned glass ceiling. The data show that the general focus on developing women leaders has not addressed the distinct challenges for Asian, black, or Hispanic women."[24]

The disparity between the representation of Asians in the professional workforce and in senior leadership is not unique to the tech industry. In law, for example, Asians are 34 percent of the graduates of the 30 top-ranked law schools, but they are the least likely of any minority group to make partner in major US law firms.[25] And although Asian women outnumber Asian men among law firm associates (54 percent to 46 percent), Asian men outnumber women by almost two times at the partner level (64 percent to 36 percent).[26]

A similar pattern of underrepresentation exists in the major Wall Street firms. According to *Bloomberg BusinessWeek*, Asians are hired on Wall Street at a much higher rate than their proportion of the general population, but they are not moving into the executive ranks at anywhere near the same rate as their white colleagues.[27] Asians are also underrepresented in senior leadership roles across corporate America. While Asians make up 12 percent of the professional workforce in the United States, they make up only 5 percent of executive-level leadership positions.[28] Thus, while Asian women are more likely than any identifiable group to have had a graduate education, they are the least likely to hold a position within three levels of the CEO or to have line or supervisory responsibilities.[29]

Reasons for Discrimination

Initially, it might be difficult to understand why Asians are not advancing into senior leadership roles at the rate their education and professional representation suggests they should. Given the stereotypes that Asians are highly intelligent, diligent, hardworking, and technically proficient, it is particularly difficult to explain why they do not advance at least comparably to white women who are not stereotyped in this positive way. However, if we look more closely at the stereotypes about Asians, the reasons for discrimination are not hard to make out. While Asians are stereotypically believed to be highly competent, they are also stereotypically characterized as very low in social skills.[30]

High Competence but Low Social Skills

A 2001 study found that because Asians are stereotyped as highly competent, other people envy them. At the same time, because they are stereotyped as having low social skills, other people feel hostile toward them.[31] A later study found that because of these two stereotypes, people were reluctant to interact with Asians or learn more about them.[32] The authors of these studies suggest that because other people are threatened by the "unfairly high" level of Asians' assumed competence, they use Asians' supposed lack of social skills as a pretext to discriminate against them. A lawsuit against Harvard College for discriminating against Asian applicants in its admission practices essentially has adopted this theory.[33]

Because of the lawsuit, we know that Harvard screens its applicants based on five categories—academic, extracurricular, athletic, personal, and overall. The ratings for academic and extracurricular categories appear to be relatively straightforward and objective. The personal category, however, appears to be anything but straightforward, with a great deal of room for subjective judgment. Qualities such as likability, helpfulness, integrity, and courage have a decidedly "eye of the beholder" quality to them. And this is the crux of the plaintiff's case. Despite Asian applicants having higher test scores, better grades, and stronger extra-curricular activities than other applicants, Asians were consistently ranked lowest in the personal category.[34]

The question, of course, is whether Harvard—or anyone—can rate a characteristic as subjective as "personality" in a way that is not infected by bias, whether consciously or not. According to the plaintiff, the low score in the personal category amounts to "the Asian American penalty," the removal of which from the admissions process would significantly increase Asian admission rates.[35]

We have no opinion as to whether Harvard's admission process ille-gally discriminates against Asians. Any admissions process that relies on factors other than objective metrics is certain to be subject to criti-cism from one perspective or another. Our concern, however, is with the apparent disparity between what might be seen as Asians' "unfairly high" academic credentials and their low rating in social skills, such as likabil-ity, helpfulness, integrity, and courage. Is this admission category a pur-poseful way of capping the percentage of Asians admitted to Harvard, or is it simply an innocent consequence of the ways in which personal ratings are assigned? Perhaps resolution of the lawsuit will enlighten us.

High Competence but Not Leaders

There is another stereotype-based explanation for the gap between Asians' representation in America's professional workforce and their presence in senior leadership. In a recent study, participants were shown identical information about a particular male leader, half of whom were identified as Asian and the other half as white. In this study, participants assessed the Asian leader as significantly lower in leadership ability than the identically described white leader. Although the Asian leader was seen as dedicated and intelligent, he was also seen as lacking in mascu-linity, charisma, and a forceful personality—stereotypical characteristics of leaders. Thus, while common stereotypes about Asians are that they are diligent, smart, well organized, motivated, and well educated—in other words, highly technically competent—they are not stereotypically deemed to be as well suited as whites for leadership roles that require a broad array of knowledge, abilities, behaviors, and interpersonal skills.

Nevertheless, when Asians—both women and men—do act like leaders—that is, assertively, forcefully, and decisively—they are penalized for violating the stereotypes that they are *supposed to be* modest and deferential to authority. Thus, Asians are caught in a familiar double bind. "If they act more dominant they will be less liked, but if they do not project dominance, they will not be seen as leaders."[36] Here is Stella's story.

Stella, an Asian insurance executive, says that when she voices an opposing or dissenting opinion, other women express disapproval that she is not being "quiet and nice." As Stella puts it, "Most of the time, they act as if I'm being overemotional and irrational. The result is that when I express a strong view on any subject, I am either ignored or treated rudely. Other women seem surprised whenever I do not play the deferential, quiet Asian part."

Tensions and Conflicts

Asian women have workplace conflicts with other women for all of the same reasons that people have workplace conflicts: disagreements about goals, methods, and priorities; differences in temperament, work habits, and tolerance for mistakes; and variations in ambition, modesty, and social ability. But Asian women also have workplace conflicts with other women that are uniquely driven by the stereotypes other women hold about them.

Model Minority

Other women—especially women of color and ethnic minorities—frequently resent Asian women because they are assumed to be more technically competent, be better educated, and come from more financially successful families. As a result, black and Hispanic women often perceive Asian women as having an unfair advantage over them, and to compensate for these feelings they may treat Asian women as socially awkward, distant, and unlikable.

The model minority stereotype is, thus, a source of workplace frustration and discomfort for Asian women: If they play the part of being highly competent and behave in a highly disciplined manner, they can be resented or taken for granted. If, on the other hand, they try to explain the difficult time they have had getting to where they are in their careers, they can be dismissed as poor-mouthing their situation or resented for not acknowledging their assumed privilege, as our friend Kim's story illustrates.

> Kim is a young lawyer. When we first met, Kim told us, "I came to the United States from South Asia with my refugee parents and siblings. As a child, I grew up in a poor neighborhood. I was the first person in my family to go to college, much less law school, and the notion of being a 'model minority' was a joke for me. Once I started to practice law, however, people assumed I came from a wealthy family, had highly educated siblings and parents, and everything I have has somehow been handed to me. People don't have a clue about the tough life I'd led or how hard I'd had to work to get where I am. When I tried recently to explain my situation to several of my women colleagues, they put me off as being disingenuous. I often feel frustrated at not being seen as the person I really am and for not being given any credit for coming as far as I have. It's as if I'm a 'trust fund' baby with no accomplishments of my own."

Tech Savvy

The stereotype that Asians are tech savvy can also bring women into conflict with other women. This can happen if they are selected to serve on teams dealing with technological issues and other women are actually better qualified. And when Asian women don't excel at technologically complex tasks, they can be criticized because others can assume they should have known how to do that. We saw this firsthand when we were at the airport with Jade, a jazz singer whose parents came to the US from India.

We were waiting for our flight when a very distraught woman rushed up to Jade. The woman was holding her laptop, and she asked Jade for help with a computer problem. Jade said she knew very little about computers and couldn't help. The woman became indignant, insisting that "of course" Jade knew how to fix computers: "After all, don't all Indians know about computers?" Jade again said she couldn't help the woman, who then left in a huff, adding very sarcastically, "Well, thank you very much!" This incident upset Jade terribly. As she said to us afterward, "Maybe I should have tried to help her."

Dragon Ladies

Another conflict-provoking stereotype about Asian women is that if they do not behave in a docile and modest manner, they are seen as overbearing,[37] demanding, aggressive, cold, strong, domineering, and deceitful.[38] Although the Dragon Lady stereotype is most often associated with East Asian women (including Chinese, Japanese, and Korean women), it is also applied to South Asian women (including Indian and Pakistani women) and Southeast Asian women (including Malaysian, Thai, and Vietnamese women). Simply by asserting themselves, demanding to be acknowledged as valuable participants, or refusing to back down when challenged, Asian women can be seen as Dragon Ladies.

Thus Asian women have their own version of the Goldilocks Dilemma: if they are docile and deferential they can be seen as "Lotus Flowers" or "China Dolls," which we discuss in the next section, but if they are agentic, they can be seen as Dragon Ladies.

Erotic Dolls

When they are referred to as China Dolls or Lotus Flowers, Asian women take on highly stereotyped erotic characteristics. A study by the Facebook dating app "Are You Interested?" found that white, black, and

Hispanic men prefer to date Asian women over women of their own race or ethnicity.[39] And in a study of public perceptions of women of color using Google's search algorithm, researchers found that Asian women were the most likely women to be fetishized.[40] Indeed, the highly sexualized stereotype of Asian women has become so pervasive that comedian Amy Schumer can get a knowing laugh with the line, "I can't compete with an Asian chick."[41] Because of this sexualized image, Asian women can be the subject of jealousy, envy, and resentment when other women in the workplace perceive them to be erotic.

Hispanic Women

Hispanics, like Asians, are not a unitary group. They (or their ancestors) came to the United States from a variety of countries in Latin America, the Caribbean, Central America, and South America. Hispanic is an ethnicity, not a race. Thus, Hispanics can be black, white, native American, Asian, and mixed-race. Hispanics differ among themselves in terms of how long they have been in the United States, what race they identify with, and what countries they (or their ancestors) were originally from.

The contrast between the socioeconomic situation of Asians and Hispanics is stark.[42] While Hispanics are the largest ethnic or racial minority group in the US, constituting 18.1 percent of the total population, they have the lowest educational attainment, personal income, and workplace leadership representation of all racial and ethnic groups.[43]

Educational Attainment

In 2015, only 15 percent of Hispanics 25 years of age or older held a bachelor's degree or higher, compared with 52.6 percent of Asians, 34.2 percent of whites, and 20.2 percent of blacks.[44] While Hispanics' educational situation is improving, it is doubtful they are receiving the same quality postsecondary education as their white counterparts. In 2016, 39 percent of Hispanics were enrolled in college, up from 22 percent in 2000.[45]

However, 72 percent of Hispanic college enrollment is in this country's 3,250 nonselective schools, where graduation rates are low (49 percent). By contrast, 82 percent of white college enrollment is in the country's 468 most selective schools, where graduation rates are much higher (82.5 percent).[46] Hispanics make up 21 percent of the total college-age population, but they account for only 12 percent of the students at selective public colleges. Selective schools spend from two to almost five times more per student than do nonselective colleges.[47] This lower per-student expenditure at nonselective schools—where the great majority of Hispanics are enrolled—translates into lower graduation rates, less access to graduate and professional schools, and less favorable labor market outcomes.[48]

Economic Situation

To a significant extent, the economic situation of Hispanics mirrors their educational attainment. In 2015, Hispanics' median personal income was $24,000, compared to $38,000 for Asians, $35,000 for whites, and $25,000 for blacks. Because Hispanics have more two-parent households than blacks, Hispanics are better situated than blacks with respect to median household income: $44,800 as opposed to $36,000. But Hispanics' median household income significantly lags behind Asians ($77,000) and whites ($61,000).[49]

Workplace Achievement

Hispanics make up 17 percent of the total US workforce,[50] while holding only 7 percent of "good jobs," as defined by the Georgetown University Center on Education and the Workplace, requiring a bachelor's degree or higher.[51] Moreover, while 17 percent of the total US workforce holds managerial, professional office, and STEM jobs, only 8 percent of Hispanics do.[52]

Working Women

Almost 14 percent of all working women are Hispanic, which is more than twice the number of working Asian women and nearly 10 percent more than the percentage of working black women.[53] Despite having higher bachelor's degree completion rates than Hispanic men (47 percent versus 37 percent), Hispanic women are the lowest-earning racial or ethnic group in the United States.[54]

At Fortune 500 companies, Hispanic women make up 6.8 percent of total employees but have the lowest representation among midlevel and senior managers than either black or Asian employees.[55]

The career difficulties that Hispanic women face are enormous, including low educational attainment, few graduate degrees,[56] severely disadvantaged economic backgrounds,[57] and lack of English proficiency.[58] Nevertheless, Hispanic women are an increasing presence at the upper end of the US employment ladder. They now make up 6.7 percent of female lawyers,[59] a 30 percent increase over the 10-year period (2004–2014); 7.5 percent of women doctors,[60] a 40 percent increase over that same time period; and 9.5 percent of all managerial professionals,[61] a 30 percent increase over the same period.[62] Between 2004 and 2014, Hispanic women increased their share of positions in medicine and management to a greater extent than either black or Asian women, and they have made good progress in both law and business.

With that said, however, even when Hispanic women possess the education, language proficiency, and economic security to compete for leadership positions, they are held back by negative stereotypes. It is these stereotypes that drive the tensions and conflicts between Hispanic women and other women in the workplace.

Stereotypes

A major 2003 study of professional Hispanic women by Catalyst provides important insights into why they find it so hard to advance in their careers. The women in the study included entry-level, midlevel, and senior-level employees; 73 percent were born in the United States; about 33 percent had graduate degrees; 78 percent were bilingual, with the remaining 22 percent speaking only English; 61 percent were raised in middle-class families; and on average, they had been with their companies for 13.5 years.

Twenty-six percent of these women held line positions with authority and responsibility for major organizational goals, and 58 percent had supervisory responsibilities.[63] Of the professional women who felt a strong connection to their community, 46 percent reported they faced negative stereotypes for women of their ethnic group. (Thirty-eight percent of all Hispanic professional women felt this way.) Of Hispanic women with a strong connection to their communities, 50 percent believed that their companies' diversity efforts had failed to address subtle racism and discrimination against their racial/ethnic group.[64]

Many negative stereotypes hold Hispanic women back: they are believed to be lazy; their intelligence is positively correlated with their English proficiency; those who dress in a feminine manner are "hot" and flirtatious ("fiery Latinas" and "hot senõritas"); and those who use a direct, assertive communication style are believed to be "angry bitchy Latinas."[65] Equally hurtful to Hispanic women's careers are the stereotypical views that they are suited for domestic and service jobs but not supervisory ones; that they are unable to perform at a high level; that they are difficult to work with; and that if they display cultural differences, they lack competence.

These stereotypes and the biases that flow from them make it difficult for Hispanic women to find women (or men) to serve as mentors and sponsors, build effective professional relationships, and gain access to informal networks. Indeed, 42 percent of professional Hispanic women believe that not having a mentor/sponsor is a significant barrier to their career advancement, and 37 percent believe the same is true because they lack access to informal networks.[66]

As is the case with most other racially and ethnically diverse women, Hispanic women feel that conforming to their organizations' accepted behavioral style is extremely important for career advancement. Only 37 percent agree or strongly agree that differences in behavioral style are encouraged in their organizations. To ensure they are perceived to fit in, 87 percent of these women reported that they maintain a conservative style of hair and makeup, and 84 percent of them reported that they conform to corporate norms in dress.[67] One Hispanic woman reported to Catalyst that when "you can disguise yourself. It's effective. The level of respect, the level of trust in your work, credibility improves."

A recent poll of Hispanic professional women found that almost a third (31 percent) feel they "must dress more conservatively" than their coworkers "to be taken seriously."[68] They also report that they avoid discussing family demands, food preferences, and celebratory practices. As a result, Hispanic women can become emotionally exhausted by trying to be someone other than who they truly are. They can lose a robust sense of their own authenticity and begin to feel as though there is an artificiality to their organization's culture. When this happens, Hispanic women may start to distrust their female colleagues, doubt their sincerity, and question their motivations.

Tensions and Conflicts

Many workplace conflicts between professional Hispanic women and other professional women are, of course, the ordinary workplace conflicts that are common to all professionals. But Hispanic women also have conflicts with other women that are the direct result of negative Hispanic stereotypes.

For example, 43 percent of professional Hispanic women believe that exceeding performance expectations is a successful strategy to overcome negative stereotypes.[69] But when they purposefully attempt to exceed expectations, other women can become resentful and hostile. Women's overt attempts to demonstrate that they are more competent, more ambitious, and more accomplished than the women with whom they work create an environment of same-gender competition that is highly hurtful to women's interpersonal relations. Such competition can lead to mutual distrust, suspicions of selfish self-promotion, and incivility.

Hispanic women's lack of mentors, sponsors, and access to valuable workplace networks also exacerbates their sense of being outsiders. While black and Asian women also experience a similar outsider status, the cultural differences between these three groups of diverse women are often too great to allow them to bond together and jointly push for access to resources and opportunities. As a result, Hispanic women who feel they are isolated within their organizations and deprived of any real allies are likely to adopt one of two directly opposing strategies.

In the first approach, Hispanic women might attempt to suck up to the other women with whom they work, do favors for them, and modify their behavior, appearance, and work patterns to be accepted and invited into the other women's informal networks. Such obsequiousness is likely to make Hispanic women feel a sense of personal diminishment and confirm the stereotype that Hispanic women are assistants, not leaders.

Many Hispanic women have shared with us their efforts to modify their behavior and appearance to fit in. But there might be a change in the air. Alexandria Ocasio-Cortez, sworn into the US Congress as its youngest member in January 2019, wore at the ceremony her "now-signature red lips and a pair of large gold hoop earrings."[70] Her appearance and her actions sent a message to other Hispanic women. As Alexa Kissinger wrote for Vox, when she had been "a young Latina staffer," she "hid who [she] was to fit in." To Kissinger the thrill is that "Ocasio-Cortez is refusing to do that."[71]

An opposing strategy is to openly behave as though they have no interest in same-gender friendships or inclusion by distancing themselves from other women. Of course, when they do this they can give the impression that they think they are superior to other women. As a result, women with whom they work are likely to regard them as unpleasant, unlikable, and unwelcome in their networks.

Thus, either response to outsider status is likely to further isolate Hispanic women from the networks and power structures to which other women, particularly white women, are likely to have greater access. Communication is an important way to increase inclusion and collegiality. Here is Angela's story.

Angela is a white marketing executive who works in a large multinational corporation with a number of Hispanic women. Angela often relies on them for her marketing projects. Initially

(Continued)

she felt uncomfortable at work because the Hispanic women always speak Spanish to each other, and they sit together at lunch. One day, to try to break the ice, Angela went up to their lunch table and asked if she could join them. After an uncomfortable silence, they agreed. Angela told them, "I have a confession to make. I don't speak Spanish, so when you speak Spanish to each other, I feel excluded." They looked surprised. Several said that because Angela is an executive and they are support staff, they assumed she didn't want to interact with them. They told her they'd try to remember to speak English when she is around. Angela told us, "We have become very friendly, and I have gotten far more support from them than I ever did before. Work is now much more comfortable for me—and I think it is for them too."

Other women, particularly white and Asian women, can feel a sense of superiority to their Hispanic female colleagues because of cultural differences and (perhaps) greater English proficiency, educational attainment, and economic achievement. Language proficiency, in particular, can be a major source of tension between Hispanic women and other women. One woman in the Catalyst study told the following story.

When I was brought here, they gave me a tutor to improve my English skills. But there was [still] the accent. So they worked with me to be able to be part of this crowd. I was supposed to change my intonation, my accent. I didn't want to do it. I said, "I want to improve my language skills, I really want to speak English and write it well, but when I open my mouth, I want them to know who I am. So I'm not changing."

While this woman's attitude is entirely understandable, even commendable, the reason her organization wanted to "improve" her speech was so that she would "fit in" better. She wanted to remain "who she is." While it is easy—and correct—to say that organizations should respect and value differences, not try to eliminate them, many organizations are not so enlightened. And when there is a clash between the effort to ensure that everyone fits in and a desire to preserve a sense of authenticity, there is a tension between the women who fit in and those who resist doing so.

Workplace tension and conflict between Hispanic women and women with different social identities is often seen as a major workplace issue.[72] This might be largely because there are so few professional Hispanic women. Yet, as they continue to advance in their careers, unless negative Hispanic stereotypes are challenged, this sort of same-gender workplace incivility will only grow.

We provide some ideas and suggestions to overcome and avoid women's same-gender conflicts with women with other social identities in chapter 10 and here.

MAKING THINGS BETTER

- In interacting with Asian women, don't make assumptions about their background, technical skills, or family situations. Asian women are—and deserve to be treated as—distinct, unique individuals. That cannot happen if they are put into the "model minority" bucket.
- In interacting with Hispanic women, don't assume they lack critical skills, educational attainment, or social skills. Remember, no group in US society other than black women faces more formidable obstacles to career advancement than Hispanic women. Be sure you don't add to their obstacles.
- Understand your privileges. Women of color and other minority women tell us that they often don't look forward to working with white women because white women so often are clueless to the privilege they have simply because they are white. They tell us that they enjoy working with those white women who understand their privilege and how much harder it is for nonwhite women to advance in their careers.

- Reach out to women who are different from you. Some women can choose to blend into the dominant white culture and fly under the radar, but other women, such as those who wear hijabs or religious symbols, cannot blend in easily. They often feel isolated and excluded unless another woman makes a concerted effort to welcome and include them.

The takeaways that follow apply to all women with social identities different from your own. These takeaways relate to LBTQ women, black women, white women, Hispanic women, Asian women, women of different ages, and women with different parental status.

- In seeking to develop stronger relationships with women with different intersectionalities, slow thinking is essential to avoid resorting to stereotypes and biases. Slow thinking requires us to be careful, weigh evidence, be logical, and resist emotional responses. As we discuss in chapter 10, Daniel Kahneman, the psychologist who won the Nobel Prize in Economics in 2002, distinguishes two modes of thinking: fast and slow.[73] Fast thinking is automatic, effortless, instinctual, and emotional. When we think fast, however, our implicit biases can affect our decisions. Unbiased decisions depend on thinking slowly because, as Kahneman puts it, the voice of our own reflective self is "much fainter than the loud and clear voice of an erroneous intuition."[74]
- We are all influenced by stereotypes and the biases that flow from them. Understanding the different and often conflicting stereotypes about women who are different from you can provide you with powerful information to build stronger workplace relationships. For example, don't stereotypically assume that a woman with an accent is incompetent, or that a non-native speaker without perfect English is lazy.
- Women with social identities different from your own need allies. Reach out to women who are not like you. Listen to them. Get to know their stories; tell them yours. And if you see them being

treated unfairly or excluded from activities or opportunities, speak up for them.

- If you are uncomfortable reaching out to women with different social identities, examine why you feel uncomfortable in *this situation*. Is it a particular person or persons? Particular intersectional characteristics? Your own status, appearance, characteristics, or background? Learn what you can do to increase your comfort in such situations. Sometimes explaining your concerns can go a long way.

- Examine your workplace networks, both formal and informal. Are they inclusive of women with different intersectionalities? What can *you* do to improve inclusiveness? Are other people preventing these networks from being inclusive? If so, what can you do about it?

- Don't allow negative interactions with one person or people of a particular race or ethnicity to negatively affect your interactions with other people from that race or ethnicity.

- Incivilities and microaggressions against women with different social identities are common. If you are the target of or a bystander to a microaggression that you cannot deal with immediately—such as through humor, calling attention to its inappropriateness, or pointing out that the comment is not true—discuss the incident at a later time with the perpetrator if you think this might be productive. Was she malicious, ignorant, clueless, inappropriately attempting to be funny, or acting on her implicit stereotypes and biases? Err on the side of pointing out the hurtful conduct or comment. Once warned, similar conduct is less likely. But be prepared for push-back, denial of the conduct, and claims that you took the comment the wrong way, that you can't take a joke, or that you are too sensitive. The important thing to remember is that the issue is not what she intended, but how you felt. Tell her you were hurt and that you expect it won't happen again.

- Mentor and support a woman with different social identities from your own. Find ways to include her in work-related and professional development opportunities. But before you offer her advice, do a good deal of listening to identify the kind of help she really wants and needs.

- Find ways to demonstrate that the women who work with you who have different social identities are valued members of your team. This can start a sea change in same-gender relationships.

Chapter 7

Racial Divides

Perhaps no group of women is more disadvantaged in their pursuit of career success than black women. As of 2015, black women constituted 12.7 percent of the women in the United States but only 5 percent of women executive officers at Fortune 500 companies.[1] As of May 2018, there were 24 women CEOs of Fortune 500 companies, none of whom was black.[2] Black women account for only 4 percent of women lawyers, 2 percent of women doctors, and 5.9 percent of tenured or tenure-track female professors at four-year colleges and universities in the US.[3]

Only 1.3 percent of executives and senior-level managers in S&P 500 companies are black women, compared with nearly 22 percent white women.[4] In 2003, Ivy League universities hired 433 new tenured and tenure-track professors, of whom 150 were women, and only 14 of those women were black.[5] Black women have lower promotion rates than comparably situated white women; more job segregation; more pressure to modify their appearance, behavior, and attitudes; and lower career expectations overall.[6]

As a result of the broad career achievement gap between black women and white women, their workplace experiences are likely to be very different. Of course, workplace experiences of all black women are not the same, any more than the workplace experiences of all white women are the same. Nevertheless, black women are likely to share some common career experiences that contrast sharply with the workplace experiences of white women as well as other women of color. In this chapter we look at these different workplace experiences; the workplace dynamics that racial stereotypes and prejudices set in motion; and why these dynamics often make it difficult for black, white, and other women of color to form close, comfortable, and mutually supportive workplace relationships.

Stereotypes

In chapter 5 we discussed the biases women encounter when they conform to traditional gender stereotypes: If they are nice, pleasant, and likable, they are not seen as tough enough to be leaders. If they violate those stereotypes by being forceful, independent, and decisive, they are not seen as sufficiently likable for other people to want to work with. Because of this double bind—what we call the Goldilocks Dilemma—women are stereotypically seen as either too soft or too hard, rarely just right. While the Goldilocks Dilemma is a common experience of white women in their pursuit of career advancement, it is not nearly so common for black women.[7] White women are stereotypically assumed to be, expected to be, and punished if they are not communal, that is, warm, caring, modest, cooperative, and so forth. In study after study, however, researchers have found that black women are not typically thought to be warm, caring, and cooperative. Quite the contrary, the most common stereotypes about black women are that they are angry, loud, assertive, and have "an attitude."[8] (We discussed the stereotypes ascribed to Asian women and Hispanic women in chapter 6 and LBTQ women in chapter 5.) The lack of congruence between the stereotypes associated with white women, on the one hand, and black women, on the other, should make us highly cautious in drawing conclusions about black women based on research that simply refers to women's characteristics, attitudes, and expectations. When this is the case, more likely than not, the women being discussed are white, not black.

Angry, Loud, Assertive

The most common stereotypes about black women—angry, loud, assertive, and having an attitude—were exemplified in an extreme form in the character of Sapphire Stevens, the wife of Kingfish on the popular *Amos 'n' Andy* minstrel-style radio and television show that ran from 1928 to 1966. Sapphire was aggressive, loud, confrontational, and domineering; she was the quintessential "angry black woman." While many people today are not familiar with the character of Sapphire, almost everyone is familiar with the stereotype that strong black women are angry. For example, former First Lady Michelle Obama, tennis star Serena Williams, and ESPN award-winning sports journalist Jemele Juanita Hill have all been characterized in the popular media as angry.

Mammy

The polar opposite of Sapphire in the gallery of stereotypes of black women is that of the mammy[9]—think Hattie McDaniel's character in *Gone with the Wind*, for which she won an Oscar. A mammy is a black woman who is selflessly unwavering in her commitment to the advancement of white interests.[10] She is amiable, contented, happy, maternal, obedient, and respectful; in other words, she is absolutely nonthreatening to the white community.

Many people will recognize mammy in the figure of Aunt Jemima, who first appeared in 1910 on a box of pancake mix. She was a large black woman with a bandanna, apron, and big smile. She put a welcoming face to a time-saving product that weary housewives could turn to. The mix was intended to conjure up a "romanticized antebellum south" that was "very gracious, luxurious, slow, and gentle...a place where there were people ready to do things for you at a moment's notice."[11] In 1989, with the product's 100th anniversary, Aunt Jemima's image changed to that of "a working grandmother," who remains a smiling, kindly, welcoming, and nonthreatening black woman.[12]

Competence

While black women are often stereotyped at these extremes—angry or subserviently helpful—black women (and men) are also stereotyped as lacking intelligence and competence.[13] The 2012 American National Election Study found, based on interviews with nearly 5,500 Americans, that 44 percent of whites believe whites are more intelligent than blacks.[14] And a 1995 study found that one of the three characteristics most commonly attributed to black people is low intelligence (the other two being athletic and rhythmic ability).[15] Here is an example of what this stereotype can look like in the workplace.

Rebekka, a black senior executive, told us that the white women she supervises often act as if their support of her is to compensate for Rebekka's supposed incompetence, rather than as a standard part of their jobs.

Goldilocks Dilemma Revisited

Because of these stereotypes, black women face a variant of the Goldilocks Dilemma as they seek to advance in their careers. White women's stereotypical challenge is to appear just right: to project confidence and competence without appearing too soft or too hard. Black women's stereotypical challenge is to be perceived as competent and confident without appearing like a mammy, on the one hand, and without being seen as angry, on the other. Thus, black women and white women face similar—but not identical—gender-based obstacles in their career advancement. But beyond these gender-based obstacles, America's shameful and pervasive (if now often implicit) racism puts up hurdles in the way of black women's advancement that are entirely unknown to white women.

Authenticity

In chapter 4 we discussed the workplace pressures on women to conform to norms, values, and expectations of gendered workplaces. Black and white women are both subject to this pressure, but black women face an additional pressure that is not part of white women's working lives: the pressure to conform to *white* norms, values, and expectations that are pervasive in gendered workplaces.

Whether black women are in corporate management, hold professional positions, serve in political office, are entrepreneurs, or are otherwise pursuing a career, they typically inhabit two distinct cultures. In their work lives, black women are immersed in the white, hierarchical, heterosexual, conservative, and middle-class culture that dominates our business, professional, political, and academic institutions. In their personal lives, black women often live in a very different culture with distinctive interpersonal communication styles, means of self-expression, attitudes toward relaxation, and forms of entertainment.

Code-Switching

As a consequence, most black professional women must "code-switch" to function effectively in these different cultures. Code-switching—moving between white organizational culture and black social culture—involves modifying behavior, appearance, language, interests, and other aspects of how one presents oneself in order to conform to the norms prevailing in any particular situation. Here is how Tanisha code-switches to try to fit in.

Tanisha, an African American midlevel corporate executive, says she keeps her hair in dreadlocks when she is not at work but she always goes into her office wearing a wig. She has never considered going to work or a workplace event without a wig. She told us, "My

(Continued)

wig is my armor that I put on to do battle in my white workplace. And, I am not alone in wearing a wig. In fact, most of my black girl-friends do the same thing. It is so much easier for us than worrying about whether our hair will distract or be disapproved of by one of our colleagues."

Former president Barack Obama, who gives soaring, formal addresses, is a conspicuous example of a truly effective code-switcher. In a 2009 video of the former president in a chili-dog restaurant in a black neighborhood in Chicago, the cashier asked him if he needed change. He replied, "Naw, we straight!"[16]

Some black women also find code-switching easy and a natural part of impression management.[17] Here is Elenore's experience.

Elenore, a prominent black entrepreneur, told us she had been born into a family that taught her "how to navigate the streets of the 'hood' as well as the subtleties of the boardrooms and the ballrooms of white America." For her, code-switching was "never a burden."

Elenore's ease with code-switching is something that Mary, a black founder of a not-for-profit, recognized when she read an earlier draft of this chapter. Mary told us,

"For whatever reason, and perhaps much like the anecdote from Elenore, I feel pretty comfortable in 'white society.' It's been a big part of my upbringing and education, so code-switching can feel less tiresome. Despite that, it is still tiring for all of us at some point. You have to read your audience and see what sticks and how far you can really go. Every day and each interaction is like a 'test' to see how you need to act around particular people (even other women of color to be honest)."

Many other successful black professional women, however, tell us they find code-switching exhausting and dispiriting. Here is Jill's story.

Jill, a midlevel manager, told us, "Every day I dress for work as if I were going to a meeting with the CEO. I am always kind and sweet to everyone, and I always smile until my cheeks hurt. I want to be sure I am not seen as an angry black woman. Every night I drop into bed exhausted from the effort.

Mixed Messages

Michelle Obama seemed to find it more difficult than her husband did to adjust to broader societal expectations. As First Lady, she encountered enormous pressure to adopt a style and personality that would make white voters more comfortable with her. She was criticized for being too aggressive, pushy, and angry.[18] Her appearance, conduct, and communication style were all under constant scrutiny. In response, she quite obviously sought to present a less forceful side, a more feminine look, and a softer conversation style. In other words, she consciously attempted to display more of her communal and less of her agentic characteristics. She writes in her recent autobiography, "I've been . . . taken down as an 'angry black woman.' I've wanted to ask my detractors which part of that phrase matters to them the most—is it 'angry' or 'black' or 'woman'?"[19] She adds, "I was exhausted by the meanness, thrown off by how personal it had become, and feeling, too, as if there was no way I could quit."[20]

There are, of course, limits to how far black women—and women with other intersectionalities—can go, or how long they will continue to try to fit into the dominant masculine white culture and still maintain a sense of authenticity. Without a strong sense of personal integrity—a conviction that her true self is aligned with the outward expression of that self—a woman's emotional well-being will suffer, her productivity will decline, and her personal satisfaction will plunge.[21] Such a sense of authenticity can be particularly difficult for black women in gendered workplaces, where they are experiencing pressure about how to dress, wear their hair, be more sociable, and not be too "ethnic."[22] Because black women's conduct and appearance are often so vigilantly policed by their white women coworkers, even highly successful black women, such as graduates of Harvard Business School, report they cannot "be themselves" at work.[23] Instead, they must continually attempt to meet other people's expectations, adeptly navigate workplace politics, and keep their emotional intelligence on high alert. As one black female academic commented, "I need to speak their language, and I have to structure my [behavior to match theirs].... It's like they don't hear me if I'm the way I am."[24]

Black Women, White Norms

White women are often strict enforcers of white cultural norms. We hear frequently about white women who apparently feel free to counsel their black female colleagues about their appearance, style, and speech. While white women may believe they are only helping black women to better fit in and avoid violating dominant (white) cultural norms, such advice can lead to an uncomfortable tension between black women and white women. Friendships, easy social relations, and open mutual support can be difficult, with sisterhood a distant prospect. For example, author Ijeoma Oluo recounted,

> I dressed like every day was a job interview. I was overpolite to white people I encountered in public. I bent over backwards to prove that I was not angry, that I was not a threat. I laughed off racist jokes as if I didn't feel the sting. I told myself that it would all be worth it one day, that being a successful black woman was revolution enough. But as I got older, as the successes I had reached for slowly became a reality, something inside me began to shift. I would try to make my voice quieter in meetings and I couldn't. I would try to laugh off the racist jokes and I couldn't. I would try to accept my boss's reasons for why I could have my promotion but not my raise, and I couldn't. And I started talking.

I started to question, I started to resist, I started to demand. I wanted to know why it was considered a bad thing that I was "opinionated," I wanted to know what exactly it was about my hair that was "unprofessional," I wanted to know what exactly it was about that joke that people found funny. And once I started talking, I couldn't stop.

I also started writing. I shifted my food blog into a "me" blog, and started saying all the things that everybody around me had always said were "too negative," "too abrasive," and "too confrontational." I started writing about my fears for my community and my family. I had started to see myself, and once you start to see yourself, you cannot pretend anymore.

It did not go over well. My white friends (having grown up in Seattle, the majority of my friends were white), some of whom I'd known since high school, were not happy with the real me."[25]

Racism

Black women's difficulties in maintaining a sense of authenticity in gendered workplaces are often due less to outright racism—the view that blacks are inherently inferior to whites—and more to the expectation that *everyone* engaged in a workplace's managerial processes must conform to the dominant, white, masculine, heterosexual norms, values, and customs. This is not to say that racism, even implicit racism, does not negatively affect black women's career experiences. It does, as is well illustrated by Edith Cooper's experiences as head of Human Capital Management at Goldman Sachs:

I am frequently asked, "What country are you from?" (I grew up in Brooklyn). I've been questioned about whether I *really* went to Harvard (I did) or how I got in (I applied). I've been asked to serve the coffee at the client meeting (despite being there to "run" the meeting) and have been mistaken as the coat check receptionist at my son's school event... People frequently assumed I was the most junior person in the room, when, in fact, I was the most senior. I constantly needed to share my credentials when nobody else had to share theirs. And, more often than not, I was the only black person—the only black *woman*—in the meeting.[26]

Cooper's unfair and cruel experiences—and undoubtedly every black woman could provide her own list of the slights and indignities she has suffered—are likely to have been motivated by ignorance and implicit stereotypes. But they also face a deeper, more intractable problem: structural racism, which we discuss in what follows.

Structural Racism

White women face severe gender-related obstacles to their career success,[27] but black women face not only those same obstacles but many race-related ones as well. A 2002 study by the John J. Heldrich Center for Workforce Development found that workplace environments operate differently for blacks than for all other racial and ethnic groups. The Center found that in comparison to white women, black women are more likely to be treated unfairly in promotions and training, to be discriminated against in advancement opportunities, and to experience the greatest sense of frustration and disengagement.[28]

The operation of racism over and above gender bias is well illustrated in a study of female firefighters at firehouses across the United States. Researchers found that when black women joined the fire companies, all of the men, regardless of race, closed ranks and purposely excluded the black women from their social networks. White women firefighters were better able to break into these male networks because of their racial identification with the dominant white male firefighters. Both the black and the white female firefighters received insufficient instruction, and they both experienced hostility, silence, lack of support, and negative stereotyping. The black women's negative experiences, however, were far more severe than those of the white women. In other words, black female firefighters were treated worse than both black men and white women. Because they were women *and* black, they faced what can be thought of as a discriminatory double whammy.[29]

A study of private law firms by the American Bar Association's Commission on Women found a similar pattern of exclusion and discrimination. The Commission found that women of color were often excluded from their firms' internal networks, were seldom offered opportunities for client contact, and received few challenging assignments. In client meetings, women of color were frequently treated as window dressing, designed to fill a quota, or put diverse clients at ease—not to play a substantive legal role. Sixty-six percent of women of color were excluded from both informal and formal networking opportunities, while the same was true for only 6 percent of white women and 7 percent of white men.[30]

Exclusion from Informal Networks

Studies show that in all types of businesses, black women experience significantly less acceptance into informal social networks than white women.[31] Not surprisingly, therefore, 40 percent of black professional women believe that their lack of access to their organization's informal networks and social systems inhibits their career advancement.[32] As we saw in chapter 2, participation in workplace social networks is a critical factor for career success and advancement.[33] And black women's lack of access to those networks is a major contributor to their underrepresentation in upper management.[34] Moreover, black women's exclusion from their organization's networks further exacerbates their separation from their other female colleagues.

Incivility

Incivility directed against black women by other women can also result from common societal stereotypes that blacks are violent and dangerous and should be feared. Here is April's story.

April, an African American management consultant, told us the following story: "I met a new client recently, and when I walked into the conference room, three white women were talking together. One of the women said she had her purse stolen earlier that week. She looked me right in the eyes and then said to the other two women, 'Of course, it was a black man who stole my purse.' I was very upset by the implication that 'of course' black people are purse snatchers. Obviously, that meeting was very stressful for me, and I was not at my best. I still get a knot in my stomach just thinking about that interaction."

An equally common source of incivility toward black women is when they supervise white women. Because of implicit racism, white women often "are not predisposed to relinquish stereotypes and feelings of racial superiority."[35] Studies show that because of a (conscious or unconscious) sense of racial superiority, many white women view reporting to black women managers as contrary to the "natural order" and, therefore, they react by disparaging their managers' competence and entitlement to leadership.[36] Such disparagement can occur in a variety of ways, such as treating their managers as beneficiaries of unjustified affirmative action or as mere tokens to evidence racial diversity. Indeed, it can be extremely difficult for white women to see their black female managers as holding management positions because of talent, hard work, and solid accomplishments.[37] Not surprisingly, therefore, black women managers often describe their workplace interactions with white women as "demeaning" and "disrespectful."[38]

When we acknowledge the exclusion, lack of respect, and slights that black women managers often experience, we can begin to understand why black women's workplace relationships with other women are so frequently marked by wariness, distance, distrust, and a dim prospect of sisterhood.

Privilege and Power

Gender bias has been the focus of the women's movement since the early 1960s.[39] As a result, white women typically see gender bias as the primary obstacle to women's career advancement.[40] They can be blind to the extraordinarily negative influence that race can have on career advancement. As *white persons*, white women have access to opportunities, activities, status, and rewards that are simply not available to black women.[41] An obvious example is white women's ability (albeit often curtailed) to participate in white men's informal networks when black women lack that opportunity.[42] Let's look at some thoughts about race, gender, and women's workplace relations from the perspective of Carol, a white executive.

Carol, a very senior white executive at a multinational manufacturing company recently told us, "I spent most of my career without any conscious awareness of my unearned white privilege. I was simply oblivious to the ways in which being white contributed to my professional status. I had been completely unaware of the central role that race played in creating many of the opportunities I enjoyed. It has only been in the last few years that I have begun to grasp the advances that simply being white, native born, educated, straight, and able-bodied has provided me; it has given me a door-opening, you're one of us, step to the front of the line status. I have now started cataloging each of the ways in which I have an unearned career advantage over my black women colleagues. I am ashamed of my cluelessness, but I am determined to do what I can to extend my privileges to the women of color with whom I work. It's daunting, because white privilege is so subtle and multifaceted, but I am trying."

Privilege is a source of personal power, and personal power determines the range of what other people regard as acceptable behavior.[43] When we stay within stereotypically acceptable behavior, other people are more likely to acknowledge, include, and listen to us. As a result, we feel comfortable, accepted, and valued. If, on the other hand, we act outside the range of what other people have determined to be acceptable behavior for us—say, by not conforming to dominant cultural norms or by flouting stereotypical expectations—we are often criticized, excluded, and disregarded.[44]

The more status, wealth, attractiveness, influence, and so forth we have, the more personal power we have and the broader the range of our acceptable behavior. All things being equal, therefore, white men—simply because they are white and men—are likely to have more power in the workplace than white women. White women—simply because they are white—are likely to have more power in the workplace than black women. And black men are likely to have more power in the workplace than black women—simply because they are men. The power imbalance between black women and *everyone else* can make it difficult for black women to have their competence, potential, and value recognized. This is why black women so often find it difficult to be accepted as legitimate leaders, and why they are so often assigned to undervalued, administrative, and routine non-career-advancing projects.[45] As long as white women are unaware of and fail to acknowledge the extent and power of their white privilege, positive and mutually supportive workplace relations between black women and white women will remain difficult.

Invisible or Too Conspicuous?

Black women are more likely than any other racial or gender group to be invisible, that is, unnoticed and unheard in the workplace.[46] As bell hooks, author and social activist, wrote, "When black people are talked about, the focus tends to be on black *men*; and when women are talked about, the focus tends to be on *white* women."[47] Here is Jessica's experience.

Jessica, a black woman account executive, told us, "It was not until a white woman supervisor started asking me about my career objectives and including me on her projects that I started to gain visibility. Other white women became more friendly with me and my abilities were taken seriously. Once this white woman signaled I was a valuable employee, things completely changed for me at work."

Of course there are black women who are noticed and whose voices are heard: Michelle Obama, Shonda Rhimes, Oprah Winfrey, Condoleezza Rice, Barbara Jordan, Coretta Scott King, Susan Rice, Anita Hill, Linda Johnson Rice, Carla Williams, Beyonce, and Whoopi Goldberg are obvious examples. But in an arresting 2010 study, researchers showed a group of white participants a set of photographs of the faces of women and men, black and white. The participants were then shown a second set of photos, some of which had been included in the first set. Researchers found that the participants had the most difficulty remembering the faces of the black women. Because participants did not have the same difficulty remembering black men's faces, researchers concluded that something more than race was affecting the participants' memories.[48] The following story, told to us by a black woman we coach, illustrates the sort of frustration black women can experience because of their apparent invisibility.

My name is Isabelle, which is easy to spell and easy to pronounce. But some of the women I work with get my name wrong all of the time. They often call me "Lynne," the name of the only other African American woman in our office. (Lynne tells me they call her Isabelle.) At first, I found it awkward to correct them because I didn't want to appear petty or embarrass them. But, I finally decided that this needed to end. So, when the next woman called me Lynne instead of Isabelle, I waited until we were alone and then

(Continued)

pointed out the error. I told her I was sure it was an honest mistake, but because it had happened more than once it made me feel as though she didn't recognize me as a serious professional. I told her I thought she was a terrific colleague and looked forward to working with her going forward. She mumbled an apology and has never made that mistake again."

In a follow-up study, the researchers found that black women's comments were more likely to be ignored or disregarded by a white audience than were the comments of white people and black men.[49] This research strongly suggests that white people don't consider black women to be as important as white people generally or as black men. As Malcolm X said, "The most neglected person in America is the black woman."[50] This explains, at least in part, why black women often find it so hard in predominantly white business and professional workplaces to be heard and to have their ideas taken seriously.[51] It may also explain why black women managers often report being mistaken for lower-status, less powerful people such as service workers, clerical employees, or domestic assistants.[52] Here is Charlotte's experience.

Charlotte, an African American senior vice president at a major financial institution, runs her organization's diversity and inclusion efforts. She explained to us that she tells young professional women of color to dress in formal business clothes, even though their workplace has a casual dress code. She cautions them that unless they look professional, people may think they are not professionals.

While black professional women can be invisible, they can also be too conspicuous. With so few senior black women in most organizations, those who are there stand out and are on constant display. Remember Edith Cooper's comment: "More often than not I was the only black person—the only black *woman*—in the meeting." And the more senior and better credentialed black women are, the more conspicuous—and unique—they become. As one C-suite executive commented, "I tick a lot of boxes for people . . . . They get a package of someone who's female, who's African-American, who has an MBA from an elite academic institution. So there I am—the purple unicorn."[53]

Because they can be so conspicuous, black women managers can feel like they live in fishbowls with other people constantly looking in, observing, scrutinizing, and judging them. Being under continuous appraisal can be emotionally exhausting, a psychological "tax" that their white female counterparts often don't have to pay.[54] As one black female academic put it, "You get it from all sides—from your colleagues AND from your students. Eventually you get exhausted with dealing with them. After a while you have to pick your battles.... You can't let it consume you, but it is still draining and demoralizing."[55]

Black women professionals can be whipsawed by an invisible/too conspicuous dilemma. They can be ignored one moment and subjected to careful policing for conformity to workplace norms the next. As a result, they can become suspicious of their white colleagues' racial attitudes, uncertain as to whom to trust, and certain that sisterhood, such as it is among their white women colleagues, is not *their* sisterhood.

Interviews with 59 senior black female executives addressed the invisibility problem. In an article in *Harvard Business Review*, the researchers found that a main driver of these black women's success "was their ability to navigate the challenge of intersectional invisibility, or the tendency to be overlooked, disregarded or forgotten due to one's status as a member of two underrepresented and devalued groups."[56] The researchers learned that these women combatted invisibility "by taking on visible, high-risk roles that helped them ascend to the upper echelons of the companies."[57]

To Be Liked or Respected?

We all care about the impressions other people have of us, and we want those impressions to line up with the ways in which we want to be perceived. Our dealings with people of other races are particularly fraught in this regard because of the stereotypes that people of one race have about people of another race. Black women are keenly aware of the stereotype that they are supposedly unintelligent and incompetent. And, white women are likely to believe that black women think they are prejudiced and closed-minded.[58] Given these beliefs about how they are regarded by women of the other race, black women and white women often attempt to forge positive relationships with each other in different, counterproductive ways.[59]

For example, in their interactions with white women, black women are likely to strive to be seen as smart, talented, valuable, and worthy of respect by maintaining a formal, professional manner. As a result, black women can come across to white women as unfriendly and aloof. In white women's interactions with black women, white women are likely to strive to be seen as unbiased, warm, friendly, and likable. Thus, white women might attempt to use humor, self-deprecation, and compliments in their interactions with black women. As a result, white women may come across to black women as patronizing and inauthentic.

When black women and white women adopt these contrasting approaches to relationship building, white women can come away believing their friendly behavior has gone unreciprocated, and black women can feel as though their efforts to achieve respect have been fruitless. This sense of mutual disappointment can be exacerbated by black women's and white women's different expectations from positive interracial relationships. Black women are likely to seek recognition as *black* women with their distinctiveness clearly accepted, acknowledged, and valued. White women, on the other hand, are likely to seek recognition based on their similarities and commonalities as *women*. Thus, when white women ignore differences and downplay race, black women can feel as if their authentic selves are not being respected, and when black women disregard similarities and raise issues of white privilege and power, white women can feel criticized and attacked. Here is Victoria's experience.

When we talked to Victoria, an African American bank executive, about her difficulties in achieving truly positive workplace relationships with white women, she told us, "Whenever I attempt to explain my concerns or clear the air by talking about our differences, my white women colleagues clam up, seek to change the subject, and appear hurt. It is as though any attempt to have a serious discussion about race is off-limits, as if it is too hot a topic to be considered. Yet, because I have not seen that they value me as a *black* woman rather than just a woman colleague, I feel depreciated. The notion that we should all be 'color-blind' is precisely the wrong approach to positive interracial relationships."

Because of their different concerns and objectives, establishing a sisterhood between black women and white women, even when the women have the best of intentions, can be difficult. Differences *and* similarities both need to be acknowledged and embraced. An interracial sisterhood is certainly possible, but it requires a good deal of communication and understanding from both sides of the racial divide.

Black and Hispanic Women

Black women and Hispanic women often report tense workplace relationships. Only 57 percent of Hispanics think that Hispanics and blacks get along very or fairly well, with 30 percent of Hispanics saying relations with blacks are strained. Even among Hispanics who have attended college, 37 percent do not believe that blacks and Hispanics get along well.

One reason for the tension between blacks and Hispanics may be the far greater sense among blacks than among Hispanics that blacks have suffered discrimination in housing, employment, college applications, and shopping or dining out. Twenty-six percent of blacks believe they face discrimination in all of these areas, while only 11 percent of Hispanics believe blacks do. And 81 percent of blacks believe they face discrimination in at least one of these areas, while only 55 percent of Hispanics believe blacks do.[60]

In many ways, the hostility between Hispanics and blacks—and particularly between Hispanic women and black women—is entirely understandable. Black and Hispanic leaders in the past have seen these two disenfranchised groups as natural political allies in the United States, a country historically dominated by whites.[61] Their alliance would thus be a natural melding of mostly poorer, often darker-skinned minorities whose struggles are—or should be—similar. But this black/Hispanic coalition has grown increasingly strained. Many blacks resent what they see as Hispanics leapfrogging over them up the economic ladder, and Hispanics increasingly see blacks as specifically targeting them for assault.[62] The result is competition between these two minority groups over power and resources, which has led to surprisingly antagonistic and uncooperative interactions. Indeed, blacks can view Hispanics as a threat to their social, economic, and political gains. And one indication of that possibility is that Hispanic household income in the United States is now about 20 percent higher than that of blacks ($40,000 versus $33,300).[63]

Black and Asian Women

Conflict between black women and Asian women generally mirrors the conflicts between black women and white women. This is so for two reasons. From the Asian side, anti-black sentiment has been ingrained in many Asian minds because "whiteness often becomes equated to success, and all the elements that have been conditioned to come with the paradigms of whiteness. One of these has been anti-blackness."[64] Thus the racism that is pervasive in white American society is also pervasive among Asians. As Diana Wong, an assistant professor and faculty fellow at NYU Gallatin, wrote, "Anti-blackness is the foundation to the creation of America. It's no secret that anti-blackness is reflected in Asian immigrant families, businesses, institutions, and interpersonal relationships on a frequent basis."[65]

Conflict with and animosity toward Asian women can be driven by black women's acceptance of the stereotype that Asians are a model minority in the United States who are believed to be superior to blacks. Moreover, the perception of universal success among Asians perpetuates the false impression that "any minority group" can succeed by just working hard and upholding "family values,"[66] thereby downplaying racism's role in the persistent social, economic, and educational difficulties faced by blacks.

While we freely acknowledge that we do not have all of the answers, we do offer some ideas and suggestions to overcome or avoid conflict to bridge the racial divide in "Making Things Better" in chapter 6, chapter 10, and here.

MAKING THINGS BETTER

- As we wrote in chapter 6 and address at length in chapter 10, don't be afraid of uncomfortable interactions and conversations with women of a different race from yours. Use these exchanges to learn more about yourself and your outlook on interpersonal relationships.
- Try to follow Gloria Steinem's advice: "If you have more power, remember to listen as much as you talk. And if you have less power, remember to talk as much as you listen."[67] This should be easy for the person with more power, but for the person with less power, it requires courage, careful impression management, and, very often, receptive—and tolerant—counterparties.
- Examine your workplace networks, both formal and informal. Are they inclusive of women of different races? If not, why not? What can *you* do to improve inclusiveness? Are there other people in those networks who keep those networks from being inclusive? What can you do about them?

- Microaggressions against black women are common. As we said in "Making Things Better" in chapter 6, if you experience a microaggression that you cannot deal with immediately—such as through using humor or calling attention to its ridiculousness—consider discussing the incident with the perpetrator later and in person.
- Don't be afraid to talk with women of different races about your workplace experiences. Ask about their experiences and recall instances of biased treatment you've experienced.
- Explore your feelings about privilege. Start a list of all of your unacknowledged privileges—and keep adding to it as you continue to think about working with women of a different race than yours. Don't just identify those privileges, acknowledge them and try to mitigate their discriminatory effects.
- Sexism and racism can be difficult to disentangle. When black women feel unfairly treated in the workplace, it can often be difficult for them to know if it is because of their gender or race or both. If you are a black woman, talk with your white women colleagues to see if they have experienced the same things. If you are a white woman, share your experiences of gender bias with your black female colleagues. By discussing these issues together, women can become clearer about just why they are experiencing specific instances of bias and be in a better position to respond accordingly.
- Mentor and support for a full year a woman of a different race than yours. Find ways to include her in work-related and professional development opportunities. And do more asking than telling. You probably don't know the sort of help she needs until you do a good deal of listening.
- Identify the norms, values, and expectations that characterize your organization and that result from its dominant culture. Are there ways that these characteristics can be changed to include more diverse perspectives?
- Both individuals and institutions need to look at decisions through an intersectional lens and acknowledge the racism and

other problems women face in the workplace. Both black women and white women need to be prepared for uncomfortable conversations that are necessary to effectuate change.

- Edith Cooper in her article "Why Goldman Sachs Is Encouraging Employees to Talk about Race—and Why as a Black Woman I Think This Is So Important" wrote that when she told her husband about the discriminatory treatment she had received, he said to her,

> 'Pick your head up. The good news is they'll never forget you.' He was right—people did remember me. From then on, I tried to turn obstacles into opportunities and focused on making an impact at work—which I could control—rather than the perceptions of others—which I could not.[68]

Cooper suggests "focusing on what you can control and taking mindful steps and positive action towards what matters to you," and she offers the following lessons from her journey, "including those difficult interactions that seemed to be based primarily on the color of my skin."

- Engage in the dialogue: don't be silent.
- Misunderstanding and miscommunication can be tempered by the simplest acts most of us learned as children: listen well, choose your words with care, and respect others.
- Focusing on our differences is easy and divisive; leveraging what we have in common is harder, but will affect positive change for all.[69]
- Conflict is not limited to women of different races and ethnicities. Women of the same race, ethnicity, and other social identities also have conflicts with each other and don't support each other in the workplace. We have been told by many women, "We cannot support each other because there is likely to be one spot available for a woman like me, so we're all in competition for that same spot. Every one of us wants to be identified with the 'ingroup' and with

the 'winners,' but we know there is only a place for one of us." Do not believe this. When women work together they can expand the opportunities for all women.

- To overcome invisibility, some senior black women are seeking organizational changes to improve the path for the next generation of black women. To do this, "many of them had taken on additional organizational roles such as managing diversity and inclusion efforts, joining boards of other (frequently non-profit) organizations, and mentoring young people."[70] This involves sharing their experiences with others, "particularly more junior up-and-coming black associates."[71]

Chapter 8

Age Matters

IN RECENT YEARS, WOMEN'S WORKFORCE participation in the United States has increased dramatically as the average age of the women in the workplace has grown progressively older. As a result, younger and older women often work side by side, with younger women increasingly supervising significantly older women. In this chapter we consider the implications of these changes, what is known about the differences between younger and older workers, and why age-based stereotypes can be so disruptive to women's same-gender workplace relationships. We wrap up with some suggestions as to how to minimize women's same-gender intergenerational conflicts.

Demographics

In 1962, only 37 percent of women aged 16 and older were working or actively looking for work. By 2016, that percentage had jumped to 57.2 percent,[1] with women making up almost half (47 percent) of all US workers.[2] In 1980, the median age of all workers was 34.6 years old, but by 2016, it had increased to 42.[3] In 2018, workers who were 55 years of age and older made up 23.1 percent of the total US workforce, up from only 16.7 percent in 1972. Workforce participation of older women has seen a particularly striking increase, growing by more than 76 percent over the past 20 years. By 2024, older women are projected to constitute 24.8 percent of the total US workforce.[4]

Workers between the ages of 21 and 36 (members of the so-called millennial generation) currently make up 35 percent of the labor force,[5] and workers 55 and older make up 27 percent of the workforce. Because of this age diversity, women are increasingly likely to be working with other women who are significantly younger or older than they are. This can yield a positive result, because studies confirm that age diversity improves productivity. Teams composed of both younger and older workers, for example, are found to be twice as likely to meet or exceed expectations as are those teams composed of people of a single age group.[6] Age diversity, however, can have a negative effect. It has been shown to increase interpersonal tensions, misunderstandings, and conflicts, which hurts effective decision making, innovation, and successful project execution.[7]

Generational Conflict

The popular press,[8] business advice books,[9] psychology and sociology journals,[10] and human resources publications[11] are filled with cautionary tales about how difficult it is for people of different ages to work together without tension and conflict. There is, however, considerable controversy about why people of different ages find it difficult to work together harmoniously. Some authors attribute these conflicts to the generations' different values, ways of working, and expectations.[12] Other authors argue that there are no significant differences in the generations' workplace values and attitudes, and that the conflicts between younger and older workers are actually due to their different stages of life development resulting from their different chronological ages.[13] Still other authors argue that both of these views are incorrect and that intergenerational conflict is primarily due to pervasive age-based stereotypes.[14]

We believe some conflicts between younger and older workers are the result of generational and life-stage differences, but that these conflicts are minimal in comparison to those caused by the societal stereotypes about the capacities, attitudes, and expectations of younger and older workers.

Generational Differences

Today's workplaces are commonly divided into five generations: the silent generation or traditionalists (born between 1922 and 1945); the baby boom generation, or boomers (born between 1946 and 1964); Generation X, or Xers (born between 1965 and 1979); Generation Y, or millennials (born between 1980 and 2000); and Generation Z, or Zers (born after 2000). Because only a few traditionalists remain in the workplace (approximately 1,682,000 or about 1 percent of the total[15] and because only a few Gen Zers have already entered the workplace (approximately 5,901,000 or about 4 percent of the total[16]), we focus exclusively on the differences among boomers, Gen Xers, and millennials and the tensions and conflicts that might be attributed to these differences.

Controversies over Generational Differences

Dividing people into generations is most often justified by the assumption that people of relatively similar ages have been imprinted with similar values and aspirations[17] because they grew up surrounded by the same cultural, economic, and historical phenomena.[18] The problem with claims suggesting that there are real differences between and among the generations is that they are frequently based on little more than speculation and anecdotal impressions.[19] Moreover, most empirical studies purporting to identify generational differences involve one-time polls or surveys given to a cross section of people of different ages. When such studies identify differences in the values, attitudes, or preferences of people of different ages, it is impossible to know whether these differences are due to their generation, chronological age, life stage, or something else.

Assessing Generational Differences

Researchers have attempted to avoid the problems inherent in one-time surveys by examining people's responses to the same questions at the same point in their life cycle.[20] Several large, annual, and nationally representative surveys can be used in this way. For example, the Monitoring the Future study of 500,000 high school students has been conducted annually since 1976; the American Freshman Survey of nine million college students has been conducted annually since 1966; and the General Social Survey of 50,000 adults has been conducted annually since 1972.[21]

By using these large longitudinal studies, social scientists have identified four empirically based generational workplace differences between boomers and millennials. First, boomers and millennials differ as to how important they expect work to be in their lives. In 1976, 74 percent of boomer high school seniors said they expected work to be "a central part" of their lives, while in 2012, only 66 percent of millennial high school seniors felt that way. Forty percent of millennial high school seniors said that the fact they do not want to work hard might prevent them from getting the job they want, while only 24 percent of boomers gave the same response when they had been the same age.[22]

Second, millennials place more value in leisure than did boomers at the same age. Almost twice as many millennial high school students as boomers at the same age rated having a job with more than two weeks of vacation as "very important." And, while 44 percent of millennials said they want a job that leaves "a lot of time for other things in your life," only 38.3 percent of boomers felt similarly when they were the same age.[23]

Third, millennials have a higher sense of their individual importance and value than did boomers. In 2012, 61 percent of millennial college students said they were "above average" in their leadership ability, compared to only 41 percent of boomers when they were the same age. And in 2012, 58 percent of the millennials thought they were "above average" with regard to being "smart," compared to only 39 percent of boomers when they were the same age.[24]

Fourth and finally, despite reporting that they don't want to work as hard as boomers, millennials report higher workplace aspirations than boomers. In 2012, 46 percent of millennial high school seniors reported wanting a job "that most people look up to and respect," compared to only 34 percent of boomers at the same age. And when entering college, 42 percent of millennials said it was important to one day be the boss, compared to only 26 percent of boomers.[25]

These findings appear to point to actual, if not dramatic, generational differences, but a few words of caution are in order. First, regardless of which category of difference we look at, there is a sizable number of people in the different generations that are more similar than different. Second, a great many subjective judgments must be made to reach these results.[26] For example, many questions must be combined and assessments made of their similarity. And third, where there are statistically significant differences in generational attitudes, these differences are generally small.

Nevertheless, the generational differences identified by the longitudinal studies may well be sources of tension and conflict between women in the workplace. For example, with around half of millennials reporting they don't want to work particularly hard, older women can be critical of this generations' effort, involvement, and engagement. Thus, in response to our own survey of women who are working with other women of different generations, we received the following comments, "Young women don't have the 'go-get-it-ness' that my generation of women had," "We can be offended by younger women who seem oblivious to what it takes to succeed," and "So many young women are slackers."

Younger women who desire more leisure time might see their organization's workplace policies as unnecessarily rigid and counterproductive. Older women, by contrast, may resent younger women's efforts to change long-standing working arrangements that the older women see as sound and productive of highly desirable organizational results.

Nevertheless, it is difficult to know whether the tensions and conflicts between younger and older women are due to actual generational differences or simply to stereotypes about women of different ages. As we discuss later in this chapter, when older women claim millennials feel "entitled" and don't want to "pay their dues," they are far more likely to feel that way because of age stereotypes about younger people rather than real generational differences.

Age-based Differences

To understand the cause of women's workplace conflicts among women of different ages, we need to know whether women's workplace performance, behaviors, and attitudes consistently change as they grow older. In other words, are the perspectives of younger and older women different simply because they are of different ages? Studies show that as people age, they undergo a number of physical, cognitive, and emotional changes that *might* lower their job performance.[27] A wide variety of behaviors, however, contribute to job performance.

One meta-analysis of 380 empirical studies found eight distinct job performance dimensions that could be negatively affected by age: core task activities, creativity, performance in training programs, organizational citizenship, safety performance, counterproductive work behaviors, on-the-job substance use, tardiness, and absence. Significantly, the researchers found that performance of core tasks—the effectiveness with which workers perform activities that advance their organization's core mission—are not affected by age. The same is true for creativity—the extent to which workers generate new and useful ways to improve organizational productivity. And performance in training programs was only weakly related to age.[28] Thus, age has little or no effect on the three job performance dimensions that are viewed as the greatest contributors to organizational productivity, innovation, and adaptability.

It is unlikely, therefore, that tensions and conflicts between older and younger women are due to differences in the quality of their job performance. Yet, workplace tensions and conflicts between women of different ages most commonly arise precisely in these areas. As we will see in the next section, people have the strongest age-related stereotypes about the quality of job performance.

The same researchers have also found that age is related to

"citizenship behaviors" and "minimum performance behaviors," with older workers being better citizens and younger workers engaging in more negative workplace behaviors.[29]

Although the changes in women's workplace attitudes and behaviors as they age are subtle, these changes can still lead to conflict between younger and older women. For example, if younger women engage in counterproductive work behaviors—such as tardiness, excessive sick days, gossiping, goofing off or just plain not getting the job done—older women can become highly critical. Likewise, because younger women are more likely to express negative emotions such as anger when compared to older female coworkers, older women might see their younger colleagues as childish, spoiled, and lacking self-discipline.[30] Older women may also resent younger women who are not doing more to help others, while younger women might criticize older women who value stability because the older women won't work for the organizational changes the younger women believe are needed. Here is Joanna's story.

> Joanna, a young sales manager, finds the leadership style of the older female managers (whom she refers to as the "old guard") stifling and toxic: "The old guard resent it when younger women speak up and express strong opinions at sales meetings. They don't want us to rock the boat. When we get excited about an idea, they criticize us for being emotional and when we take time off they become upset, even though our work is done. And when we object to rigidities in the organization's policies, they call us troublemakers."

Age-based Stereotypes

A large multicountry survey found that employees in all age groups, generations, organizational levels, and geographic regions have significant age-based stereotypes. Younger workers are likely to think they are more creative and efficient multitaskers than older workers. Older workers are more likely to think they have a stronger work ethic than younger workers and that younger workers demand unjustified recognition.[31] Thirty percent of hiring managers say older employees are difficult to train; 34 percent say they are unable to adapt to new technologies; and 36 percent say they are too cautious. On the flip side, 79 percent of hiring managers view younger workers as less reliable than older workers.[32]

Moreover, people commonly believe that older workers are poor performers,[33] resist change,[34] are unlikely to learn new things,[35] and are more expensive to employ.[36] By contrast, younger workers are commonly thought to be entitled, lacking loyalty, overly reliant on technology, and too dependent on constant feedback.[37] Other common stereotypes about older people are that they are less potent, active, decisive, and autonomous than younger people.[38] In addition, older workers are thought to be physically more tired, not as mentally agile, unable to leverage technology, and less willing to change and adapt. Younger workers, on the other hand, are assumed to be flexible, open-minded, and naturally tech savvy.[39]

Older Workers

Based on a synthesis of more than 100 studies of workplace age-related stereotypes, researchers concluded that stereotypes about older workers have four principal themes. First, older workers are believed to have lower ability, less energy (mental and physical), less motivation, and less productivity than younger employees. Second, older workers are believed to be resistant to change, to be less adaptable and flexible, and to have less ability to learn new skills than younger workers. Third, older workers are believed to have less potential for development and are assumed to be less willing to keep up with technology than younger workers. And fourth, older workers are believed to be costlier to an organization than younger workers because they are paid more, use more benefits, and are closer to retirement.[40]

For the most part, these stereotypes about older workers are not accurate. For example, exhaustion at work does not go up with age. In fact, more women under the age of 45 reported they were exhausted (43 percent) than did those over 45 (35 percent), with women over 60 the least exhausted of all.[41]

Obviously, the negative stereotypes about older workers have serious discriminatory consequences. Older workers with similar qualifications or attributes as younger workers commonly receive lower ratings in interviews and performance appraisals.[42] Although there are positive stereotypes about older workers—they are more dependable, stable, honest, trustworthy, loyal, and committed to the job—these positive stereotypes are not nearly as pervasive, strong, or harmful as are the negative stereotypes.

Younger Workers

Negative stereotypes about younger workers are:

- they want to dictate when and how they work,
- they feel entitled to praise and advancement without paying their dues,
- they think their organizations are lucky to have them,
- they think their bosses can learn a lot from them,
- they think they know more than they actually do,
- they don't want to work hard,
- they are excessively self-absorbed,
- they are not responsible or dependable,
- they are job-hoppers who lack loyalty and needy narcissists who crave constant positive feedback,
- they are easily distracted by technology,
- they lack focus and dedication, and
- they want special privileges.[43]

Because of these negative stereotypes, younger workers experience age-based discrimination in their careers, often finding it difficult to be taken seriously, to have their ideas accepted, to be assigned to important projects, and to have their technological skills appreciated. In fact, biased treatment of younger workers is quite common, with subjective performance appraisals particularly susceptible to age bias.[44]

Obviously, the negative stereotypes about younger workers have serious discriminatory consequences. Take, for example, the common stereotype that millennials are lazy, "easily bored, crave instant gratification and would rather hop from gig to gig."[45] Comprehensive studies in the United States and United Kingdom, however, show that the opposite is true: "It turns out, millennials are just as committed as their elders were at the same age, if not more so. What's more, they're not being rewarded for that loyalty."[46] Resolution Foundation reported these results with respect to the United Kingdom, and Pew Research Center published similar findings with respect to the United States.[47]

Technology Gulf

Perhaps the age-based stereotypes causing the most workplace tension and conflict between younger and older women concern the use of and reliance on technology. Younger women grew up immersed in technology and are often thought of as "digital natives."[48] As a result, younger women are generally thought to prefer electronic and digital communication techniques, are quick to embrace new technologies,[49] and are continually connected with family and friends through their smartphones, blogs, instant messaging, texting, and social media tools.

Older women, by contrast, are generally thought to prefer communicating face-to-face, by telephone, and by email. They are less likely—at least in the work context—to use blogs, social networking sites, texting, or instant messaging.

The age-based technology gap is real. For example, 74 percent of millennials believe technology makes their lives easier, compared to just 18 percent of boomers.[50] Here is Marissa's experience.

Marissa told us that she and her millennial colleagues find the communication preferences of their older female boss to be cumbersome and ineffective. They started communicating with each other by text and with their boss by email. This worked for a while,

(Continued)

but eventually they found that this created extra work and a serious problem when an important conversational string was dropped from an email and not fully vetted by the boss. Marissa went to the boss to see if she would start texting, but her boss said she didn't want to work on her phone and that Marissa and her colleagues should start using their computers more so that there will be a better record of the exchanges.

Tension and conflict between younger and older women with respect to technology can be greatly exacerbated because of the stereotypes surrounding age and technology. Thus, younger workers are assumed to be computer savvy, while older workers are assumed to be (at best) grudging participants and (at worst) clueless. These stereotypes can disrupt key aspects of workplace collaboration: communication, learning, leadership, and decision making.[51] As a result, age-based stereotypes about the value and appropriate use of technology can easily foster tension and conflict with respect to authority, management style, values, and outlook. Age-based stereotypes can also negatively affect:

- team collaboration,
- creation of joint documents,
- how information and data are incorporated into strategic decisions,
- expansion of the organization's relationship with its customers and suppliers, and
- the creation of new processes to simplify task performance.

Here is Charlotte's perspective.

Charlotte is one of the oldest women in the midsized accounting firm where she is a partner. She told us recently that she enjoys surprising the young people with whom she works about her computer savvy

(Continued)

and technological expertise. She said, "People who don't know my skills assume I will be the least tech-savvy person in the room, and I use this to my advantage. When accounting graduates start working at our firm every year, I find an opportunity to work with them one-on-one. Once the younger accountants understand just how tech savvy I am, I get more respect, attention, and a better work product."

Older women can become resentful when they see their everyday work habits and organizational culture disrupted by technological innovations. At the same time, younger women can resent older female managers who insist on traditional approaches that deny them the opportunity to use their skills or restrict their access to basic technological tools with which they are comfortable.

Some older women can also see younger women as obsessively absorbed in technology: taking notes on smartphones, preferring to meet by Skype, and staying in touch through social media such as Twitter, Instagram, Snapchat, and Facebook. Younger women can view older women as inflexible and out of date, because of their preferences for paper and pencil, face-to-face meetings, email, and telephone calls. Here is Azu's story.

Azu, a senior manager at a major bank, told us her team was charged with developing new policies for a complex operational area. The older workers wanted to do this in face-to-face meetings and through an email listserv. Azu and her younger colleagues wanted to set up a collaborative website for the team with a document repository, thread discussion groups, instant messaging, contact management, and a shared calendar. The older women were highly resistant to this approach and only agreed to it after Azu said she would post everything herself and individually walk the older team members through the process. She told us the entire process left her resentful and doubtful about the leadership abilities of the older managers on her team.

The increasing reliance on technology in the workplace has created an enormous demand for workers with technical skills. Yet here again, age-based stereotypes create intergenerational conflict. The assumption that younger workers are actually tech savvy while older workers are tech clueless, means that older women often see employment opportunities for which they might be fully qualified going instead to younger, less experienced women. Younger women can refuse to deal with older women on tech-related issues because they assume that the older women either don't understand the issues and possibilities or are hostile to technological innovation. Younger workers are more likely than older ones to push for mobile, virtual, and remote workplaces with more flexibility and work-life balance. As a result, older workers might see younger workers as lazy.

As women age, they face additional workplace problems. Age stereotypes combine with gender stereotypes to create a "double whammy" for older women. Thus, when 55-year-old women are compared to 55-year-old men, younger women, and younger men, they are viewed as the least adaptable group of employees.[52] This means that expectations and beliefs about older women's character and likely behavior are strongly shaped by stereotypes associated with age and gender.[53] Not only are the stereotypes about older people predominantly negative, they are also deeply held. Indeed, there is strong evidence that because of age-based stereotypes, older women are seen in more negative terms than younger people (women or men).[54] Here is Robyn's story.

When 56-year-old Robyn moved across the country, she didn't think twice about finding a new job. As a successful architect, she thought she'd be able to step into a new firm and pick up where she left off. She was deeply shaken to find that she was seen as too old for a new architectural position and that her skills and experience were discounted. Over a two-year period, Robyn never once got an interview for an architectural job. Instead, she was considered only

(Continued)

for building management positions that did not require her architecture degree, and even those positions always went to younger job candidates.

Younger Bosses

Age-based stereotypes are particularly disruptive when older women work for younger women. A survey conducted by CareerBuilder found that 16 percent of US workers have a boss who is 10 or more years younger than they are.[55] Such younger boss–older subordinate relationships can shake up stagnant hierarchies, introduce fresh talent, and make clear performance is valued over longevity. On the other hand, such relationships can create negative dynamics because of the lack of congruence between women's ages and status.

When they find themselves in such situations, older women are forced to consider that they may lack the talent to keep pace. A study of more than 8000 workers in 61 German companies found that workers who were supervised by younger people reported more negative emotions, such as anger and resentment, than did those workers whose managers were older than they were.[56] Here is Dee's experience.

Dee has worked at the same company for 35 years, receiving promotions over the years as well as salary increases. When a woman 30 years younger than Dee was hired as her new supervisor, Dee started to question her career success; she felt inadequate. Now Dee wonders what she should have done differently to have had a more successful career. She has become so discouraged that she has started to plan her retirement.

In addition to experiencing an increase in negative emotions, older women can engage in counterproductive behaviors, such as failing to cooperate with, or providing little support for, their younger bosses. Thus, when women are in younger boss–older subordinate situations, their relationships can be strained and quite negative.[57] As a result, when older women report to women who are significantly younger than they are, older women frequently rate their younger bosses' leadership skills lower than younger workers rated their younger bosses, younger workers rated their older bosses, or older workers rated their older bosses.[58]

Obviously, when older women have a low regard for the leadership skills of their significantly younger female bosses, there is a ready source of workplace conflict between them. Older women are likely to show less respect, work less hard, and be more critical than they would be if they worked for an older boss, whether a woman or a man. And younger female bosses are likely to be aware of their older subordinates' attitudes, leading them to evaluate the older women's performance more harshly than they would otherwise do. All in all, unless managed carefully, the younger female boss-older female subordinate relationship is a recipe for a tension–filled workplace. Here is Ashley's story.

Ashley is a successful millennial manager who was promoted over a large group of older managers to implement an important initiative. She assumed she would have difficulty with the older women on her team, so she took the initiative and met one-on-one with each of them. She directly addressed their age disparity by acknowledging that they had more experience than she did and that she would need their help if their team was going to be successful. She also asked about their personal career objectives and what she could do to help them realize their goals. Ashley told us that this worked well with all but one of her female subordinates, a woman who has subsequently left the company. As a result of her efforts, Ashley was able to build an extremely close-knit team of women with a wide range of ages.

Meta-Stereotype

A *meta-stereotype* is a stereotype that one group holds about the way they believe they are stereotypically viewed by other people. Conflicts between women due to age-based stereotypes can be accentuated because of meta-stereotypes. Research suggests that people are aware of the stereotypes that others hold about them because of the groups they fall into[59] and that people expect others will view them in terms of those stereotypes.[60] Of course, just as the stereotypes that people have about the characteristics of people of any particular group are likely to be invalid when applied to individual members of that group, the same is true for meta-stereotypes. How people *think* other people view them does not necessarily reflect what other people *actually* think of them. Interestingly, in a 2012 study of age-based meta-stereotypes, researchers found that older workers (50 and over) thought that younger workers (30 and younger) were far more likely to attribute negative characteristics to them, such as being boring, stubborn, and grumpy, than the younger workers actually did.[61] Nevertheless because older workers believed they were being viewed negatively by younger workers, the older workers sought to avoid interactions with the younger workers. This avoidance becomes a self-fulfilling prophecy that increases the tensions and conflicts between the age groups.

Further, the younger workers had even more negative meta-stereotypes about older workers' view of them. Younger workers thought that older workers viewed them almost entirely in terms of negative stereotypes such as being immature, clueless, and brash. In fact, only 7.5 percent of the traits the younger workers thought older workers ascribed to them were positive. In fact, Younger workers seemed to entirely lack any recognition that older workers thought any of their workplace traits were positive. Younger workers' negative meta-stereotypes caused them to distance themselves from their older colleagues, thus causing further age segregation, which also becomes a self-fulfilling prophecy that makes it even harder for younger and older women to work together comfortably.

While these age-based conflicts often exist in the workplace, they are not insurmountable. We provide some ideas and suggestions to overcome or avoid these conflicts in chapters 10 and 11 and in the section that follows.

MAKING THINGS BETTER

- The popular press would have us all believe that generational differences are dramatic and create significant workplace conflicts. Yet many of these supposed differences and conflicts are not supported by research. The unfortunate result is that younger and older women are likely to react to negative age stereotypes rather than to actual differences between them.
- Younger women often believe that technological changes are being made too slowly in the workplace. The answer is not to harbor resentments about older women but rather to make the business case to older women about appropriate technological changes.
- Avoid workplace age segregation. Encourage programs, activities, and project teams that provide opportunities for open communication between women of different ages and career levels.
- Keep an open mind. Learning is a lifelong process. Younger and older female colleagues can provide a wealth of information, life experiences, and workplace knowledge for each other. As a respondent to our age survey said, "We need to hear each other's stories before we formulate opinions about other people."
- Treat older female colleagues as your peers, not as your mother; and treat younger female colleagues as your peers, not as if they were children.
- Understand the reasons behind possible tensions and negative emotions between younger supervisors and older subordinates. If an older subordinate tries to circumvent a younger supervisor's authority, this must be addressed firmly but respectfully. Younger supervisors also need to acknowledge that they can learn from

older subordinates, want to earn their respect, and appreciate their maturity and experiences.

- Don't get trapped by meta-stereotypes. Take the time to get to know other women who are significantly older and younger than you are. You might be surprised to see how similar your career aspirations actually are.
- Younger supervisors should learn what motivates their older subordinates and find ways to inspire their teams.
- Older supervisors need to be willing to learn from younger subordinates and remain open to different points of view.
- Acknowledge and recognize the unique contributions that women of different ages bring to the workplace.

Chapter 9

Mothers and Others

I T IS HARDLY NEWS THAT it is extremely difficult for women in the United States to have successful, satisfying, guilt-free careers (what we will call "Careers") *and* equally successful, satisfying, and guilt-free child-rearing experiences (what we will call "Families").[1] It is often assumed that this difficulty arises because once women have children, their maternal instincts outweigh their career ambition such that they cannot effectively manage the competing demands of Careers and Families.[2] In fact, these competing demands are most often made unmanageable by structural factors that are entirely external to women's actual needs and desires. It is these structural factors—not women's maternal instincts—that make it so hard for women in the United States to pursue challenging jobs *and* to be certain their children are in healthy, safe, nurturing environments where their children can develop in sound academic, emotional, and spiritual ways.

Mothers' Rocky Workplace Road

As *New York Times* columnist Gail Collins has pointedly observed,

> The feminist movement of the late twentieth century created a new United States in which women ran for president, fought for their country, argued before the Supreme Court, performed

heart surgery, directed movies, and flew into space. But it did not resolve the tensions of trying to raise children and hold down a job at the same time.[3]

The tensions Collins points to are caused primarily by the lack of convenient, affordable, quality childcare; the pressures on mothers to parent "intensively"; the strong and pervasive workplace stereotypes and biases against mothers; and the masculine norms and expectations of gendered workplaces. Together, these factors create a toxic environment for women attempting to have both Careers and Families at the same time.

Childcare

Some women would never be comfortable relying on third parties for any part of their children's care. They believe their fundamental role and responsibility is the care, nurturing, and guidance of their children: that they—and only they—can do this the way it *should be done*. Many more women, however, agree with Betty Friedan, who wrote, now so many years ago, "The only way for a woman, as for a man, to find herself, to know herself as a person, is by creative work of her own."[4] For these women, creative work means work outside of the home, and that means relying, to one degree or another, on others to help with childcare. The problem, however, is that finding such help is often a major challenge.

Unlike every other industrialized nation, the United States provides little (if any) assistance with childcare. Beginning with maternity leave, the United States does not guarantee paid leave for newborn care. While federal law guarantees up to 12 weeks of job-protected maternity leave, this leave does not have to be paid.[5] The United States is, thus, in a very exclusive club, because only the US, Liberia, Papua New Guinea, and Swaziland do not have any form of guaranteed *paid leave* for newborn care.[6]

With respect to sick leave, the United States also holds an exclusive position as the only one of the world's 21 wealthiest nations that does not mandate paid sick days.[7] And, perhaps most damaging of all to women's efforts to combine Careers and Families, the United States has the most-underfunded, poorest-quality, most-chaotic system of childcare among all industrialized countries.

It is hard to exaggerate the inadequacy of third-party childcare in the United States. A majority of all mothers with young children work outside of the home, and less than one-third of all American children have a full-time, stay-at-home parent.[8] As a consequence, childcare services must be found for the great majority of the 12 million American children under the age of 5.[9] Unfortunately, availability, cost, and quality of childcare services are all major problems facing American families.

Availability

In a comprehensive 2016 study, the Center for American Progress looked at childcare services in a group of eight representative US states. It found that in those states, 42 percent of all children under 5 years of age ("young children") live in "childcare deserts," that is, zip codes with at least 30 young children but either no childcare center or so few centers that there are more than three times as many young children as there are available spaces.[10] In these eight states alone, 1.8 million young children live in childcare deserts: 55 percent of those in rural areas, 36 percent of those in suburban areas, and 49 percent of those in urban areas.[11]

Cost

Even in places where childcare services are available, the cost is often prohibitive. On average, it costs more to send young children to a daycare center than it does to send a grown child to an in-state college: $9,589 a year for daycare as opposed to $9,410 a year for in-state college.[12] Even so, the cost of sending a child to daycare pales in comparison to the cost of in-home care by a caregiver or nanny—the preferred childcare service of many mothers with demanding careers. The average cost of such an in-home service is $28,353 a year, which is 53 percent of the US median household income.[13]

The US government does provide grants to the states from the Child Care and Development Fund to issue vouchers for childcare services to low-income parents.[14] However, "low income" is typically defined as having a household income at or below 75 percent of a given state's median income, and very few women pursuing Careers qualify for this assistance.[15] There is also a federal tax credit for childcare expenses, but if a mother's annual family earned income is $43,000 or more, she receives a credit of only 20 percent of her childcare expenses up to $3,000 for one child or $6,000 for two or more children.[16] A tax credit of $600 or $1,200 is hardly significant assistance for women paying more than $10,000 per year for childcare.

Despite working mothers' obvious need for assistance with their childcare responsibilities, US businesses do little to help, providing subsidies for only 1 to 4 percent of total childcare costs.[17] Ellen's experience is typical.

When we interviewed Ellen for this book, she told us she had had a very successful and satisfying career. Her one child, a daughter, was in a five-days-a-week daycare facility near her home. She and her husband took turns dropping their daughter off and picking her up. When her daughter was two years old, Ellen had twin boys. After three months of maternity leave, Ellen found it very difficult to find quality childcare for all three children. She thought about a nanny, but concluded they could not afford one. She tried three different childcare arrangements, but found them all unsatisfactory because of their poor quality and high cost. Ellen finally concluded that she and her husband could not juggle their careers and childcare for three kids in their current location. Ellen put her career on hold and moved back to her hometown to be closer to her family. Her husband was able to quickly find a new job, but Ellen decided to take a short break from her career to care for the children. Her children are now all in school and Ellen has been trying for about a year to get a new position. To date, her efforts to restart her career have proved far more difficult than she had ever anticipated. As she said to us, "I doubt I will ever be able to have a career of the sort I had before the birth of the boys."

Quality

Because childcare is an extremely low-profit service, US childcare is typically of poor quality. Factoring in real estate, supplies, insurance, and labor costs, childcare center expenses are high, particularly in states that require one caregiver for every three or four children. Despite their high costs, childcare centers find it very difficult to raise their prices because most of their customers are already paying all they can afford. As a result, childcare centers have an incentive to provide only bare-bones services, in barely adequate facilities, by people with minimal training who are paid very low wages. Consequently, only 11 percent of childcare establishments in the United States are accredited by the National Association for the Education of Young Children or the National Association for Family Childcare.[18]

Commenting on the childcare situation in the United States, Brigid Schulte, one of the authors of the New America study entitled "Our Fragmented, Patchwork Care System," stated, "The thing to remember about childcare is that the market really doesn't work.... [Childcare] has to be subsidized. It has to be seen as a public good."[19] Why the market for childcare doesn't work and how it could be fixed are vitally important issues.[20] Our concern at the moment, however, is not with how to fix our country's abominable childcare system, but to make clear that the lack of affordable, quality childcare is one of the main reasons why so many women find it so hard to simultaneously have Careers *and* Families.

Intensive Mothering

The prevailing ideology in the United States as to what is required to be a good mother is inconsistent with a mother pursuing a Career. Mothers are continuously told by the media and the popular press that a mother's care is unique and irreplaceable, and that regardless of a mother's other interests, needs, or obligations, her children must always come first.[21] Thus this ideology that good mothering equals intensive mothering rests on the belief that good mothers are not employed.[22]

The nature of intensive mothering, and the fallacies underlying the idea, were first spelled out by Sharon Hays in her 1996 book, *The Cultural Contradictions of Motherhood*.[23] Hays argued that intensive mothering was "the socially dominant form of child rearing in the contemporary United States."[24] More than 20 years later, intensive mothering is still the dominant parenting ideology in the United States.[25] While there are competing models of mothering, none has anywhere near the cultural influence of intensive mothering. Indeed, when both the French approach to parenting[26] and the Free Range approach[27] were first proposed, they were met with strong negative reactions, anger, and resistance. The French approach, set out in *Bringing Up Bebe*, "helps kids eat normal foods, behave themselves, and sleep all night."[28] The Free Range approach encourages parents to instill independence in young children by accurately assessing the risks that their children face and then helping them make choices and develop independence.[29]

Intensive mothering is more likely to be practiced by those women with the luxury to expend extravagant amounts of time, energy, and money on their children.[30] But the belief in the inherent "rightness" of intensive mothering is common among women of all socioeconomic classes.[31] Indeed, mothers in less affluent circumstances often "feel guilty that they don't earn enough to get their kids private music lessons or academic tutoring. They feel guilty that they aren't sacrificing more of their time shuttling their kids to extracurricular activities. They worry about how they will ever afford to send their kids to college."[32]

The belief that children's physical, emotional, and intellectual well-being depends on their spending as much time with their mothers as possible is clearly widespread. Mothers in 2018 spent 40 percent more time with their children than mothers did in 1965.[33] Professional women are leading this trend, with women with college degrees spending about 25 percent more time on child-rearing responsibilities than mothers without such a degree. In fact, these highly educated women are now spending about twice as much time on child-rearing responsibilities as their counterparts did 50 years ago.[34]

Intensive mothering is now so widely accepted that two popular terms are frequently used to describe the women who practice it: *helicopter moms* and *lawnmower moms*. Helicopter moms are "preoccupied with and overprotective of their children," while lawnmower moms take their preoccupation and overprotection to the next level by actually intervening in their children's lives to constantly "prevent [them] from facing any kind of adversity."[35] Lawnmower moms are so named because they "mow down all of their children's challenges, discomforts and struggles."[36]

Despite spending more time than ever before on child rearing, professional women with young children are often dissatisfied with the parenting job they are doing. More often than not, they feel guilty because their careers are preventing them from being truly "good" mothers.[37] For these women their inability to "conform to the intensive mothering ideal" is a source "of anxiety, depression, and self-blame."[38]

This guilt is entirely unjustified. As we discussed in *Breaking Through Bias*, there is no empirical support for the belief that intensive mothering is beneficial, much less essential for children's healthy development.[39] In fact, when mothers work outside the home, their children actually benefit.[40] Nevertheless, so long as the ideology of intensive mothering continues to hold sway, many women will continue to find it impossible to combine Careers and Families in a truly satisfying way.

Motherhood Bias

As if the lack of quality, affordable childcare and our society's expectation of intensive mothering did not create sufficiently formidable obstacles to mothers having both Careers and Families, when mothers are at work they are often treated quite badly. Women with small children are discriminated against with respect to assignments, compensation, and promotions; they are subjected to dispiriting incivilities and microaggressions; and they are excluded from valuable social interactions and networks. This biased treatment of mothers is by no means exclusively by men, as Julie's story illustrates.

Julie is an executive at a West Coast manufacturing firm. She recently told us. "When my son was young, I was the only mother in a work group that included six women. The other women would occasionally go out for drinks after work and never included me. One day as they were getting ready to leave together, I asked if I could join then. 'Oh no,' said one of the women, 'you need to get home to your family.' With that, they all walked out laughing."

Studies show that mothers earn 5 percent less per hour per child than women without children.[41] Mothers are 79 percent less likely to be hired; are half as likely to be promoted; when hired they are offered $11,000 less in salary; and are held to higher performance standards than women without children.[42] This discriminatory treatment of mothers is even worse for mothers who are racially or ethnically different from the workplace's dominant (typically white) social identity group. Indeed, one study found that a higher percentage of black and Hispanic women with children were likely to downsize their ambitions (59 percent) than were similar women without children (40 percent).[43]

Communal Women Par Excellence

The discriminatory treatment of mothers is due, in large part, to straightforward gender bias. Women, simply because they are women, are deemed to be less agentic and more communal than men, and therefore less suited for assignments, projects, and careers associated with high competence, decisiveness, and emotional toughness.[44] In relation to other women, however, mothers are assumed to be quintessentially communal and nonagentic. They are thought to be the kindest, nicest, and most modest of all women, and, therefore *even less* suited for challenging assignments, projects, and careers than are women without children.

The pervasive depreciation of mothers' competence and emotional toughness has been demonstrated in numerous studies. For example, when participants in one such study were presented with identical profiles of fictitious management consultants that varied only by gender and parental status, participants (both women and men) rated female consultants with children—but not male consultants with children—as less likely to be hired than their same-sex counterparts without children.[45] In another study, when identical résumés (except for parental status) were submitted for actual open positions, women with children were called back about half as often as women without children.[46] And in yet another study, participants (both women and men) were shown a video of a woman interacting with others in a work scenario. In half of the videos, the woman appeared to be pregnant and in the other half she did not appear to be pregnant; otherwise the videos were identical. When participants were asked to evaluate the woman's performance and work commitment, they consistently rated the apparently pregnant woman lower than they did the identical woman when she did not appear to be pregnant.[47]

Successful Women, Bad Mothers

Apart from mothers being discriminated against because they are viewed as quintessentially communal and nonagentic, mothers are also discriminated against because of the proscriptive and prescriptive stereotypes about mothers. Because of the historical separation of women's and men's societal roles and the more recent ascent of the ideology of intensive mothering, it is stereotypically assumed that mothers (but not fathers) *should be* responsible for childcare and mothers (but not fathers) *should not be* working outside the home. Given these stereotypes, one research study found that women who had left high-status professional jobs consistently reported receiving little support from their colleagues and employers when they initially returned to work after having had a child, but they received substantial praise and encouragement when they ultimately left the workplace to care for their children full-time.[48] Such experiences are a product of colleagues and managers so often seeing working mothers as bad mothers.

Women trying to combine Careers and child raising are also negatively evaluated when they unambiguously demonstrate a high level of competence and career commitment. A 2010 study asked female and male participants to evaluate mothers and fathers with identical credentials, performance ratings, and job commitments. Female evaluators consistently rated the mothers—but not the identically credentialed fathers—as having undesirable interpersonal qualities. Female evaluators penalized the mothers in their recommendations for promotion, hiring, and salary. Significantly, these penalties were not correlated with how the female evaluators rated the mothers' competence and commitment but were correlated with their presumed interpersonal deficiencies. Interestingly, male evaluators did not penalize these high-achieving mothers relative to the other hypothetical candidates.[49]

This study does not mean that only women but not men are biased against working mothers. Rather, both women and men presume that mothers are not as well suited for leadership roles as fathers, but when mothers *did* attain leadership roles and unambiguously demonstrated their competence and commitment, women evaluated them more negatively than men did. While the reason for this is not entirely clear, we believe that female evaluators felt threatened by or resentful of high-achieving mothers who set a difficult or impossible standard for other women to meet. This may explain why women so often view high-achieving mothers as cold, selfish, and unlikable—so as to remove them from interpersonal comparison.

Workplace Culture

As we discussed in chapter 4, our workplaces tend to be highly gendered with decidedly masculine norms concerning appropriate work patterns, conversational and managerial styles, and relational behaviors. People in management far more than others are expected to conform their conduct to these norms. For people in management, the pressure to conform to these norms of conduct is exceptionally high. As difficult and stressful as it often is for women generally to do this, women with children face substantial additional challenges. Typical of these masculine workplace norms are the assumption that work and home are separate nonoverlapping spheres, that long hours are the appropriate sign of career commitment, and that participation in after-work socializing is a condition for inclusion in workplace networks.

Separate Spheres

In the United States, at least among urban middle- and upper-middle-class socioeconomic groups, it used to be commonly assumed that men should work outside the home as the breadwinners, while women worked inside the home, managing all things domestic. In this traditional view, work and home are separate, nonintersecting life spheres. Thus, when men are at work, they are assumed not to have worries about, much less have to deal with, domestic matters such as cleaning, shopping, and child rearing. Managers—particularly senior managers—simply should not be concerned about or interrupted by nonwork tasks. This view of work and home as distinct nonoverlapping spheres prevails at almost all Fortune 500 companies, where 75 percent of men in executive positions do not have to worry about domestic concerns because they have spouses or partners who are not employed and tend to home and children.[50]

For mothers seeking or holding senior leadership positions, however, work and home are often difficult to separate so neatly. Such women are unlikely to have stay-at-home partners, and their work life is likely to be a continuous battle to maintain the illusion that their work and home lives are separate, with neither interfering with the other. As a result, many women either conceal the fact that they have children or lead others to believe their children's needs and interests are of little concern for them.[51] The problem that mothers have in maintaining this illusion is that they— far more than fathers—typically have the primary responsibility for dealing with their children's well-being.[52] Therefore, children's unanticipated needs—sickness, school closings, canceled daycare—can be unwelcome occurrences that make it all too apparent to their colleagues and managers that their home life is not a separate and distinct sphere from their work life. For this reason, several women have told us that they tell their employers that *they* are sick when their children are in order to maintain the illusion that their ability to devote themselves 100 percent to their career is unburdened by domestic responsibility. Of course, the effort to maintain the appearance that their lives can be neatly divided into non-overlapping spheres can be highly stressful. Nevertheless, in gendered workplaces, a mother's career success often depends on her behaving in ways that demonstrate that her career and all other aspects of her life can be kept apart.

Long Hours

Organizational expectation that senior managers will work long hours *at the office* is particularly hard for most mothers to meet. When such managers are also expected to be constantly available, childcare arrangements can reach the breaking point. Yet these two demands—long hours and 24/7 availability—are expected of people with high-status, high-paying, highly interesting careers. In fact, for many such careers, productivity, work quality, and efficiency can actually be less important for continual success than long, highly visible hours in the office.

Mothers, despite their ambitions and career aspirations, can reach a point where they feel a need to set limits on how much of their child rearing responsibilities they are willing to off-load to others. Therefore, they face a clear double bind: remaining a fully involved mother and forgoing desirable career opportunities, or submitting to the demands of long hours and constant availability and giving up personally satisfying parenting relationships. Unless mothers can find a way to avoid or overcome this double bind, they have little chance of successfully having both Careers and Families.[53] We discuss flexible work arrangements in chapter 10 as a way to help women successfully manage Careers and Families.

Socializing

In gendered workplaces, out-of-the-office socializing is often an expected part of relationship building and informal networking. Such socializing, particularly drinks, sports, and evening events, is not just an occasion for relaxation and good times, but essential to cultivating mentoring possibilities, strengthening interpersonal relationships, and learning of leadership opportunities. Because most senior men can easily keep the spheres of work and home separate, participating in such social events is little more than an extension of their workday. It is not nearly as easy for time-constrained mothers. Long, inflexible hours are bad enough, but the further expectation that they stay away from home for drinks, client entertaining, or marketing excursions may simply be impossible to meet given their child-rearing responsibilities. But when mothers fail to participate in such out-of-office activities, they often miss out on important career-enhancing opportunities. In gendered workplaces, mothers' inability or unwillingness to participate in these activities can increase their isolation and separation from men and other women without children.

Mothers' Same-Gender Conflicts

The tensions and conflicts between mothers and other women in the workplace are due, in large part, to the combination of mothers' rocky workplace road and the pervasive stereotypes about mothers and about women without children and the career advantages these women enjoy. Whether because of jealousy or resentment with respect to childcare arrangements, disapproval of particular parenting practices, hostility over preferential treatment given to women without children, or frustration with their inability to fit into masculine work patterns, mothers pursuing careers are both the dispensers and recipients of disapproval, anger, and disparagement. While mothers can criticize other mothers for their parenting practices,[54] mothers can also criticize women without children as being somehow incomplete, selfish, and self-centered. To hear some mothers talk about women without children, it is as though they are doomed to live out the rest of their lives full of regret and loneliness.

Katie, a sales manager in her 40s, told us she does not have any children, and at work she is "treated by the mothers I work with as if I am of a lesser status than they are. It is as if they do not see me as

(Continued)

a complete woman. They treat me with pity, tell me what a terrible decision I made not to have children, and warn me to plan for an old age with no one to take care of me."

Established workplace relationships between women are likely to change once one of them becomes a mother. Take, for example, the situation that developed between Jessica, a new mother, and her boss, Dora.

Jessica would leave work in time to feed her baby and put him to bed before going back online to handle end-of-day items. While she was feeding her son, Dora started calling Jessica with questions that could easily have waited until after Jessica's son was asleep or the next morning. Jessica was getting frustrated and angry about Dora's inconvenient calls. One night she answered the phone and told Dora she was busy "right now" but would be happy to call Dora back "in a few hours." Dora simply said they could discuss it in the morning. Jessica realized then that Dora had only wanted to be reassured that Jessica was still available to her now that Jessica was a mother. After Jessica made clear she had no intention of reducing her commitment to the job, their relationship went back to the comfortable way it had been before Jessica's son was born.

Incivility

Workplace incivility takes the form of rude or discourteous behavior. Unfortunately, incivility is common in many organizations. In large-scale surveys between 71 and 79 percent of all employees report having had uncivil encounters at work.[55] Mothers, however, appear to be particularly subject to workplace incivility. Here is one example of how such incivility can arise.

Madeline, a senior executive in a midsized financial services firm, told us, "A couple of weeks ago, Jill, a promising financial analyst, returned early from her company-paid maternity leave to handle a major project. Lauren, one of Jill's colleagues, told Jill she had no business being back at work and that she should be home with her baby. Jill responded by saying that her baby was in good hands. The discussion, however, got quite heated. At that point, another female colleague, Rossy, stepped in and told Lauren that it was none of her business what Jill did. Then Lauren turned on Rossy, repeating that Jill should not be at work and that Rossy should mind her own business. Rossy called Lauren's views stupid, old-fashioned, and out of date. Lauren told Rossy her views showed what's wrong with society today. Lauren stormed off, and Lauren has not talked to Jill or Rossy since."

Precisely because mothers' competence and commitment are so routinely questioned, mothers frequently encounter incivility in their efforts to be acknowledged as valuable team members. But mothers can also treat women without children in rude and disrespectful ways. Take, for example, Leslie's story.

Leslie, a very successful tax accountant, told us, "The 'kid factor' in my experience definitely causes deep conflicts between women who have kids and women who don't. There are many dynamics that enter into this, including the assumption that women without kids (like me) chose not to have children. I went through massive fertility treatments but ultimately to no avail. When I was going through these treatments, I received infinitely more support, understanding, and compassion from the men I worked with than from the women I worked with. In fact, many mothers treated me

(Continued)

with open disrespect, telling me that the reason I couldn't get pregnant was because I was working too hard and was under too much stress. The truth of the matter was that my husband and I were using state-of-the-art fertility technology, and my not becoming pregnant had nothing to do with stress and everything to do with biology. Nevertheless, many of the mothers I worked with consistently treated me as though it was my fault."

Another major source of conflict between mothers and other women is the frequent assumption by mothers that women without children should be available to fill in for them simply because they don't have childcare demands. Women without children tell us that the mothers they work with often assume they can cover for them simply because the demands on their time are not "as important" as those on mothers' time. As we were told by one of our women survey respondents, "If women want to raise children and have a career, that's fine with me, but they shouldn't expect any special breaks—and I let them know it." And in a survey we conducted about younger and older women working together, one of our female respondents told us, "I resent younger women using their kids as a constant excuse not to come to work, to leave 'on time,' or to get in late."

Microaggressions

Microaggressions convey a derogatory or negative view or opinion. Some of the microaggressions directed against mothers that have been related to us are, "You have kids so you're not suited for the manager job that has just opened up," "Joe asked if you'd like to be on the XYZ account but I told him you can't handle it because you need to get home," and "Was your pregnancy planned?" Microaggressions directed against women without children about which we have been told include "When are you having kids?", "Let me fix you up with my friend's son," "You don't understand what it is to be a woman until you have children," "You could always adopt a baby," and "It must be unsatisfying not to have children." Here is Jo's experience.

Jo, a lesbian who is not "out" at work, keeps pictures of her dog in her office, none of her wife and their children. The other women she works with don't know anything about her personal life, which often makes Jo feel uncomfortable. They always talk about their families and tell Jo how much she is missing without having a husband and children. As Jo told us, "Sometimes I feel like making up a fake boyfriend just so they will stop giving me pitying looks when I don't accept their offers to fix me up on dates."

Claire, a woman without children, shared with us the following story about meeting her new boss.

Claire is a senior manager at an engineering firm. When she was introduced to her new boss, Martha, Martha shook her hand and said, "Claire, so how many kids do you have?" When Claire said, "None," Martha was silent for a few long seconds. Claire saw this as a microaggression because "Martha had attempted to validate me based on my status as a mother, rather than about my work-related experiences."

Isolation

Mothers—because they are different from most of the male leaders in gendered workplaces and different from women without children—can be purposefully excluded from their colleagues' networks and social activities. Exclusion, however, can work both ways. Mothers can disparage women without children and exclude them from *their* networks and informal activities. Here is Meg's story.

Meg told us that in recent years her close group of workplace female colleagues has drifted into two groups—the mothers and the others. Without any discussion, the mothers and the women without children have even stopped having lunch together.

Mothers of small children and women without children can frequently seek to maintain sufficient distance between them to avoid being painted with what each group sees as the other group's negative characteristics: in the case of mothers, their supposed lack of competence and commitment, and in the case of women without children, their supposed lack of femininity and completeness. In addition, in our experience mothers and other women often assume that the other group is not interested in the same things that they are interested in.

Although these conflicts can seem insurmountable, there are ways to overcome or avoid them. We make some suggestions in chapter 10 and here.

MAKING THINGS BETTER

- Don't buy into the concept of intensive mothering. It's another stereotype that holds mothers back in their careers.
- Women's perceptions about having children change at different career and life stages. In the report "Cracking the Code," for example, the researchers found that

     at or close to, the time of starting a family, women are highly sensitive to the interconnections of their personal and professional responsibilities. They are also aware of the career implications of motherhood. 36% of women interviewees believe their career progression had decelerated—on average by 4 years—as a result of taking maternity leave. 13% describe this deceleration as helpful in allowing them to adjust to balancing home and work commitments. 19% are less positive about what they believe are unhelpful organizational responses to them starting a family.[56]

- With hindsight, senior women leaders report being less concerned about the impact on their careers of having children. Twenty-four percent describe the positive effects of having a family on their career progression to include broadening their perspective, enhancing their personal and organizational skills, developing their empathy for other colleagues with families, and making them more determined to succeed.[57]

- Organizations need to make efforts to accommodate mothers with small children (and provide paternity leave as a way of encouraging men to take up a greater share of childcare responsibilities). Women in most American families are expected to perform more childcare and housework than their spouses or partners. Businesses need to ensure that these differences do not trigger discriminatory career consequences. For example, women who take maternity leave should not lose career ground, and mothers should receive the same career opportunities and face the same workplace demands as their male coworkers. Women who take time out should have on-ramp opportunities available when they return.

- Organizations can help women with children get to the top in their leadership ranks by following the advice in "Cracking the Code":

  Organizations need to take a long view about the career paths for their female talent. Sensible career management is of immense value to women throughout the early stages of their career. Challenging women in the middle stages of their career to revisit their short and medium term aspirations in light of personal growth as a result of having a family could add some fresh perspectives on who should be in the talent pool. More dynamic data could help organizations to build a clearer picture of the impact that time out from work has on both men and women.[58]

- Mothers should not assume that women without children are available to step in to cover for their personal scheduling needs, or that women without children have more flexible schedules than those of mothers.
- Women without children should not assume that mothers are less committed to their careers because of their children.
- All women need to recognize that assumptions about mothers and careers are based on stereotypes and biases that have no more validity than other stereotypes and biases.
- Mothers should not make assumptions about why other women do or do not have children. These are personal decisions that can be affected by many complicated factors.
- Women should speak up when they see mothers being treated in discriminatory or dismissive ways.
- Mothers should not imply or suggest that women without children are missing out on an important life experience. Other women have their own reasons for their decisions.
- Mothers and women without children working together can build a strong and effective sisterhood.

PART IV

Going Forward

Chapter 10

Overcoming Women's Identity Conflicts

WOMEN, APART FROM HAVING WORKPLACE conflicts that are no different from men's, do have conflicts with the women they work with that are distinctive and quite unlike men's workplace conflicts. But contrary to many authors' claims, women's distinctive workplace conflicts are not due to some unique personality characteristics that lead them to be mean to, competitive with, or antagonistic toward each other. Women are not programmed (by nature, nurture, or both) to be hostile to their same-gender colleagues. Quite to the contrary, such empirical evidence as is available points to women's strong desire to bond with and support other women—to build sisterhoods.

As we have argued throughout this book, women's distinctive same-gender workplace conflicts are the direct result of biases that exist in the workplace. These biases are of two sorts: biases pervasive in gendered workplaces—affinity and gender bias—and women's own biases about women with different social identities (what we will call Identity Bias). Women's identity biases are a result of stereotypes, internalized from their cultural, family, and workplace environments, about women with different social identities—race, ethnicity, age, sexual orientation, gender identity, or parental status. As a result of these stereotypes, women often ascribe characteristics to "different" women that imply they are difficult to work with, lack essential interpersonal skills, or possess undesirable personality characteristics. In this chapter we discuss how to minimize women's identity conflicts—their discomfort with, suspicion of, and wariness of women with different social identities by fostering candid, constructive, nondefensive conversations among and between women whose distinctive social identities are different from their own.

In chapter 11 we discuss how best to attack affinity bias and gender bias in gendered workplaces, namely by significantly increasing the gender diversity in its senior leadership.

Women's Identity Biases

In chapters 5 through 9, we discussed the unique workplace difficulties women experience because they have different social identities. As a result of these differences, women often have quite different life and workplace experiences, perspectives on career opportunities and prospects, and attitudes toward other people with distinctive social identities. Women can, and often do, come into conflict with other women simply because, despite their common gender, they are "different" from each other (conflicts of this sort we call "Identity Conflicts"). Men most certainly also have Identity Conflicts, but women's Identity Conflicts deserve special attention because in gendered workplaces women, because they are women, are a conspicuous outgroup. Therefore, when women with one distinctive social identity have conflicts with, distance themselves from, behave with incivility toward, or are openly hostile to women with different social identities, they are pushing those women even farther away from their organizations' centers of power; they are calling into question those women's qualifications for leadership; and they are making it even more difficult for those women to participate in key social and professional networks. When women have conflicts with women of a different race, ethnicity, age, or sexual orientation, for example, they are sending the signal that even women think less of these "different" sorts of women.

If our workplaces were more inclusive, respectful, and valuing of people with distinctive social identities, Identity Conflicts would be greatly diminished. Unfortunately, most of our workplaces have a great deal of work to do before they are truly welcoming of all different sorts of people, and women's workplace Identity Conflicts need to be addressed now. Fortunately, women can do a great deal to end their own Identity Conflicts by improving the nature of the conversations they have with women who are different from them.

What Needs to Be Understood

Women's views of women who have intersecting social identities that are different from their own are multilayered attitudes resulting from the internalization of cultural, family, and workplace stereotype-driven biases. All of us are socialized, albeit to different degrees, to have Identity Biases of various sorts about people with different racial, ethnic, age, and sexual identities. Such biases are ubiquitous and difficult, if not impossible, to eliminate entirely. Nevertheless, women work every day with women whose social identities are different from their own. Based on our years of coaching and counseling, we believe most of them would prefer to build sisterhoods with these different women than to separate from them in uncivil standoffs. The creation of such sisterhoods and the avoidance of incivility depends on women of different social identities being able to have open, candid, and respectful conversations with each other about their attitudes toward, experiences with, and expectations of each other. The problem, of course, is that such conversations are difficult to have and are often very uncomfortable. This is typically because they can implicate our own biases or prejudices, causing us to become defensive if not offended. These conversations can exacerbate rather than reduce Identity Conflicts. The trick, therefore, is to find ways to talk about Identity Bias without defensiveness, ways that increase understanding, appreciation, and respect and that incline us more toward sisterhood.

Women's Conversations with Themselves

Regardless of our particular social identities, we all have biases about people who belong to different identity groups, and we all believe in the value and importance of our distinctive identity. Many of us, however, find it very difficult to acknowledge our biases, preferring to maintain the illusion that we are bias-free, firm believers in and practitioners of universal equality, and value people who are different from us. Since that is an illusion, a useful first step toward becoming ready to have positive conversations with women whose social identities are different from their own is for women to have frank conversations with themselves about their beliefs, feelings, and attitudes concerning social identity.

One such conversation should involve women asking themselves what makes them uncomfortable in dealing with women of a different race or ethnicity. Why do they find it difficult to relate as easily with such women as they do with women of their same social identity? What specific characteristics of such women do they admire or dislike? Do they think these women are less cooperative, accomplished, or intelligent than women like them? Are such women more hostile, disagreeable, cliquish, or disrespectful? Do they have any evidence that their views in this respect are justified? If so, how good is it? If not, where did their views come from? Are they proud of the way they feel? Would they want it generally known that they feel this way? Would they become defensive if someone accused them of having such attitudes? Are they prepared to discuss their attitudes with the women about whom they have them?

A second such conversation with themselves should involve how women feel about themselves and their own social identity. Do they have privileges (or disadvantages) because of that identity? What are they? Are these privileges (or disadvantages) fair? Would they want them removed? Because of their social identity, do they (consciously or unconsciously) act toward people who are different from them in hostile, antagonistic, or demeaning ways? If so, why, and are they proud of that behavior? When they interact with people who are like them, do they disparage, exclude, or demean people with different social identities? What are their personal qualities and characteristics that have allowed them to get where they are (or prevented them from getting there)? Are they prepared to talk about these personal qualities and characteristics with people who are not like them?

It is very difficult to have these conversations with ourselves, not least because no one wants to admit that they have Identity Biases. Often such conversations are possible only after a close friend or colleague has called our attention to an insensitive remark we have made or an action we have taken; we have witnessed clearly biased behavior on the part of someone we respect; or we have gotten the result after having taken the Implicit Attitude Test for race or ethnicity at Harvard's Project Implicit.[1] Whatever result we get, however, until we acknowledge our own biases and have done our best to have conversations with ourselves about those biases, we are not going to be able to make much progress at ending our workplace Identity Conflicts.

Women's Conversations with Other Women

Once women have come to terms—to the extent they are able on their own—with their Identity Biases, they should be in a position to start to have conversations with different women that hold the promise of ending workplace Identity Conflicts. But even after women have thoughtfully analyzed their own Identity Biases, having constructive conversations with other women about identity, bias, and workplace opportunities can be tricky and fraught with the possibility of making things worse rather than better. Therefore, keep in mind that words matter. Depending on what women say and how they say it, they can either blow up relationships or move them forward. When women are not alert to the sensitivities of the people with whom they are talking, it is easy to say stupid, hurtful, and disrespectful things. Women attempting to have serious conversations with other women about their Identity Conflicts need to be prepared for some rough sailing, at least at first. In her book, *So You Want to Talk about Race*, Ijeoma Oluo writes that when you attempt to have such conversations, "You're going to screw this up royally. More than once. But you should have these conversations anyway."[2]

In order to maximize the chances that women's conversations with other women about identity conflicts are productive and move toward sisterhood, we offer a number of suggestions based on our own experiences and the discussions in *So You Want to Talk about Race* and the Catalyst Research Project, "Flip the Script."[3]

1. **Be clear (at least to yourself) about why you are having this conversation**. Once you are clear about your objective in entering into a conversation about social identities and why they so often make women's same-gender relationships difficult, you should be on guard that the woman with whom you are having the conversation might have an incompatible objective to your objective. Women's conversations about their attitudes, feelings, and beliefs about identity differences can very easily result in resentment and hostility if there has been a serious misunderstanding about why a conversation is happening.

2. **Do not become defensive and don't provoke defensiveness**. If you are talking about a sensitive identity difference and feel the need to defend yourself—"I am not a racist," "I have many LGBTQ friends"— stop and ask yourself why do you feel threatened? Has your objective shifted from what you wanted it to be to protecting your own ego? If you allow yourself to become defensive, you are unlikely to understand what is being said and you are unlikely to say what you meant to say.

By the same token, you should avoid saying anything that is likely to cause the other person to become defensive. For example, saying, "I'm sorry you feel that way," devalues the other person's feelings by suggesting her feelings may not be justified. Instead, a better thing to say would be, for instance, "I certainly did not mean to offend you or make you uncomfortable, but I see that I did. Please help me to be certain I don't do it again."

3. **The problem is bigger than your feelings**. Identity Conflicts are the result of Identity Biases that are systemic in our society and

workplaces. While your personal feelings are certainly involved, keep in mind that the biases you have found in yourself are likely to be experienced by your conversational partner on a daily basis, and she is likely to be subjected to slights and incivilities from many other people in many other situations. So don't make the conversation all about the way *you* feel.

4. **Your aim should be to understand, not to demonstrate you are a good person.** Whatever your objective in entering into the conversation in the first place, you should be consistently working to understand where the other woman is coming from, what vulnerabilities she may be reluctant to reveal, and how you can make clear that it is safe for her to proceed with this conversation with *you*.

It is precisely because women with different social identities have had such different experiences and hold such different perspectives that Identity Conflicts occur. You should strive to understand and to be seen as seeking to understand, not to demonstrate that you are not biased or hostile or disapproving. Forget about establishing the validity of your own point of view. Your aim should be to do better, not to prove you are a good person.

5. **Color-blind is difference blind**. Thinking, or worse saying, "The world would be a better place if all of us were color-blind" is not only dumb—the world is never going to be color-blind—but also highly insensitive to the fact that the woman with whom you are talking probably takes great pride in her racial or ethnic identity and does not want it ignored but acknowledged and valued. Suggesting we should be color-blind is a prescription for Identity Conflict, not a way to build a sisterhood of women with different social identities.

6. **Don't talk about identity conflicts unless you are ready.** Effective conversations about Identity Conflict depend not only on the women involved having, at least, a dawning awareness of their biases, but also on their willingness to listen to what may be disconcerting or uncomfortable comments without taking offense. Saying something like, "Let's not go there, it will only make things more difficult," is worse than not starting the conversation in the first place. Conversations between

two women about their Identity Conflicts should seek to achieve a deep, profound understanding of the reasons for those conflicts. Identity Conflicts will not end if women feel that certain topics are off-limits, must be tiptoed around, or involve "walking on eggshells." Therefore, instead of avoiding certain topics, trying something like, "I know this is difficult even painful to talk about, but I am prepared to if you are."

7. **Show interest**. When a woman is trying to talk with another woman about their Identity Conflicts, she needs to have and *to show* genuine interest in the other woman's feelings, experiences, perspectives, and expectations. If both women have such an interest and are prepared to listen to the criticism and hostility that may well come out, a lasting resolution of their Identity Conflicts is possible. If they are not, there is no possibility of such a resolution.

8. **Be prepared to express your desire for sisterhood.** Key to constructive conversations about Identity Conflicts is your aligning yourself with the woman with whom you are speaking, not increasing the distance between you. If you want to have solid, positive, supportive relationships with women whose social identities are different from your own, you can't be afraid to acknowledge that you very much want to provide and find safe spaces within which different women can speak about themselves, express their frustration and anger, and drop their "we are all alike" masks.

9. **Some sure fire conversation killers**. There are several things that should never be said in conversations about Identity Conflicts. Among them are, "No offense, but . . . ," "Don't be so sensitive," "Can't you take a joke?", "I am not a racist," "I have many black (Asian/Hispanic/LGBTQ) friends," and "You are different." Statements such as these shut down conversations, not open them up. You may not want to say, "I want to be your sister," but you can say, "I want you to help me do a better job of managing our relationship."

10. **Take responsibility for what you have said and done**. If you are ready to talk with another woman about your Identity Conflicts, you should also be ready to learn how you have, in some way, offended, hurt, or humiliated that other woman. When you do learn, don't say something

like, "I certainly didn't mean to do that," but rather something like, "I am truly sorry. That was unkind of me, and I will try to never do that again." Acknowledge your own biases and lack of sensitivity and admit what you did was a microaggression. Conversations about Identity Conflicts should force you out of your comfort zone and into a place where you are ready to acknowledge and own your unsisterly conduct.

Chapter 11

Attacking Workplace Bias

IN GENDERED WORKPLACES THERE IS a strong, if unconscious, preference on the part of members of the managerial ingroup (primarily white, heterosexual men) to work with, support, and advance people who are like them (affinity bias), and an equally strong, if also unconscious belief that men are more competent, capable, and effective than women at performing tasks requiring decisiveness, independence, and leadership ability (gender bias).

In this chapter we discuss how best to attack affinity bias and gender bias in gendered workplaces by significantly increasing the gender diversity of its senior leadership.

Operation of Affinity and Gender Biases

Affinity and gender biases exist because of the gendered nature of our workplaces: men's dominance over organizational leadership and their ability and (often unconscious) desire to perpetuate masculine cultural norms, values, and expectations. In such workplaces, these biases create serious obstacles to women's career advancement and situational dynamics that force women to compete with one another because of the limited number of women's seats at leadership tables, to battle with one another by restricting access to needed career resources, and to elbow one another aside to obtain recognition in situations where masculine characteristics are valued and feminine ones are depreciated. Therefore, to remove these obstacles and change these dynamics, a way must be found to change the gendered nature of our workplaces. In our view, the most effective way to do this is by increasing the number of women in an organization's senior leadership until women make up a critical mass of its leaders.

Seven-Step Initiative

We believe that the best way to accomplish this is for an organization to undertake a seven-step initiative. First, establish an educational program for executives and managers, women as well as men, focusing on how and why affinity and gender bias impose serious obstacles to women's career advancement. Second, implement policies for hiring, evaluation, and advancement based on the principle of "blind auditions." Third, adopt practices and procedures that force executives and managers to use "slow thinking" when making career-affecting decisions. Fourth, impose definitive requirements that eliminate or reduce discretionary decisions. Fifth, introduce a reason-neutral, results-flexible work policy. Sixth, commit to a program of small, achievable steps toward a quantified diversity goal. And seventh, enlist senior men as active allies in the effort to achieve significant gender diversity in senior leadership.

Education

All the education, workshops, and bias training in the world will not on their own increase an organization's gender diversity. Nevertheless, properly focused, a gender-related education initiative that is sustained over a reasonable period of time is a necessary first step toward that goal. Such education needs to be of two sorts. The first involves making executives and managers aware of just how much harder it is for women than it is for men to advance in gendered workplaces. The second involves learning why this is so; that is, how gender stereotypes arise, operate to create implicit biases, and result in leaders (generally quite innocently) making discriminatory career-affecting decisions.

Neither part of such an educational initiative can be accomplished in a single session or uncoordinated series of workshops. If an organization's leaders are to gain a deep and lasting appreciation of the reality of gender discrimination and the persistence of the stereotypes that foster it, they need to be exposed to a carefully constructed series of interactive educational programs conducted over an extensive period of time. The content and design of such programs should be specifically tailored to each organization's unique history, workplace practices, and current gender diversity makeup. Assuring that an organization's educational programs accomplish their intended objective, however, can be challenging. If they are fluffy and cliche-ridden, the programs will accomplish nothing; if they are heavy-handed and preachy, the programs can make matters worse by provoking male backlash.

Properly structured and presented, however, an educational initiative can equip executives and managers with the information they need to identify where, when, and how implicit affinity and gender biases are adversely affecting the fairness of their organization's hiring, evaluation, promotion, compensation, and retention processes. Once that identification has been made, executives working at the organizational level and managers working at the local level will be in positions to attack gender discrimination with the tools provided by the next three parts of our suggested diversity initiative: blind auditions, slow thinking, and the elimination of discretion.

Blind Auditions

The first tool to be put into the hands of those tasked with increasing gender diversity relies on the concept of "blind auditions." This concept is modified from the practice of major symphony orchestras in the United States. In the 1970s, women constituted only about 10 percent of such orchestras' members. About that time, these orchestras started conducting auditions from behind screens so that the judges would be blind to the performers' gender. As a result, the gender mix of major symphony orchestras is now almost 50 percent women and 50 percent men.[1]

Business and professional organizations can apply the basic principle underlying blind auditions in a surprising variety of ways to prevent consideration of employee characteristics that *should not be relevant* when making decisions that affect other people's careers. For example, before considering job applications, the human resources department or some other group that is not charged with making hiring decisions can rewrite résumés to remove all indications of gender, race, and other stereotyped social identities. The same can be done when assignment, compensation, and promotion decisions are made on the basis of written materials, as long as familiarity with the person under consideration is not a critical element of the decision.

The concept underlying blind auditions is that our subjective feelings, beliefs, and attitudes should not affect our supposedly merit-based decisions. Thus, any steps that can be taken to reduce the role of subjectivity in career-affecting decisions are all to the good. Evaluation processes that permit evaluators to rely on their gut instincts, comfort level with the person being evaluated, or perception of her or his fit with the organization's culture, are bad; evaluation processes that limit evaluators to providing objective information about the quality of an individual's performance, specific examples of her or his leadership abilities and accomplishments, and comparative information about similarly situated colleagues are good. To the extent reasonably possible, all decisional processes that have career-affecting consequences should require decision makers to justify their judgments in terms of job-related competencies and accomplishments, not personal preferences, likes or dislikes, social connection, or commonality of interests.

It is surprising how many aspects of an organization's evaluation processes are structured to permit, even encourage, subjective judgments. It is also surprising how easy it is to reduce that subjectivity once executives and managers are tasked with doing so and they know what to look for.

Slow Thinking

The second tool to be used in increasing gender diversity is "slow thinking." Daniel Kahneman, a psychologist who won the Nobel Prize in Economics in 2002, distinguishes two modes of thinking: fast and slow.[2] Fast thinking is automatic and effortless; it is based on experiences, impressions, instincts, and feelings. We think fast most of the time, for we normally allow ourselves to be guided by our impressions and feelings, confident that our intuitive judgments are usually justified. Indeed, if we didn't use fast thinking, we wouldn't be able to get dressed, go to work, and get done much of what we have to do in the time available.

Kahneman, however, identifies many reasons why we are prone to make systematic errors when we use fast thinking. These errors recur predictably in circumstances when our judgments are affected by our feelings of liking and disliking, comfort and discomfort, and familiarity and unfamiliarity. Thus, when executives and managers use fast thinking in making career-affecting decisions, those decisions will be influenced by their implicit affinity and gender biases. It doesn't matter that these executives and managers believe they are the least biased, fairest, most merit-oriented individuals in the world; if they use fast thinking in making career-affecting decisions, they will favor people who are like them. They will favor those who their feelings and instincts tell them are better qualified than others to be selected, promoted, or given a raise. In gendered workplaces, when executives and managers think fast, men are favored over women, white people are favored over people of color, and straight people are favored over people who identify as LGBTQ.

If an organization's career-affecting decisions are not to systematically discriminate against women, executives and managers need to make these decisions using slow thinking. Slow thinking is careful, deliberative, fact-based, and logical. It is difficult because, as Kahneman puts it, the voice of our rational, reflective self is "much fainter than the loud and clear voice of an erroneous intuition."[3] Individuals making critical decisions for an organization will not use slow thinking just because they are told to do so; they need to be forced to do so by the circumstances in which those decisions are made. For example, when executives and managers make such critical decisions—say, about hiring, promotion, or compensation—they should be encouraged, or required, to make them only after they have explained to another person how and why they are inclined to make the decision a particular way and after they have listened to how and why the other person is inclined to make that same decision. Such a two-person, back-and-forth deliberative process forces the participants to think critically, logically, and objectively, with an awareness that another person will be assessing whether they have *good reasons* for making the decision in the way they propose to do.

Another way to encourage slow thinking is to require career-affecting decisions to be made on a comparative basis. When executives and managers can make important assignments, major promotions, or significant salary adjustments only after consideration of at least two viable candidates *and* articulation for why they have chosen one over the other, they are forced to focus specifically on the objective differences in the candidates' talents and accomplishments.

A third way to force slow thinking is to let executives and managers know that the justifications they give for their career-affecting decisions will be reviewed by an independent person or group. Knowledge of such a review process forces slow thinking because the decision makers want to appear fair, careful, and objective. (It is also an effective way of monitoring decision making for indications of implicit bias.)

Eliminating Discretion

The third tool for increasing gender diversity is, where possible, to eliminate decision-making discretion. Mahzarin R. Banaji and Anthony G. Greenwald, developers of the Implicit Attitude Test (IAT) administered at Harvard's Project Implicit, refer to implicit biases as "mind bugs" that are "dauntingly persistent."[4] As we have argued, simply being aware of our implicit biases will not prevent them from doing their discriminatory mischief. In Banaji and Greenwald's terms, we need to find ways to "outsmart the mind bugs" that reside within our heads by devising "techniques that will allow us to override unintended results of our automatic, reflexive patterns of thought," and thereby eliminate the discriminatory consequences of our implicit biases.[5]

A key way to outsmart mind bugs is to adopt firm guidelines that eliminate discretion from decisions that might otherwise be influenced by implicit bias. An example of such a discretion-eliminating guideline might be a requirement that all project development teams—or trial, architectural, investment banking, any sort of teams—have an equal number of women and men. Another technique might be to require that all employees at specified stages of their careers be assigned to, complete, and be evaluated with respect to projects of specific sorts.

Another technique that might be used to outsmart our mind bugs would be to adopt some variation of the so-called Rooney Rule. This rule, named for Dan Rooney, the former owner of the Pittsburgh Steelers, was adopted by the National Football League in 2003. It requires pro football teams to interview at least one minority candidate before filling senior coaching and operations positions.[6] While the Rooney Rule does not *require* teams to actually hire minority candidates, the NFL has seen a marked increase in minority coaches and general managers since its adoption.[7] A variation of the Rooney Rule has been adopted by a number of major law firms in the form of the Mansfield Rule, named after Arabella Mansfield, the first woman lawyer in the United States.[8]

Business and professional organizations might use a variation of the Rooney Rule to outsmart mind bugs by mandating that when career-enhancing projects are being assigned or significant positions are being filled, women *must be* among the candidates considered. As with the NFL, this would not guarantee that women would be selected or promoted but it would at least eliminate affinity and gender bias from the candidate selection process, thereby increasing the prospects for greater gender diversity.

A fourth way in which mind bugs might be outsmarted is to take personal choice entirely out of the project assignment process. This is likely to be strongly resisted by the individuals making assignments; they know who has done a good job for them in the past, and they will want to work with those same people in the future. The problem with a selection system is that it can short-change women in gendered workplaces. Because many more men than women give out assignments, select team members, and choose who is to make a client presentation, this selection process is likely to be skewed in men's favor. As a result, when the time comes that women should be ready to move up the leadership ladder, they often have not had the experiences they need to be seen as qualified to do so. Organizations will, undoubtedly, have to find some sort of compromise here, between allowing the assignment process to be entirely discretionary and eliminating discretion entirely. For example, executives and managers could be given wide latitude in making most assignments but required periodically, on some predetermined basis, to work with people whom they had not personally selected. Another approach might be to require executives and managers to make assignments only after the consideration of at least two candidates, one selected by them and the other selected in an objective, neutral way.

Flexibility

Education, blind auditions, and processes that force slow thinking and eliminate unnecessary discretion go a long way toward moving an organization to a true merit-based system of career advancement. Unfortunately, workplace gender equality may not result in gender equity. By this we mean that it may still be much harder for women than for men to keep their work life and their home life separate, not continuously impinging on one another. As we discussed in chapter 9, the workplace pressure on and expectations of mothers are very different from those that fathers experience. Undoubtedly, in an ideal world, domestic responsibilities as well as career opportunities would be equal for women and men. As Amelia Earhart said in the early 1930s, "The work of married men and women should be split. She should taste the grind of earning a living—and he should learn the stupidity of housework."[9] But that is no more the world women live in today than it was in the 1930s. Consider the following statistics.

- 37 percent of wives with successful careers help with children's homework, while only 9 percent of men do.
- 51 percent of these wives take time off from work if a child is sick, but only 9 percent of men do.
- 45 percent of such wives clean the house, while only 9 percent of the husbands do.
- 50 percent of such wives prepare meals, but only 9 percent of the husbands do.
- 51 percent of such wives shop for groceries, while only 7 percent of the men do.
- 43 percent of these high-achieving women feel their husbands create more household work for them to do than their husbands contribute.[10]

The 2015 McKinsey study "Women in the Workplace" found that among women in entry-level executive positions, 44 percent report they do more home chores and 45 percent report they do more childcare than their partner or spouse.[11] It is particularly at this entry level that women need to present themselves as fully committed to their careers; it is very hard to do this if your partner or spouse is not sharing equally in domestic duties.

Gender equity thus depends on some sort of recognition and accommodation of women's far more burdensome domestic responsibilities. The obvious solution is to provide flexible work arrangements to women with children. But such a policy specifically created for mothers is not likely to improve their workplace situations and is likely to make their workplace situations worse. Mothers taking advantage of such a policy are likely to be viewed with suspicion as not being fully committed to their careers. Many mothers are unwilling to take advantage of flexible arrangements for fear it will result in negative work consequences such as wage penalties, lower performance evaluations, and fewer promotions.[12] And women without children often find that their managers are more understanding of a mother's need for flexibility, while expecting them to pick up the slack because they "have no life."[13]

Nevertheless, mothers often need flexible work arrangements to be able to compete at the top of their game for career advancement, and such arrangements are a highly attractive benefit to most people in the workplace. When the American Institute of Certified Public Accountants conducted a study of the effects of flexible work arrangements in accounting firms, it found that 89 percent of the firms surveyed had instituted one or more types of modified work arrangements.[14] Of those firms, 96 percent of them thought that these flexible arrangements help retain talent.

The clear benefits of flexible workplace policies for mothers and others—whether it is the ability to work from home, to tailor workplace hours, or take on a reduced schedule—are clear: workplace satisfaction increases, productivity increases, and employee retention improves.[15] With that said, however, it is impossible to have a one-size-fits-all approach to flexibility. Each organization should let its workplace managers—the same ones who identify the areas of gender bias—figure out what works best for their workplace, as long as those workplaces deliver excellent work, on time. As researchers reported in the *Harvard Business Review*, "When done right, flexibility results in a happier, healthier, and more productive workforce. And it helps attract the best employees, and makes them want to stick around."[16]

The only thing that is essential for any workplace flexibility arrangement is that it be reason-neutral and open to everyone—not only mothers. Such an arrangement, while benefiting everyone, constitutes a major step toward gender equity—while giving all employees a highly desirable career benefit.

Small Changes

Even the best-intentioned organization can view the achievement of significant gender diversity, particularly at its senior leadership level, as a daunting challenge. The belief is that significant gender diversity can only be achieved with fundamental, culture-altering changes—changes that are far too radical to be seriously considered. As a result, gender diversity is most commonly pursued with bias training, policy pronouncements, and cheerleading-type encouragements—techniques that hold little if any likelihood of doing much to change the fundamental gendered nature of our workplaces. But it is a mistake to see achievement of gender diversity as a single overarching and virtually intractable problem. Rather, it should be thought of as a series of relatively small problems that if addressed consecutively can be solved over time. Indeed, achievement of real gender diversity is possible if it is pursued through a series of what Shelley Correll, director of the Clayman Institute for Gender Research at Stanford University, calls "small wins." Correll argues that realistically possible changes "are often small and imperfect."[17] Thus, to make gendered workplaces "more inclusive and meritocratic," the most effective approach is to take "concrete, implementable actions... of moderate importance [that] produce visible results."[18] When a small win is achieved, "it often creates new allies and makes visible the next target of change."[19]

Small wins in the battle against affinity and gender biases might include starting a flexible work program by making Fridays flex days and monitoring the effect on morale and productivity; if the results were positive a day at a time might be added to the flex program. Another approach to obtaining a small win might be to institute one of the blind audition, slow thinking, or discretion-eliminating techniques and monitor whether it has a noticeable impact on the selection or evaluation of women; if so, the technique could be expanded. Of course, a more direct approach might be taken, say, requiring that 15 to 20 percent of project teams be led by women, or establishing a mandatory mentoring program that involved an equal number of women and men as both mentors and mentees.

The nature of the possible small wins and the order in which they are pursued will vary from organization to organization depending on its traditions, current practices, employee mix, and prevailing attitudes toward gender diversity. But in every organization, there are small wins to be had, and every small win opens up the possibility for the next one. It is important, however, that in determining how to proceed, an organization does so with a view to the eventual achievement of a specific, clearly articulated, quantified long-term diversity goal. Achieving significant gender diversity is a little like achieving a fleet of fuel-efficient automobiles. Neither will happen unless a specific future goal is set and small, incremental, practical steps are taken each year toward that goal.

Men as Allies

Gendered workplaces are gendered because the men who typically control them want (often unconsciously) these workplaces to continue to be controlled and shaped by men and masculine behavioral norms. As a result, in gendered workplaces, there is likely to be less-than-enthusiastic support for adopting a comprehensive program for achieving gender diversity of the sort we have just laid out—education, application of the principle of blind auditions, processes that force slow thinking, guidelines that eliminate discretion, establishment of flexible working arrangements, and pursuit of a plan of small wins toward a quantified future diversity objective. Something beyond a committed sisterhood will be needed if this seven-step initiative or anything like it is to be implemented in organizations with strongly gendered workplaces. We do not want to appear overly pessimistic, but unless the CEO or a substantial number of the senior men around him can be enlisted into the effort to achieve meaningful gender diversity, the prospects for ending the discriminatory consequences of affinity and gender bias are slim. But in our experience, there are men at or near the top of virtually every organization who are people of goodwill committed to doing the smart thing to advance their business's long-term best interest. The trick is to convince these men that diversifying senior leadership is the smart thing and to turn them from fair-minded leaders into active, committed allies. There are three serious impediments to doing this: a lack of appreciation of the problem, the prevalence of traditional marriages, and the pressure to conform to prevailing masculine norms.

Appreciation of the Problem

The Boston Consulting Group found that most of the men aged 45 and older who typically lead decision making in corporate and professional organizations significantly underestimate the obstacles women face in advancing in their careers.[20] Indeed, only 25 percent of these men think women face workplace obstacles that are more severe than those men face.[21] These male leaders typically believe their workplaces are far less biased than they actually are, and they have little or no appreciation of the benefits to their bottom lines that diversification would bring.[22]

There is much that can be done to increase senior male leaders' appreciation of the problems resulting from affinity and gender bias. An educational program of the sort we have recommended is an obvious way to do this. Very often, however, it is precisely the senior men, those who most need such a program, who are most resistant to participating in it. That is why in chapter 2 we recommended that in seeking allies for their diversity initiatives, woman should approach senior men on a one-on-one basis. The same holds true here. A direct nonconfrontational one-on-one pitch to senior male leaders by women who work with them about their organization's bias and the importance of their participation in the educational program holds the greatest promise for overcoming such men's reluctance to participate. It may not be possible to get through to all senior male leaders, but if several powerful, highly regarded men do participate—the CEO and C-suite occupants most of all—in the education initiative, it will make an enormous difference in the extent to which and enthusiasm with which other men participate.

Marriage Structure

Research has found that senior male managers whose wives are not employed outside the home are "pockets of resistance" to increasing gender diversity.[23] In a study of 993 married, heterosexual male managers, researchers found that

> men in traditional marriages [married to women who are not employed] tend to view the presence of women in the workplace unfavorably, perceive that organizations with a higher number of female employees operate less smoothly, find organizations

with female leaders are unattractive, and are more likely to deny qualified female employees opportunities for promotions.[24]

Given that 75 percent of men in executive positions have a spouse or partner who is not employed,[25] a very sizable proportion of senior male leaders are unlikely—regardless of their organization's educational programs—to become active allies in an effort to achieve a critical mass of women executives in their organizations. Nevertheless, given the link between marriage structure and attitudes toward gender diversity, there is a strong possibility that senior male leaders whose wives have their own careers can be enlisted as vigorous and active supporters of the sort of diversity program we have outlined.

Peer Pressure

In chapter 4, we discussed the pressure women face in gendered workplaces to conform their behavior and management style to dominant masculine norms, values, and expectations. Senior male leaders are also under pressure not to deviate from these dominant cultural norms. A fundamental if unacknowledged objective of gendered workplaces is to perpetuate male control and masculine values. Therefore, men who openly and actively support the advancement of women, seek to assure a safe environment within which women can forcefully express their views, and call out sexist or discriminatory comments and behavior can often be seen as violating gender expectations, failing to be team players, and deserving exclusion from the inner circles of power.

This institutional pressure on men to conform to the unspoken agenda of gendered workplaces may further limit the pool of viable male allies, but it does not eliminate it entirely. In almost all organizations, there are strong senior men who are sufficiently secure in their positions not to be dissuaded from helping women advance once they are convinced it is the right thing to do. Women need to identify these men, reach out to them, bond with them, and work with them to build a critical mass of senior women leaders.

Putting It All Together

The program we are suggesting for attacking affinity and gender bias involves education, tools to prevent those biases from having discriminatory consequences for women, and an effort to achieve gender equity, not just gender equality. It also involves a long-term, incremental "small wins" game plan and the active support of male allies who are in senior leadership. This is unquestionably an ambitious undertaking. We have not, however, suggested any action specifically directed at reducing or eliminating organizations' dominant masculine norms, values, and expectations. While we did make some suggestions in this regard in various of the "Making Things Better" sections of individual chapters— women joining men's informal networks, the formation of strong women's advocacy groups, and cross-gender mentoring—we are firmly convinced that the only truly effective, permanent way to change organizations' masculine cultures is the presence of a critical mass of women in senior leadership roles—precisely the goal of the diversity program we have laid out.

It has been almost 20 years since sociologist Joan Acker argued that organizations themselves are gendered, reflecting and reproducing male advantages. She theorized—and we have attempted to demonstrate— that all aspects of our gendered workplaces, including their practices, procedures, and hierarchies, reflect long-standing distinctions between men and women, masculinity and femininity, and power and domination that aid the reproduction and maintenance of gender inequality.[26] Despite the wide acceptance of Acker's views, there has been considerable controversy concerning how the gendered nature of our workplaces can be ended. On one side, some researchers have argued that women's presence in leadership positions will allow them to "rock the boat" and "disrupt the gender order."[27] On the other side, researchers have argued that when women gain access to positions of authority, their ability to influence inequality at levels below them will be limited either because they will be "willing to do gender in expected ways"[28] or because their power will be constrained by the strength of existing organizational norms.[29]

While the presence of only token women in leadership positions is unlikely to do much to dismantle the gendered practices in our workplaces, we are convinced that once a sufficiently large number of women are in senior leadership positions (filling at least 20 percent of them), such women will be able to effectively promote gender equality with regard to hiring, project assignment, compensation, promotion, and retention. Moreover, with a critical mass of women in positions of power, junior women's opportunities for effective social networking, mentoring, and sponsorship will increase, thereby improving *their* career advancement prospects and those of the women who will follow.

Our conviction that a critical mass of women in senior leadership positions will facilitate the systematic dismantling of the masculine behavioral norms in our workplaces is strongly supported by an extensive study of the consequences for gender equality. Researchers studied 81 Texas-based Fortune 100 companies, with a total of 5,679 discrete workplaces.[30] They found that greater representation of women in leadership positions at both the corporate level—executive officers and board members—and workplace level—managers—is significantly associated with less gender segregation in an organization's nonmanagerial workforce. In other words, women's presence at the top of organizational hierarchies and as managers within specific workplaces is associated with less gender segregation among subordinates. Moreover, and most significantly to us, there is a positive and significant correlation between the percentage of women who are corporate executives and the percentage of women who are managers.

The effectiveness of a critical mass of women in senior leadership at undoing the gendered nature of a workplace is further confirmed by a qualitative study involving 255 senior executives in 19 Australian organizations, where women constitute about 30 percent of the top three levels of executive leadership. The researchers found that "both women and men clearly agreed that the presence of women in senior roles had changed management cultures and influenced methods of decision-making."[31] As one male executive commented, women's presence in senior leadership "has broken down the male clubbing. So that's so much less a feature of business in this organization than it used to be."[32] The researchers found that both women and men welcomed what they consider to be more friendly and collegial work environments. Overall the study found

> the consequences for managerial culture arising from the presence of women in a critical mass is a closer alignment with the ideals of contemporary leadership [which] should be seen as desirable. The women . . . actively sought to create work environments that sustained them, simultaneously enacting a range of [changes to] cultural norms, [that were] accepted by their male colleagues."[33]

While the prospects for making real change in gendered workplaces are good if a sufficient number of women can join senior leadership, the obvious problem is how to get women there. The seven-part plan we have laid out will accomplish that if organizations will only adopt it. Their decision to adopt it or not will depend on an effective alliance between a committed sisterhood and active male allies. With such an alliance, we have every confidence that true diversification of leadership will result.

Conclusion

Women will always have workplace conflicts with other women, just as men will always have workplace conflicts with other men. But, if the affinity and gender biases inherent in gendered workplaces are remedied—and women have the essential but difficult conversations with other women about their Identity Biases—we believe we will be able to stop talking about women's distinctive, same-gender conflicts and focus simply on quickly resolving the interpersonal conflicts that all of us have.

GLOSSARY

The following glossary of definitions of the key terms used in this book is designed to provide a useful reference guide.

Affinity bias: An implicit or explicit preference for people in one's own social identity group (often thought of as the *ingroup*) over people in different identity groups (often *outgroups*). A woman can be in an ingroup in dealing with other women as a group but in the outgroup in gendered workplaces. See *gendered workplaces*.

Agentic: A word derived from *agency*. A person with agentic characteristics exhibits stereotypically masculine traits, such as being aggressive, assertive, competitive, independent, self-confident, proactive, strong, forceful, loud, stable, unemotional, and risk-taking. Leaders are stereotypically seen as agentic.

Bias: We use the word *bias* to refer to the predisposition to engage in discriminatory behavior as the result of stereotypes of one sort or another. Bias can manifest itself in many ways, for example, by treating people in one stereotyped group less favorably than people in another group. Bias can also be demonstrated by preferentially advancing, providing more opportunities for, or compensating more generously people in one stereotyped group over another, or by refusing to hire, interact with, or consider for particular tasks or projects a person from a stereotyped group. Bias can also be displayed by viewing stereotyped people as having decidedly unpleasant or objectionable personal qualities.

Cisgender (or Cis): A cisgender person identifies with the biological sex assigned at birth. It does not refer to gender expression or to sexual orientation. See *sexual orientation*.

Communal: A word derived from *community* and *communion*. A person with communal characteristics exhibits stereotypically feminine traits, such as being nurturing, kind, sympathetic, concerned with the needs of others, socially sensitive, warm, approachable, understanding, solicitous of others' feelings, emotional, sentimental, gentle, domestic, family-focused, good with children, modest, and friendly. A communal person is stereotypically seen as a good assistant or helper, not as a leader.

Conflict: We use the word *conflict* to refer to all interpersonal workplace difficulties, tensions, disagreements, altercations, feuds, aggressions (covert and open), and hostilities. There are obviously distinctions between these interpersonal difficulties. For example, Merriam-Webster defines *tension*, in the sense relevant here, as "a state of latent hostility or opposition between individuals or groups,"[1] while it defines *conflict* as "competitive or opposing actions of incompatibles: antagonistic state or action (as of divergent ideas, interests, or persons), a conflict of principles."[2]

By using *conflict* as a catchall word for all interpersonal difficulties, we are not making a judgment about the nature or severity of the workplace stresses women experience or the consequences to their harmonious relations with other women. People have conflicts whenever they perceive that their needs, wants, or objectives are inconsistent with those of someone else and that only one party—absent compromise or some other resolution—can realize her or his preferred outcome.

Conflicts can arise because of differing views about how best to accomplish a task or complete an assignment or because of personal dislike, distrust, or distaste. Conflicts can be trivial and quickly resolved or serious and long-lasting. Conflicts can be addressed through open disagreement (good-natured or hostile); with humor or negative emotions (anger, frustration, antagonism, aggression, or disgust); or by open verbal or physical attacks. They can also be addressed by ignoring them or by nursing them until they turn into long-running grudges. They can be experienced as emotional discomfort, with or without any outward sign to other people of that discomfort. People can seek to resolve conflicts or dig in their heels and insist on "my way or the highway."

In other words, interpersonal conflicts come in all shapes and sizes, and there is nothing distinctive about the frequency or intensity of women's same-gender conflicts when compared to men's. What sets women's conflicts apart from men's is women's own responses to same-gender conflicts, the way other people evaluate those conflicts, and the workplace stereotypes and biases that fuel so many of them.

Discrimination: The unequal treatment of members of different groups of people based on their race, ethnicity, gender, social class, sexual orientation, gender identification, physical ability, religion, and so on.

Double bind: A psychological state in which a person receives conflicting messages and faces a negative outcome, no matter which of two available behaviors that person adopts. For an example see *Goldilocks Dilemma*.

Exclusion: An environment where a person is set apart from other people, not allowed to take part in an activity, or denied resources for reasons of bias.

Explicit bias: A negative attitude or preconception about people in a particular social group that a person holds consciously and explicitly endorses.

Feminine stereotypes: The traditional, often unconscious, belief that women are and should be communal and should not be (very) agentic.

Gender: Socially constructed roles, behaviors, norms, attitudes, characteristics, and activities that are viewed as appropriate and expected for women and men. The term *feminine* refers to women's socially approved characteristics and *masculine* refers to men's socially approved characteristics, as opposed to females and males as differentiated by their biological sex.[3] Not all individuals and groups of people, however, "'fit' established gender norms."[4] In this book, we attempt to be sensitive to individuals and groups with gender identities other than female and male, such as nonbinary, gender non-conforming, queer, and gender-fluid individuals.

Gender identity: A person's identification as a female, male, both, neither, or another gender entirely. Gender identity is different from a person's sexual orientation. See *sexual orientation*.

Gendered workplaces: Workplaces and organizations that are overwhelmingly led by men and have decidedly masculine cultures that are perpetuated by pervasive affinity and gender biases. Gendered workplaces include businesses, the professions, academia, and government organizations.

Goldilocks Dilemma: The double bind women face because they suffer adverse career consequences for being either communal or agentic. If a woman is communal she is viewed as likable but not as a leader; if she is agentic she is viewed as competent but also as unpleasant, cold, and unlikable. We refer to this double bind as the Goldilocks Dilemma because women are frequently viewed as too soft (too communal) or too hard (too agentic) but rarely just right.

Heterosexism: The view that heterosexual people are the norm for both gender identity and sexual orientation, and that, therefore, it is desirable and appropriate for all people to be heterosexual and not LGBTQ. See *LGBTQ*.

Identity threat: The psychological state in which a person fears the loss of power or competence because of belonging to a particular social identity group.

Implicit bias: A person's automatic, unconscious attribution of a stereotypical characteristic to members of particular groups.

Impression management: A person's conscious effort to behave—or to communicate—so as to shape or change the impressions other people will have of that person.

Incivility: Incivility is rude or discourteous behavior that can be experienced in a variety of ways, including condescending comments; having one's competence disparaged; and social and professional snubs, such as being excluded or ignored, curtly dismissed, criticized brusquely, dealt with sarcastically, interrupted or talked over, contradicted rudely, or treated with a lack of regard. Incivility is a relatively mild form of what is often referred to as *counterproductive workplace behavior*. More severe forms of such behavior include interpersonal aggression, bullying, and deliberate social and professional undermining. These hostile behaviors are typically undertaken with the unambiguous intent to harm another person. Workplace incivility, by contrast, is not necessarily designed to harm someone else as much as it is to express disapproval, displeasure, or distaste at another person's conduct, appearance, or intentions.[5] Incivility is common in many organizations, with between 71 percent and 79 percent of all employees reporting that they have had uncivil encounters at work.[6] Microaggressions are a form of incivility. See *microaggressions*.

Inclusive: An environment that welcomes, respects, values, and supports people despite their different characteristics and social identities. Inclusive workplaces make people feel welcome, comfortable, and part of their group.

Ingroup bias: See *affinity bias*.

Institutional racism: The ways in which structural policies and practices create different outcomes for different racial groups; for example, in the United States white people have social, educational, and economic advantages over other racial groups.

Intersectionality: The intersection of the distinct social identities with a woman's gender. Such identities include race, age, disability, ethnicity, gender identity, religion, and sexual orientation. A woman's intersectional characteristics contribute to her unique experiences and perspectives.

LBTQ: The initialism used to refer to a woman, for purposes of this book, who is a lesbian, bisexual, transgender, or queer or questioning.

LGBTQ: The initialism used to refer to a person who is a lesbian, gay, bisexual, transgender, or queer or questioning.

Masculine stereotypes: The traditional, often unconscious, assumption that men are and should be agentic and that they should not be (very) communal.

Masculine workplaces: See *gendered workplaces*.

Microaggressions: A form of incivility involving a comment or action (often unconscious or unintentional) that expresses a prejudiced attitude toward someone who is a member of a marginalized person or group (such as a woman, a racial or ethnic minority, or an LGBTQ person).[7] Microaggressions are slights that convey a derogatory or negative view or opinion about a marginalized person or group. See *incivility*.

Outgroup: See *affinity bias*.

Prejudice: An unjustifiable attitude (usually negative) about members of a different social group from one's own. Such negative attitudes are typically based on stereotypes that disparage people's distinctive differences rather than regard them as unique and valuable characteristics.

Sex: Biological and physiological characteristics that define women as *female* and men as *male*.[8]

Sexual orientation: A person's attraction (physical, emotional, romantic, or otherwise) to another person. A person can be straight, lesbian, gay, bisexual, asexual, pansexual, queer, or another orientation entirely. Sexual orientation is different from a person's gender identity. See *gender identity*.

Sisterhood: Women's workplace relationship with other women that might not involve actual friendships but that is positive, understanding, supportive, and encouraging.

Social identity: A person's sense of oneself as a member of a social group or groups—such as race, ethnicity, gender, social class, sexual orientation, gender identification, physical ability, or religion—that creates for that person both ingroups and outgroups. Social identity is how people classify themselves and others as belonging to specific social groups.

Social identity threat: A psychological state in which a person's performance is inhibited or impaired because that person is aware that particular tasks have a strong negative association with a social identity with which she or he identifies.

Stereotype: We use the word *stereotype* to refer to a characteristic or set of characteristics that people ascribe to people (including themselves) based on their particular distinctive social identities, such as gender, sexual orientation, gender identity, race, ethnicity, age, and motherhood. When people believe (consciously or unconsciously) without actual credible information, that a person of a particular social group has the stereotypical characteristics associated with that group, they are making a biased or prejudiced evaluation that can lead to discriminatory consequences. Stereotypes are overly broad and unsupported generalizations about characteristics supposedly shared by members of the stereotyped group. Stereotypes function as scripts for behavior—prescribing how people should be evaluated and regarded and how others tend to relate to them. Such scripts frequently result in discriminatory behavior.

Stereotype threat: A psychological state in which a person's performance is inhibited or impaired because that person is aware that particular tasks have a strong positive association with the social group of which a person is not a member, or a strong negative association with a social group of which the person is a member.

Systemic racism: See *institutional racism*.

Transgender (or Trans): A term used for a person with a gender identity different from the biological sex assigned to that person at birth.

Unconscious bias: See *implicit bias*.

NOTES

Introduction

1. Leah D. Sheppard and Karl Aquino, "Sisters at Arms: A Theory of Female Same-Sex Conflict and Its Problematization in Organizations," *Journal of Management* 43, no. 3 (March 1, 2017): 691–715.
2. Sheppard and Aquino, "Sisters at Arms," 691–715.
3. Felicia Pratto et al., "Social Dominance Orientation: A Personality Variable Predicting Social and Political Attitudes," *Journal of Personality and Social Psychology* 67, no. 4 (1994): 741–63.
4. For example, Allison Joy, "Queen Bees Sting: How Good Are Female Leaders at Mentoring the Next Generation?" *Comstock's*, May 2, 2016, https://www.comstocksmag.com/commentary/queen-bees-sting; Peggy Drexler, "Americans Prefer Their Bosses Male," *Psychology Today*, August 14, 2014, https://www.psychologytoday.com/us/blog/our-gender-ourselves/201408/americans-prefer-their-bosses-male; Grace Bonney, *In the Company of Women: Inspiration and Advice from over 100 Makers, Artists, and Entrepreneurs* (New York: Artisan, 2016), 9.
5. Pam Kruger, "The Myth of the Office Bitch," *CBS News*, April 14, 2011, Money Watch, https://www.cbsnews.com/news/the-myth-of-the-office-bitch.

Chapter 1

1. Erika Holiday and Joan I. Rosenberg, *Mean Girls, Meaner Women: Understanding Why Women Backstab, Betray and Trash-Talk Each Other and How to Heal* (California: Orchid Press, 2009), 34.
2. Michelle Villalobos, *The Stiletto in Your Back: The Good Girl's Guide to Backstabbers, Bullies, Gossips & Queen Bees at Work (the Good Girl's Guide to Getting Ahead)* (2013), chap. 2, Kindle.

3. Kelly Valen, *The Twisted Sisterhood: Unraveling the Fallout of Aggression among Girls and Women, Pushing for a More Mindful Civility* (New York: Ballantine Books, 2010), part 2, Kindle.

4. Anh Tan et al., "The Human Hippocampus Is Not Sexually-Dimorphic: Meta-Analysis of Structural MRI Volumes," *NeuroImage* 124, part A (January 2016): 350–366; Christopher Bergland, "The Male and Female Brain Are More Similar than Once Assumed," *Psychology Today*, November 2, 2015, https://www.*psychologytoday*.com/us/blog/the-athletes-way/201511/the-male-and-female-brain-are-more-similar-once-assumed.

5. Susan Shapiro Barash, *Tripping the Prom Queen: The Truth about Women and Rivalry* (New York: St. Martin's Griffin, 2006).

6. Cheryl Dellasega, *Mean Girls Grown Up: Adult Women Who Are Still Queen Bees, Middle Bees, and Afraid-to-Bees* (Hoboken, NJ: John Wiley & Sons, 2005).

7. Holiday and Rosenberg, *Mean Girls, Meaner Women.*

8. Leora Tanenbaum, *Catfight: Women and Competition* (New York: Seven Stories Press, 2011).

9. Katherine Crowley and Kathi Elster, *Mean Girls at Work: How to Stay Professional when Things Get Personal* (New York: McGraw Hill, 2013).

10. Meredith Fuller, *Working with Bitches: Identify the Eight Types of Office Mean Girls and Rise Above Workplace Nastiness* (Boston: Da Capo Press, 2013).

11. Phyllis Chesler, *Woman's Inhumanity to Woman* (Chicago, Illinois: Lawrence Hill Books, 2009).

12. Cathi Hanauer, *The Bitch in the House: 26 Women Tell the Truth about Sex, Solitude, Work, Motherhood, and Marriage* (New York: William Morrow Paperbacks, 2003).

13. Villalobos, *Stiletto in Your Back.*

14. Chesler, *Woman's Inhumanity*, 1.

15. Barash, *Tripping the Prom Queen*, 5–7 (Emphasis in the original).

16. Valen, *The Twisted Sisterhood*, introduction.

17. Villalobos, *The Stiletto in Your Back*, introduction.

18. Kristen Wong, "Are Women Afraid to Compete with Each Other at Work?" *Glamour*, July 5, 2018, Culture, https://www.glamour.com/story/are-women-afraid-to-compete-with-each-other-at-work; Olga Khazan, "Why Do Women Bully Each Other at Work?" *Atlantic*, September 2017, https://www.theatlantic.com/magazine/archive/2017/09/the-queen-bee-in-the-corner-office/534213.

19. Olga Khazan, "Why Don't More Women Want to Work with Other Women?" *Atlantic*, January 21, 2014, Business, https://www.theatlantic.com/business/archive/2014/01/why-don't-more-women-want-to-work

-with-other-women/283216; Meredith Fuller, "Why Are Women Nasty to Other Women?" *Psychology Today*, August 4, 2013, https:// www.psychologytoday.com/U.S./blog/working-btches/201308/why-are-some-women-nasty-other-women; Emma Gray, "Women at Work: Jealousy and Envy Impact Women Differently than Men," *Huffington Post* (blog), May 6, 2012, The Blog, https://www.huffingtonpost.com/emma-gray/women-at-work-jealousy-envy-men_b_1480030.html.

20. Letty Cottin Pogrebin, "Competing with Women," *Ms.*, July 1972, in *Competition: A Feminist Taboo? eds.* Valerie Miner and Helen E. Longino (New York: The Feminist Press, 1987), 21–37.

21. Dellasega, *Mean Girls Grown Up*, 13.

22. Holiday and Rosenberg, *Mean Girls, Meaner Women*, 130.

23. Crowley and Elster, *Mean Girls at Work*, 184.

24. Valen, *The Twisted Sisterhood*, part 2.

25. Villalobos, *The Stiletto in Your Back*, chap. 1.

26. Villalobos, chap. 1.

27. Villalobos, chap. 4.

28. Villalobos, chaps. 1 and 4.

29. Villalobos, chap. 6.

30. Chesler, *Woman's Inhumanity*, ix.

31. Chesler, 79.

32. Chesler, 172.

33. Chesler, 2.

34. Dellasega, *Mean Girls Grow Up*, 13.

35. Dellasega, 13.

36. Holiday and Rosenberg, *Mean Girls, Meaner Women*, 27.

37. Holiday and Rosenberg, 25.

38. Holiday and Rosenberg, 25.

39. Holiday and Rosenberg, 145.

40. Holiday and Rosenberg, 145.

41. Barash, *Tripping the Prom Queen*, 33.

42. Barash, 33 (Emphasis in the original).

43. Barash, 33.

44. Barash, 33.

45. Barash, 158.

46. Chesler, *Woman's Inhumanity*, 2.

47. Holiday and Rosenberg, *Mean Girls, Meaner Women*, 8.

48. Tanenbaum, *Catfight*, 47.

49. Holiday and Rosenberg, *Mean Girls, Meaner Women*, 27.

50. Tanenbaum, *Catfight*, 19.

51. Tanenbaum, 26.

52. Tanenbaum, 177.

53. Jeannette McGlone, "Sex Differences in Human Brain Organization," *Behavioral and Brain Sciences* 3, no. 2 (June 1980): 217–27, 226, https://www.cambridge.org/core/journals/behavioral-and-brain-sciences/article/sex-differences-in-human-brain-asymmetry-a-critical-survey/93B49551A4D139B20E39C7F2019CC57D; see also Daphna Joel and Cordelia Fine, "Can We Finally Stop Talking about 'Male' and 'Female' Brains?" *New York Times*, December 2, 2018, https://www.nytimes.com/2018/12/03/opinion/male-female-brains-mosaic.html.

54. Carol Tavris, *Mismeasure of Woman: Why Women Are Not the Better Sex, the Inferior Sex, or the Opposite Sex* (New York: Touchstone, 1992); "Men and Women: No Big Difference," American Psychological Association, October 20, 2005, https://www.apa.org/research/action/difference.aspx.

55. Barbara J. Risman, "Intimate Relationships from a Microstructural Perspective: Men Who Mother," *Gender and Society* 1, no. 1 (March 1987): 6–32, https://journals.sagepub.com/doi/10.1177/089124387001001002.

56. Nancy J. Chodorow, *The Reproduction of Mothering* (Berkeley, CA: University of California Press, 1978).

57. Carol Gilligan, *In a Different Voice: Psychological Theory and Women's Development* (Boston: Harvard University Press, 1982).

58. Gilligan, *In a Difference Voice*, 8.

59. Tavris, *Mismeasure of Woman*, 83.

60. Susan D. Cochran and Letitia Anne Peplau, "Value Orientations in Heterosexual Relationships," *Psychology of Women Quarterly* 9, no. 4 (December 1985): 477–88, https://journals.sagepub.com/doi/10.1111/j.1471-6402.1985.tb00897.x.

61. Rosabeth Moss Kanter, *Men and Women of the Corporation* (New York: BasicBooks, 1977), 161 (Emphasis in the original).

62. Tavris, *Mismeasure of Woman*, 91.

63. Leah D. Sheppard and Karl Aquino, "Sisters at Arms: A Theory of Female Same-Sex Conflict and Its Problematization in Organizations," *Journal of Management* 43, no. 3 (March 2017): 691–715.

Chapter 2

1. Robin Morgan, *Sisterhood Is Powerful: An Anthology of Writings from the Women's Liberation Movement* (New York: Vintage Books, 1970).

2. Marjorie J. Spruill, *Divided We Stand: The Battle over Women's Rights and Family Values that Polarized American Politics* (New York: Bloomsbury, 2017), 24.

3. Spruill, *Divided We Stand*, 24.

4. Lorraine Boissoneault, "The 1977 Conference on Women's Rights that Split America in Two," *Smithsonian*, last modified February 15, 2017, https://www.smithsonianmag.com/history/1977-conference-womens-rights-split-america-two-180962174/.

5. Spruill, *Divided We Stand*, 7.

6. Charlotte Perkins Gilman, *Herland: A Lost Feminist Utopian Novel* (New York: Pantheon, 1979), 69.

7. Keith O'Brien, *Fly Girls: How Five Daring Women Defied All Odds and Made Aviation History* (New York: Houghton Mifflin Harcourt, 2018), chap. 10, Kindle.

8. O'Brien, *Fly Girls*.

9. Madeleine Albright, "Speech at New Hampshire Campaign Rally for Hillary Clinton," filmed February 6, 2016, https://www.washingtonpost.com/video/politics/madeleine-albright-stumps-for-clinton/2016/02/06/f42095dc-cd1e-11e5-b9ab-26591104bb19_video.html?utm_term=.3ea70248c6aa.

10. Sophia A. Nelson, "Time to Put the 'Sister' Back in 'Sisterhood,'" *Huffpost*, updated February 10, 2014, https://www.huffingtonpost.com/sophia-a-nelson/what-is-sisterhood-really_b_4410051.html.

11. Christina Radish, "'Tomb Raider' Screenwriter Geneva Robertson-Dworet on Rethinking Lara Croft & 'Captain Marvel'," *Collider*, March 19, 2018, http://collider.com/tomb-raider-geneva-robertson-dworet-interview/.

12. Emma Bowman, "Female Breakout 'Captain Marvel' Screenwriter Is Disrupting the Superheroine Trope," *NPR*, September 9, 2018, Movie Interviews, https://www.npr.org/2018/09/09/645703206/female-breakout-captain-marvel-screenwriter-is-disrupting-the-superheroine-trope.

13. Mia Galuppo, "3 Female Screenwriters on Crashing the Blockbuster Boys Club: I Want to See a Female Darth Vader," *Hollywood Reporter*, December 11, 2017, Movies, https://www.hollywoodreporter.com/news/3-female-screenwriters-crashing-blockbuster-boys-club-i-want-to-see-a-female-darth-vader-1063482.

14. Galuppo, "3 Female Screenwriters."

15. "The 'Masculine' and 'Feminine' Sides of Leadership and Culture: Perception vs Reality," *Knowledge@Wharton*, October 5, 2005, http://knowledge.wharton.upenn.edu/article/the-masculine-and-feminine-sides-of-leadership-and-culture-perception-vs-reality/; S. N. Crites, Kevin E. Dickson,

and A. Lorenz, "Nurturing Gender Stereotypes in the Face of Experience: A Study of Leader Gender, Leadership Style, and Satisfaction," *Journal of Organizational Culture, Communications and Conflicts* 19, no. 1 (January 2015): 1–23.

16. Robin J. Ely, Herminia Ibarra, and Deborah M. Kolb, "Taking Gender into Account: Theory and Design for Women's Leadership Development Programs," *Academy of Management Learning & Education* 10, no. 3 (September 2011): 474–93.

17. Ely, Ibarra, and Kolb, "Taking Gender into Account,"474–93.

18. Ely, Ibarra, and Kolb, 475.

19. Andrea S. Kramer and Alton B. Harris, *Breaking Through Bias: Communication Techniques for Women to Succeed at Work* (New York: Bibliomotion, Inc., 2016).

20. Colleen Chesterman, Anne Ross-Smith, and Margaret Peters, "The Gendered Impact on Organisations of a Critical Mass of Women in Senior Management," *Policy and Society* 24, no. 4 (2005): 69–91.

21. Michelle Myers, "Women Wanted—Building a Strong Network for Women in Your Workplace," *Progressive Women's Leadership*, November 23, 2015, https://www.progressivewomensleadership.com/women-wanted -building-a-strong-network-for-women-in-your-workplace/.

22. Saundarya Rajesh, "How Networking Benefits Women in Their Career," *People Matters* (blog), July 12, 2016, https://www.peoplematters.in/blog/ diversity/how-networking-benefits-women-in-their-career-13649?utm _source=peoplematters&utm_medium=interstitial&utm_campaign= learnings-of-the-day.

23. Ellyn Shook and Julie Sweet, *When She Rises, We All Rise* (Accenture, 2018), https://www.accenture.com/es-es/_achmedia/PDF-73/Accenture-which -she-rises-we-all-rise.pdf.

24. University of Notre Dame, "Women, Your Inner Circle May Be Key to Gaining Leadership Roles," *Science Daily*, January 22, 2019, https://www .sciencedaily.com/releases/2019/01/190122133334.

25. Yang Yang, Nitesh V. Chawla, and Brian Uzzi, "A Network's Gender Composition and Communication Pattern Predict Women's Leadership Success," *Proceedings of the National Academy of Sciences of the United States of America* 116, no. 6 (February 2019): 2033–38.

26. Yang, Chawla, and Uzzi, "A Network's Gender Composition," 2033–38.

27. Kelsey Vuillemot, "These Nine Women Lawyers Love Two Things: Dancing, and Makin' It Rain," *National Association of Women Lawyers* (blog), January 29, 2016, https://www.nawl.org/p/bl/et/blogaid=405; Katherine

Larkin-Wong, "Ms. JD and Levo League Partnership—The DQs Show Us Why Women Helping Women Works! "*Ms. JD* (blog), January 23, 2012, https://ms-jd.org/blog/article/ms-jd-and-levo-league-partnership-olgs -show-us-why-women-helping-women-works. The Dancing Queens is the actual name of the group Andie belongs to.

28. Center for Women and Business at Bentley University, "Taking Employee Resource Groups to the Next Level," Fall 2016, https://www.bentley.edu/ files/2017/03/17/Bentley%20CWB%20ERG%20Research%20Report%20 Fall%202016.pdf.

29. Center for Women and Business at Bentley University.

30. For a discussion about the differences between "outputs" and "outcomes," see Deborah Mills-Scofield, "It's Not Just Semantics: Managing Outcomes vs. Outputs," *Harvard Business Review*, November 26, 2012, https://hbr .org/2012/11/its-not-just-semantics-managing-outcomes.

31. Shawn Achor, *Big Potential: How Transforming the Pursuit of Success Raises Our Achievement, Happiness, and Well-Being* (New York: Currency, 2018).

32. Jessica Bennet, "Do Women-Only Networking Groups Help or Hurt Female Entrepreneurs?" *Inc.*, September 21, 2017, https://www.inc.com/ magazine/201710/jessica-bennett/women-coworking-spaces.html. Some of these groups include Heymama, Women's Inspiration and Enterprise ("WIE"), Wing, Riveter, Ellevate Network, theli.st, Create & Cultivate, Sally, SheWorx, Girlboss Media, Muse, and Bumble Bizz.

33. Shawn Achor, "Do Women's Networking Events Move the Needle on Equal-ity?" *Harvard Business Review*, February 13, 2018, https://hbr.org/2018/02/ do-womens-networking-events-move-the-needle-on-equality.

34. Matt Egan, "Still Missing: Female Business Leaders," *CNN*, March 24, 2015, Business, https://money.cnn.com/2015/03/24/investing/female-ceo -pipeline-leadership/index.html.

35. Herminia Ibarra, Robin J. Ely, and Deborah M. Kolb, "Women Rising: The Unseen Barriers," *Harvard Business Review*, September 2013, https://hbr .org/2013/09/women-rising-the-unseen-barriers.

36. David R. Hekman et al., "Does Diversity-Valuing Behavior Result in Diminished Performance Ratings for Non-white and Female Leaders?" *Academy of Management Journal* 60, no. 2 (2017): 771–97.

37. Stephanie K. Johnson and David R. Hekman, "Women and Minorities Are Penalized for Promoting Diversity," *Harvard Business Review*, March 23, 2016, https://hbr.org/2016/03/women-and-minorities-are-penalized-for -promoting-diversity.

38. Johnson and Hekman, "Women and Minorities."

39. Johnson and Hekman, "Women and Minorities."

40. Anne Welsh McNulty, "Don't Underestimate the Power of Women Supporting Each Other at Work," *Harvard Business Review*, September 3, 2018, https://hbr.org/2018/09/dont-underestimate-the-power-of-women-supporting-each-other-at-work.

41. McNulty, "Don't Underestimate."

42. Boston Consulting Group, "Fixing the Flawed Approach to Diversity," January 17, 2019, Matt Krentz, Justin Dean, Jennifer Garcia-Alonso, Frances Brooks Taplett, Miki Tsusaka, and Elliot Vaughn, https://www.bcg.com/enus/publications/2019 /fixing-the-flawed-approach-to-diversity.aspx

43. "#MentorHer," Why Mentoring Matters, LeanIn, accessed February 11, 2019, https://leanin.org/sexual-harassment-backlash-survey-results.

44. Brenda F. Wensil and Kathryn Heath, "4 Ways Women Can Build Relationships When They Feel Excluded at Work," *Harvard Business Review*, July 27, 2018, https://hbr.org/2018/07/4-ways-women-can-build-relationships-when-they-feel-excluded-at-work; Andrea S. Kramer and Alton B. Harris, "The Impropriety Bias," Andie&Al (blog), August 30, 2017, https://andie-andal.com/the-impropriety-bias/.

45. Steve Andersen, "How Men Can Be a Great Ally for Women by Breaking Patterns," April 22, 2017, https://goodmenproject.com/ethics-values/how-men-can-be-a-great-ally-for-women-by-br..., accessed on December 31, 2018.

46. KPMG, *Leadership Study: Moving Women Forward into Leadership Roles*, 2015, https://home.kpmg/content/dam/kpmg/ph/pdf/ThoughtLeadership Publication/KPMGWomensLeadershipStudy.pdf.

47. Catalyst, "Paying It Forward Pays Back for Business Leaders," 2012, https://www.catalyst.org/media/paying-it-forward-pays-back-business-leaders.

48. Ellen Galinsky et al., *Leaders in a Global Economy: A Study of Executive Women and Men* (Families and Work Institute, 2003), http://familiesand work.org/downloads/LeadersinaGlobalEconomy.pdf.

Chapter 3

1. Belle Derks et al., "Gender-Bias Primes Elicit Queen-Bee Responses among Senior Policewomen," *Psychological Science* 22, no. 10 (2011): 1243–49. The discussion of measuring the strength of women's gender identification through an analysis of their responses to a series of statements is based on this article.

2. Kim Parker, Juliana Menasce Horowitz, and Renee Shepler, "How Do Your Views Compare on Gender Compared with Those of Other Americans?," *Pew Research Center*, December 5, 2017, http://www.pewresearch.org/fact -tank/2017/12/05/how-do-your-views-on-gender-compare-with-those-of -other-americans/.

3. Derks et al., "Gender-Bias," 1243–49.

4. Derks et al., "Gender-Bias," 1243–49.

5. Derks et al., "Gender-Bias," 1243–49.

6. Derks et al., "Gender-Bias," 1243–49.

7. Jolien A. van Breen et al., "A Multiple Identity Approach to Gender: Iden- tification with Women, Identification with Feminists, and Their Interac- tion," *Frontiers in Psychology* 8:1019 (June 30, 2017); Carola Leicht et al., "Counter-Stereotypes and Feminism Promote Leadership Aspirations in Highly Identified Women," *Frontiers in Psychology* 8:883 (June 2, 2017).

8. van Breen et al., "A Multiple Identity Approach"; Leicht et al., "Counter- Stereotypes and Feminism."

9. van Breen et al., "A Multiple Identity Approach"; Leicht et al., "Counter- Stereotypes and Feminism."

10. Leicht et al., "Counter-Stereotypes and Feminism."

11. Alice H. Eagly and Blair T. Johnson, "Gender and Leadership Style: A Meta-Analysis," *Psychological Bulletin* 108, no. 2 (1990): 233–56, https:// opencommons.uconn.edu/cgi/viewcontent.cgi?referer=https://www .google.com/&httpsredir=1&article=1010&context=chip_docs.

12. Marjorie J. Spruill, *Divided We Stand: The Battle over Women's Rights and Family Values that Polarized American Politics* (New York: Bloomsbury, 2017), 31.

13. Shelah Gilbert Leader and Patricia Rusch Hyatt, *American Women on the Move: The Inside Story of the National Women's Conference, 1977* (Lan- ham, MD: Lexington Books, 2016).

14. Caroline Bird et al., *What Women Want: From the Office Report to the President, the Congress and the People of the United States* (New York: Simon and Schuster, 1977), 17.

15. Spruill, *Divided We Stand*, 12.

16. Tanya Melich, *The Republican War against Women: An Insider's Report from Behind the Lines*, updated ed. (New York: Bantam Books, 1998), 37.

17. Phyllis Schlafly, *Feminist Fantasies* (Dallas: Spence Publishing Company, 2003), 79.

18. Gloria Steinem, "Address to the Women of America" (speech, National Women's Political Caucus, July 10, 1971).

19. "Hillary's Vision for America," Office of Hillary Rodham Clinton, accessed December 17, 2018, https://www.hillaryclinton.com/issues/.

20. "Making America Great Again," accessed December 17, 2018, https://www.DonaldTrump.com/.

21. Jill Filipovic, "Our President Has Always Degraded Women—And We've Always Let Him," *Time*, December 5, 2017, time.com/5047771/donald-trump-comments-billy-bush/.

22. Molly Ball, "Donald Trump Didn't Really Win 52% of White Women in 2016," *Time*, October 18, 2018, Politics, http://time.com/5422644/trump-white-women-2016/.

23. Phyllis Schlafly, Ed Martin, and Brett M. Decker, *The Conservative Case for Trump* (Washington, DC: Regnery Publishing, 2016).

24. Elizabeth A. Sharrow et al., "Gender Attitudes, Gendered Partisanship: Feminism and Support for Sarah Palin and Hillary Clinton among Party Activists," *Journal of Women, Politics & Policy* 37, no. 4 (2016): 394–416.

25. American Psychological Association, "1 in 4 Employees Negatively Affected by Political Talk at Work This Election Season, Finds New Survey," press release, September 14, 2016, https://www.apa.org/news/press/releases/2016/09/employees-political-talk.aspx.

26. American Psychological Association, "Political Talk Plagues Workers Months After U.S. Election," press release, May 3, 2017, https://www.apa.org/news/press/releases/2017/05/political-talk.aspx.

27. Juliana Menasce Horowitz, Kim Parker, and Renee Stepler, "Wide Partisan Gaps in U.S. over How Far the Country Has Come on Gender Equality," *Pew Research Center*, October 18, 2017, http://www.pewsocialtrends.org/2017/10/18/wide-partisan-gaps-in-u-s-over-how-far-the-country-has-come-on-gender-equality/.

Chapter 4

1. George Guilder, "Women in the Work Force," *Atlantic*, September 1986, https://www.theatlantic.com/magazine/archive/1986/09/women-in-the-work-force/304924/.

2. Esteban Ortiz-Ospina and Sandra Tzvetkova, "Working Women: Key Facts and Trends in Female Labor Force Participation," *Our World in Data* (blog), October 16, 2017, https://ourworldindata.org/female-labor-force-participation-key-facts.

3. United States Department of Labor, Bureau of Labor Statistics, *Women in the Labor Force: A Databook*, (BLS Report, November 2017), https://

www.bls.gov/opub/reports/womens-databook/2017/home.htm; "Changes in Women's Labor Force Participation in the 20th Century," United States Department of Labor, Bureau of Labor Statistics, February 16, 2000, https://www.bls.gov/opub/ted/2000/feb/wk3/art03.htm?view_full.

4. "Labor Force, Female (% of Total Labor Force)," World Bank, September 2018, https://data.worldbank.org/indicator/SL.TLF.TOTL.FE.ZS.

5. "Labor Force."

6. Judith Warner, Nora Ellmann, and Diana Boesch, *The Women's Leadership Gap*, Center for American Progress, November 20, 2018, https://www.americanprogress.org/issues/women/reports/2018/11/20/461273/womens-leadership-gap-2/. They now earn about 57 percent of undergraduate degrees, 59 percent of master's degrees, 48.5 percent of law degrees, 47.5 percent of medical degrees, and 38 percent of MBAs.

7. Catalyst, *2009 Catalyst Census: Fortune 500 Women Executive Officers and Top Earners*, December 9, 2009, https://www.catalyst.org/system/files/2009 fortune 500 census women executive officers and top earners.pdf.

8. Elizabeth Travis, "Academic Medicine Needs More Women Leaders," *AAMC News*, January 16, 2018, https://news.aamc.org/diversity/article/academic-medicine-needs-more-women-leaders/.

9. "Tracking the 2018 Governors Race Results," *Governing: The States and Localities*, last updated November 7, 2018, http://www.governing.com/governor-races-2018.

10. Warner, Ellmann, and Boesch, *The Women's Leadership Gap*.

11. Jeff Green and Jordyn Holman, "Men Are Replacing Women as CEOs in a Step Backward on Diversity," *Bloomberg*, August 5, 2017, https://www.bloomberg.com/news/articles/2017-08-03/men-replacing-women-as-ceos-marks-big-step-backward-on-diversity?eminfo=%7b%22EM AIL, Andrew Ross Sorkin, "When a Female C.E.O. Leaves, the Glass Ceiling Is Restored," *New York Times*, August 6, 2018, https://www.nytimes.com/2018/08/06/business/dealbook/indra-nooyi-women-ceo.html.

12. Yeoman Lowbrow, "You've Come a Long Way, Baby: Virginia Slims Advertising Year-by-Year," *Flashbak*, October 3, 2016, https://flashbak.com/youve-come-a-long-way-baby-virginia-slims-advertising-year-by-year-365664/.

13. Katie Abouzahr et al., "Dispelling the Myths of the Gender 'Ambition Gap,'" Boston Consulting Group, April 5, 2017, https://www.bcg.com/en-us/publications/2017/people-organization-leadership-change-dispelling-the-myths-of-the-gender-ambition-gap.aspx

14. Nancy M. Carter and Christine Silva, *The Myth of the Ideal Worker: Does Doing All the Right Things Really Get Women Ahead* (New York: Catalyst, 2011), https://www.catalyst.org/system/files/The_Myth_of_the_Ideal_Worker _Does_Doing_All_the_Right_Things_Really_Get_Women_Ahead.pdf.

15. Catalyst, "Catalyst Study Explodes Myths about Why Women's Careers Lag Men's," press release, https://www.catalyst.org/media/catalyst-study -explodes-myths-about-why-womens-careers-lag-mens.

16. Sue R. Madsen, *On Becoming a Woman Leader: Learning from the Experiences of University Presidents* (San Francisco: Jossey-Bass, 2008), 207.

17. Robin J. Ely, Herminia Ibarra, and Deborah Kolb, "Taking Gender into Account: Theory and Design for Women's Leadership Development Program," *Academy of Management Learning & Education* 10, no. 3 (September 2011): 12–14, https://flora.insead.edu/fichiersti_wp/inseadwp2011/ 2011-69.pdf.

18. Herminia Ibarra, Nancy M. Carter, and Christine Silva, "Why Men Still Get More Promotions than Women," *Harvard Business Review*, September 2010; Herminia Ibarra, "Women Are Over-Mentored (but Under-Sponsored)," interview by Julia Kirby, *Harvard Business Review*, 2010, https://hbr.org/2010/08/women-are-over-mentored-but-un.

19. Rhona Rapoport et al., *Beyond Work-Family Balance: Advancing Gender Equity and Workplace Performance* (San Francisco: Jossey-Bass, 2001), xiii.

20. Lisa A. Mainiero and Sherry E. Sullivan, *The Opt-Out Revolt: Why People Are Leaving Companies to Create Kaleidoscope Careers* (Mountain View, CA: Davies-Black Publishing, 2006), 75.

21. Lisa A. Mainiero and Sherry E. Sullivan, "Kaleidoscope Careers: An Alternate Explanation for the 'Opt-Out' Revolution," *Academy of Management Executive* 19, no. 1 (February 2005): 106–23.

22. Felicia Pratto, Jim Sidanius, and Shana Levin, "Social Dominance Theory and the Dynamics of Intergroup Relations: Taking Stock and Looking Forward," *European Review of Social Psychology* 17, no. 1 (January 2006): 271–320.

23. Robin J. Ely, "The Effects of Organizational Demographics and Social Identity on Relationships among Professional Women," *Administrative Science Quarterly* 39, no. 2 (June 1994): 203–238.

24. In 2015, of the total number of claims by the EEOC that alleged harassment of employees, approximately 45 percent alleged harassment on the basis of sex. Ending Secrecy about Workplace Sexual Harassment Act, H.R. 4729, §1(b)(2), 115th Cong. (2017). In 2015, companies paid out more

than $295 million in public penalties over sexual harassment, which does not include private settlements and internally resolved complaints. Ending Secrecy about Workplace Sexual Harassment Act, §1(b)(5). Allegations of harassment on the basis of sex have been increasing. In fiscal year 2018, the EEOC "filed 66 harassment lawsuits that included allegations of sexual harassment. That reflects more than a 50 percent increase in suits challenging sexual harassment over fiscal year 2017." U.S. Equal Employment Opportunity Commission, "EEOC Release Preliminary FY 2018, Sexual Harassment Data," press release, October 4, 2018, https://www.eeoc.gov/eeoc/newsroom/release/10-4-18.cfm. The EEOC's preliminary findings for 2018 note that "charges filed with the EEOC alleging sexual harassment increased by more than 12 percent from fiscal year 2017." "EEOC Releases Preliminary FY 2018."

25. Chai R. Feldblum and Victoria A. Lipnic, *Select Task Force on the Study of Harassment in the Workplace* (United States Equal Employment Opportunity Commission, June 2016), 9.

26. Feldblum and Lipnic, *Select Task Force*, 9.

27. For a particularly chilling account of the discriminatory consequences of pervasive inappropriate sexual behavior, see Ellen Pao, *Reset: My Fight for Inclusion and Everlasting Change* (New York: Spiegel & Grau, 2017).

28. Feldblum and Lipnic, *Select Task Force*, 26.

29. Andrea S. Kramer and Alton B. Harris, "How Do Your Workers Feel about Harassment? Ask Them," *Harvard Business* Review, January 29, 2018, https://hbr.org/2018/01/how-do-your-workers-feel-about-harassment-ask-them, reprinted in *HBR's 10 Must Reads, On Women and Leadership* (Boston: Harvard Business Review 2018), 130–37.

30. Daniel Goleman, "Sexual Harassment: It's about Power, Not Lust," *New York Times*, October 22, 1991, Archives.

31. Feldblum and Lipnic, *Select Task Force*, 8–9.

32. Goleman, "Sexual Harassment."

33. M. L. Sam Ruckwardt, "Opting Out of Law Practice and Opting Back In," *GPSolo Magazine*, September 26, 2018, https://www.americanbar.org/groups/gpsolo/publications/gp_solo/2012/september_october/opting_out_law_practice_back_in/.

34. Quora, "Why Women Leave the Tech Industry at a 45% Higher Rate than Men," *Forbes*, February 28, 2017, https://www.forbes.com/sites/quora/2017/02/28/why-women-leave-the-tech-industry-at-a-45-higher-rate-than-men/#1b38ef0b4216.

35. Lisa Belkin, "The Opt-Out Revolution," *New York Times Magazine*, October 26, 2003, http://www.nytimes.com/2003/10/26/magazine/the-opt-out-revolution.html.

36. Tanya Byker, "The Opt Out Continuation: Education, Work, and Motherhood from 1984 to 2012," *RSF: The Russell Sage Foundation Journal of the Social Sciences* 2, no. 4 (August 2016): 34–70.

37. PriceWaterhouseCoopers, PWC Time to Talk 2018, https://pwc.blogs.com/gender_agenda/2018/06/rising-levels-of-female-career-ambition.html.

38. Julie Coffman and Bill Neuenfeldt, "Everyday Moments of Truth: Frontline Managers Are Key to Women's Career Aspirations," Bain & Company, June 17, 2014, https://www.bain.com/insights/everyday-moments-of-truth.

39. Bonnie Marcus, "It's Obstacles Women Face in the Workplace Not a Lack of Ambition that Causes Them to Opt Out," *Forbes*, August 15, 2016, https://www.forbes.com/sites/bonniemarcus/2016/08/15/its-the-obstacles-women-face-in-the-workplace-not-a-lack-of-ambition-that-causes-them-to-opt-out/#7d9601e12667.

40. Robin J. Ely, Pamela Stone, and Colleen Ammerman, "Rethink What You 'Know' about High-Achieving Women," *Harvard Business Review*, December 2014, https://hbr.org/2014/12/rethink-what-you-know-about-high-achieving-women.

41. Andrea S. Kramer and Alton B. Harris, *Breaking Through Bias: Communication Techniques for Women to Succeed at Work* (New York: Bibliomotion, 2016).

42. Julia Malacoff, "Why Women Are Becoming Increasingly Dissatisfied with Their Workplace over Time," *kununu US*, March 6, 2017, https://www.kununu.com/us/kununu-us/news/why-women-are-becoming-increasingly-dissatisfied-with-their-workplace-over-time.

43. G. Coates, "Integration or Separation: Women and the Appliance of Organizational Culture," *Women in Management Review* 13, no. 3 (1998): 114–24.

44. Judy Wajcman, *Managing like a Man: Women and Men in Corporate Management* (Cambridge, UK: Blackwell Publishers, 1998), 107.

45. Ridhi Tariyal, "To Succeed in Silicon Valley, You Still Have to Act like a Man," *Washington Post*, July 24, 2018, https://www.washingtonpost.com/news/posteverything/wp/2018/07/24/to-succeed-in-silicon-valley-you-still-have-to-act-like-a-man/?utm_term=.386045c03507.

46. Shawn Andrews, *The Power of Perception: Leadership, Emotional Intelligence, and the Gender Divide* (New York: Morgan James, 2018), chap. 6, Kindle.

47. Kramer and Harris, *Breaking Through Bias*.

48. Olivia A. O'Neill and Charles A. O'Reilly III, "Reducing the Backlash Effect: Self-Monitoring and Women's Promotions," *Journal of Occupational and Organizational Psychology* 84, no 4 (2010): 825–32.

49. O'Neill and O'Reilly, "Reducing the Backlash Effect."

50. Kramer and Harris, *Breaking Through Bias.*

51. Kramer and Harris, *Breaking Through Bias.*

Chapter 5

1. Angeline Goh, "An Attributional Analysis of Counterproductive Work Behavior (CWB) in Response to Occupational Stress" (dissertation, University of South Florida, November 21, 2006), http://digital.lib.usf.edu/content/SF/S0/02/62/13/00001/E14-SFE0001895.pdf.

2. Allison S. Gabriel, Marcus M. Butts, and Michael T. Sliter, "Women Experience More Incivility at Work Especially from Other Women," *Harvard Business Review*, March 28, 2018, https://hbr.org/2018/03/women-experience-more-incivility-at-work-especially-from-other-women.

3. Alex C. Milam, Christiane Spitzmueller, and Lisa M. Penney, "Investigating Individual Differences among Targets of Workplace Incivility," *Journal of Occupational Health Psychology* 14, no. 1 (2009): 58–69.

4. Milam, Spitzmueller, and Penney, "Investigating Individual Differences."

5. Milam, Spitzmueller, and Penney, "Investigating Individual Differences."

6. Allison S. Gabriel et al., "Further Understanding Incivility in the Workplace: The Effects of Gender, Agency, and Communion," *Journal of Applied Psychology* 103, no. 4 (2018): 362–82.

7. Saera R. Khan and Alan J. Lambert, "Ingroup Favoritism versus Black Sheep Effects in Observations of Informal Conversations," *Basic and Applied Social Psychology* 20, no. 4 (1998): 263–69.

8. Carol T. Kulik and Mara Olekalns, "Negotiating the Gender Divide: Lessons from the Negotiation and Organizational Behavior Literatures," *Journal of Management* 38, no. 4 (July 2012): 1387–1415.

9. Leah D. Sheppard and Karl Aquino, "Sisters at Arms: A Theory of Same-Sex Conflict and Its Problematization in Organizations," *Journal of Management* 43, no. 3 (March 2017): 691–715.

10. Jane Ann Hurst, "It's All about Relationships: Women Managing Women and the Impact on Their Careers" (dissertation, Massey University, Albany, New Zealand, 2017).

11. Sharon Mavin, "Venus Envy: Problematizing Solidarity Behaviour and Queen Bees," *Women in Management Review* 21, no. 4 (June 2006): 264–76.

12. Hurst, "It's All about Relationships."

13. Pat Heim, Susan Murphy, and Susan K. Golant, *In the Company of Women: Indirect Aggression among Women: Why We Hurt Each Other and How to Stop* (New York: Jeremy P. Tarcher/Putnam, 2001), 53–54.

14. Alice H. Eagly and Maureen Crowley, "Gender and Helping Behavior: A Meta-Analytic Review of the Social Psychological Literature," *Psychological Bulletin* 100, no. 3 (1986): 283–308.

15. Jean Baker Miller, *Toward a New Psychology of Women*, 2nd ed. (Boston: Beacon Press, 1986).

16. Olga Khazan, "Why Don't More Women Want to Work with Other Women?" *Atlantic*, January 21, 2014, https://www.theatlantic.com/busi ness/archive/2014/01/why-dont-more-women-want-to-work-with-other -women/283216/#disqus_thread; Lizzie Crocker, "Why Do Women Say They Don't Like Working for Female Bosses?" *Daily Beast*, November 13, 2013, https://www.thedailybeast.com/why-do-women-say-they-dont-like -working-for-female-bosses.

17. Marianne Cooper, "For Women Leaders, Likability and Success Hardly Go Hand-in-Hand," *Harvard Business Review*, April 30, 2013, https://hbr .org/2013/04/for-women-leaders-likability-a.

18. Susan T. Fiske, "Stereotyping, Prejudice and Discrimination," in D.T. Gilbert, S.T. Fiske, and G. Lindzey, eds., *The Handbook of Social Psychology*, 4th ed. (New York: McGraw-Hill, 1998), 378.

19. Madeline E. Heilman et al., "Penalties for Success: Reactions to Women Who Succeed at Male-Gender-Typed Tasks," *Journal of Applied Psychology* 89, no. 3 (2004): 416–27.

20. Madeline E. Heilman and Tyler G. Okimoto, "Why Are Women Penalized for Success at Male Tasks? The Implied Communality Deficit," *Journal of Applied Psychology* 92, no. 1 (January 2007): 81–92.

21. Madeline E. Heilman, Caryn J. Block, and Richard F. Martell, "Sex Stereotypes: Do They Influence Perceptions of Managers?" *Journal of Social Behavior & Personality* 10, no. 6 (1995): 237–52; Madeline E. Heilman, "Sex Stereotypes and Their Effects in the Workplace: What We Know and What We Don't Know," *Journal of Social Behavior and Personality* 10, no. 6 (1995): 2–26; Heilman, "Penalties for Success."

22. Philip Brickman and Ronnie Janoff-Bulman, "Pleasure and Pain in Social Comparison," in *Social Comparison Processes: Theoretical and Empirical Perspectives*, eds. Jerry M. Suls and Richard L. Miller (Washington, DC: Hemisphere Press, 1977), 149–86.

23. Elizabeth J. Parks-Stamm, Madeline E. Heilman, and Krystle A. Hearns, "Motivated to Penalize: Women's Strategic Rejection of Successful Women," *Personality and Social Psychology Bulletin* 34, no. 2 (December 4, 2007): 237–47, https://journals.sagepub.com/doi/10.1177/0146167207310027.

24. Melissa Davey, "Workplaces that Consider Themselves Meritocracies 'Often Hide Gender Biases,'" *Guardian*, August 24, 2016, https://www .theguardian.com/australia-news/2016/aug/24/workplaces-that-consider -themselves-meritocracies-often-hide-gender-biases; Emilio J. Castilla and Stephan Benard, "The Paradox of Meritocracy in Organizations," *Administrative Science Quarterly* 55, no. 4 (December 1, 2010): 543–676.

25. "Trading Action for Access: The Myth of Meritocracy and the Failure to Remedy Structural Discrimination," *Harvard Law Review* 121, no. 8 (June 2008): 2157.

26. Castilla and Benard, "The Paradox of Meritocracy," 543–76.

27. Castilla and Benard, "The Paradox of Meritocracy," 543–76.

28. Castilla and Benard, "The Paradox of Meritocracy," 543–76.

29. Mindi D. Foster and E. Micha Tsarfati, "The Effects of Meritocracy Beliefs on Women's Well-Being after First-Time Gender Discrimination," *Personality and Social Psychology Bulletin* 31, no. 12 (December 2005): 1730–1738.

30. Belle Derks et al., "Do Sexist Organizational Cultures Create the Queen Bee?" *British Journal of Social Psychology* 50, no. 3 (March 2011): 519–35; Belle Derks et al., "Gender-Bias Primes Elicit Queen Bees Responses among Senior Policewomen," *Psychological Science* 22, no. 10 (October 2011): 1243–9.

31. Joan C. Williams, Rachel Dempsey, and Anne-Marie Slaughter, *What Works for Women at Work: Four Patterns Working Women Need to Know* (New York: New York University Press, 2014), 179.

32. Hanna Rosin, "Why Doesn't Marissa Mayer Care about Sexism?" *XXfactor* (blog), *Slate*, July 16, 2012, https://slate.com/human-interest/2012/07/new-yahoo-ceo-marissa-mayer-does-she-care-about-sexism.html.

33. Leora Tanenbaum, *Catfight: Women and Competition*, (New York: Seven Stories Press, 2002), 201.

34. "Gender Identity (Female, Male, or Non-Binary)," California Department of Motor Vehicles, accessed January 1, 2019, https://www.dmv.ca.gov/portal/dmv/detail/dl/gender_id; Laurel Wamsley, "Oregon Adds a New Gender Option to Its Driver's Licenses: X," *NPR*, June 16, 2017, https://www.NPR.org/sections/thetwoway/2017/06/16/533207483/Oregon-adopt _December 18, 2018.

35. "What You Should Know about EEOC and the Enforcement Protections for LGBT Workers," U.S. Equal Employment Opportunity Commission, accessed January 9, 2019, https://www.eeoc.gov/eeoc/newsroom/wysk/enforcement_protections_lgbt_workers.cfm.

36. Frank Newport, "In U.S., Estimate of LGBT Population Rises to 4.5%," *Gallup*, May 22, 2018, Politics, https://news.gallup.com/poll/234863/estimate-lgbt-population-rises.aspx. Most of the data available with respect to LGBTQ people refers to them as LGBT, so we will use LGBT, where appropriate, to track the data.

37. Data on LGBTQ adults is not collected in a consistent manner, nor are the number of LGBTQ adults tracked by any governmental agency. There is substantial variation among the generations with respect to those identifying as LGBTQ: 1.4 percent of traditionalists report being LGBT, 2.4 percent of baby boomers do, 3.5 percent of Generation X do, and 8.2 percent of millennials do. Unless we assume that with each passing year more people in the US population are becoming LGBTQ—a highly unlikely explanation—a more likely explanation is that young people are far more comfortable with publicly acknowledging their sexual orientation and gender identification than are older people. The Pew Research Center has found that only one-third of all employed LGBTQ adults believe all or most of the people they work with are aware of their sexual orientation or gender identity. Pew Research Center, "A Survey of LGBTQ Americans: Attitudes, Experiences and Values in Changing Times," June 13, 2013, http://assets.pewresearch.org/wp-content/uploads/sites/3/2013/06/SDTLGBT-Americans 062013.pdf. Moreover, the Human Rights Campaign has found that slightly more than half (53 percent) of employed LGBT adults are entirely "closeted" or only a few people know of their sexual orientation or gender identity.

38. Newport, "In U.S., Estimate of LGBT."

39. Samantha Allen, "Just How Many LGBT Americans Are There?" *Daily Beast*, January 14, 2017, https://www.thedailybeast.com/just-how-many-lgbt-americans-are-there.

40. "Quick Facts," U.S. Census Bureau, accessed January 8, 2018, https://www.census.gov/quickfacts/fact/table/US/RHI425217.

41. U.S. Commission on Civil Rights, *Working for Inclusion: Time for Congress to Enact Federal Legislation to Address Workplace Discrimination against Lesbian, Gay, Bisexual, and Transgender Americans* (Washington, DC: November 2017), http://www.washingtonblade.com/content/files/2017/11/Report-Final.pdf.

42. NALP, "LGBT Representation among Lawyers in 2017," *NALP Bulletin*, January 2018, https://www.nalp.org/0118Research.

43. "FORTUNE 500 Non-Discrimination Project," Equality Forum, accessed December 20, 2018, https://equalityforum.com/fortune500.

44. Derald Wing Sue, *Microaggressions in Everyday Life: Race, Gender, and Sexual Orientation* (Hoboken, NJ: John Wiley & Sons, Inc., 2010), 191.

45. Lauren Zurbrügg and Kathi N. Miner, "Gender, Sexual Orientation, and Workplace Incivility: Who Is Most Targeted and Who Is Most Harmed?" *Frontiers in Psychology* 7 (May 2016), 2, https://www.ncbi.nlm.nih.gov/pmc/articles/PMC4851979/pdf/fpsyg-07-00565.pdf.

46. Fred George Macoukji, "Gay, Straight, or Slightly Bent? The Interaction of Leader Sexual Orientation and Gender on Leadership Evaluations" (dissertation, University of South Florida Scholar Commons, January 2014), 30–31, https://scholarcommons.usf.edu/cgi/viewcontent.cgi?referer=https://www.google.com/&httpsredir=1&article=6458&context=etd.

47. Macoukji, "Gay, Straight."

48. Evan Urquhart and Parker Marie Molloy, "Can Cis Lesbians and Trans Women Learn to Get Along?" *Slate*, February 16,2015, https://slate.com/human-interest/2015/02/cisgender-lesbians-and-trans-women-how-to-mend-the-rift.html; Tracy Baim, "The Battle Within, Cis and Trans Women, Can We Get Along," *Windy City Times*, August 1, 2018, http://www.windycitymediagroup.com/lgbt/ESSAY-The-Battle_Within_Cis-and_Trans-Wo.

49. Urquhart, "Can Cis Lesbians."

50. Urquhart, "Can Cis Lesbians."

51. Urquhart, "Can Cis Lesbians."

52. Sue, *Microaggressions in Everyday Life*, 190.

53. Federal law is in flux and needs to be consulted to determine possible application of Title VII of the U.S. Civil Rights Act. Civil Rights Act of 1964 (Title VII), 42 U.S.C. § 2000e et seq. Although Title VII does not protect transgender people, it does protect individuals from discrimination based on sex stereotypes and gender nonconformity. EEOC and Woodward v. A&E Tire, 325 F.Supp 3d 1129 (D. Colo. 2018); See also Scott M. Wich, "Federal Law Protects Stereotyped Transgender Employees," *Society for Human Resource Management*, December 18, 2018, https://www.shrm.org/resourcesandtools/legal-and-compliance/employment-law/pages/court-report-protection-stereotyped-transgender-employees.aspx. See CNN, "Woman Fired After Coming Out Transgender Could Take Case to the Supreme Court," *NBC26 Green Bay*, August 29, 2018, https://www

.nbc26.com/news/national/woman-fired-after-coming-out-transgender
-could-take-case-to-the-supreme-court.

54. Sue, *Microaggressions in Everyday Life*, 204–5.

55. Sue, *Microaggressions in Everyday Life*, 197.

56. Sue, *Microaggressions in Everyday Life*, 204–5.

57. Wade C. Rowatt et al., "Associations among Religiousness, Social Attitudes, and Prejudice in a National Random Sample of American Adults,"
Psychology of Religion and Spirituality 1, no. 1 (2009): 14–24.

58. "State Maps of Laws & Policies," Human Rights Campaign, updated January 11, 2019, https://www.hrc.org/state-maps/employment.

59. Obergefell v. Hodges, 135 S. Ct. 2584 (2015).

60. Nicole Torres, "Women Can Benefit when They Downplay Gender," *Harvard Business Review*, July-August 2018 https://hbr.org/2018/07/women
-benefit-when-they-downplay-gender.

61. Sue, *Microaggressions in Everyday Life*, 205–06.

Chapter 6

1. Kimberle Crenshaw, "Mapping the Margins: Intersectionality, Identity
Politics, and Violence against Women of Color," *Stanford Law Review*, 43,
no. 6 (July 1991), 1241–1299.

2. Sheryl Sandberg and Adam Grant, "Sheryl Sandberg on the Myth of the
Catty Woman," *New York Times*, June 23, 2016, Opinion, https://www
.nytimes.com/2016/06/23/opinion/sunday/sheryl-sandberg-on-the-myth
-of-the-catty-woman.html.

3. "Facts on U.S. Immigrants, 2016: Statistical Portrait of the Foreign-Born
Population in the United States," Pew Research Center Hispanic Trends,
September 14, 2018, http://www.pewhispanic.org/2018/09/14/facts-on-u
-s-immigrants/.

4. "Facts on U.S. Immigrants."

5. "Facts on U.S. Immigrants."

6. "Facts on U.S. Immigrants."

7. "Facts on U.S. Immigrants."

8. "Quick Take: Women of Color in the United States," Catalyst, November 7,
2018, https://www.catalyst.org/knowledge/women-color-united-states-0;
U.S. Equal Employment Opportunity Commission, *2015 Job Patterns for
Minorities and Women in Private Industry*, accessed December 19, 2018,
https://www.eeoc.gov/eeoc/statistics/employment/jobpat-eeo1/.

9. U.S. Equal Employment Opportunity Commission, *2015 Job Patterns for Minorities and Women in Private Industry*, accessed December 19, 2018, https://www.eeoc.gov/eeoc/statistics/employment/jobpat-eeo1/.

10. Pew Research Center, *The Rise of Asian Americans*, updated ed., April 4, 2013, 2, http://www.pewsocialtrends.org/2012/06/19/the-rise-of -asian-americans/; Unless otherwise noted, all statistics about the economic, educational, and personal characteristics of Asian Americans and their achievements relative to other racial and ethnic groups are from the Pew Research Center's report.

11. Gustavo López, Neil G. Ruiz, and Eileen Patten, "Key Facts about Asian Americans, a Diverse and Growing Population," *Pew Research Center*, September 8, 2017, http://www.pewresearch.org/fact-tank/2017/09/08/key -facts-about-asian-americans/.

12. U.S. Census Bureau, *Highest Median Household Income on Record*, September 12, 2018, https://www.census.gov/library/stories/2018/09/highest -median-household-income-on-record.html; Pew Research Center, "Life in the United States," chap. 2 in *The Rise of Asian Americans*, June 19, 2012, http://www.pewsocialtrends.org/2012/06/19/chapter-2-life-in-the-united -states/. Fifty-two percent of Asian Americans say their personal financial situation is excellent or good, while only 24 percent of Hispanics and 35 percent of the general public agrees as to their personal financial situations. Eighty-eight percent of Asian Americans think that compared with other racial and ethnic minority groups, they have been more or equally successful. Sixty-nine percent of Asian Americans believe people can get ahead if they are willing to work hard, a view shared by just 58 percent of the American public as a whole.

13. López, Ruiz, and Patten, "Key Facts about Asian Americans."

14. Jack Linshi, "The Real Problem When It Comes to Diversity and Asian-Americans," *Time*, October 14, 2014, http://time.com/3475962/asian -american-diversity/.

15. Buck Gee and Denise Peck, "Asian Americans Are the Least Likely Group in the U.S. to Be Promoted to Management," *Harvard Business Review*, May 31, 2018, https://hbr.org/2018/05/asian-americans-are-the-least-likely-gro up-in-the-u-s-to-be-promoted-to-management.

16. Lilian Wu and Wei Jing, "Real Numbers: Asian Women in STEM Careers: Invisible Minority in a Double Bind," *Issues in Science and Technology* 28, no. 1 (Fall 2011). All statistics in this paragraph are from this article.

17. Wu and Jing, "Real Numbers: Asian Women." Of the scientists and engineers employed by the government, only 28 percent of Asian women are

managers compared with 36 percent of white women, 37 percent of black women, and 36 percent of Hispanic women.

18. Wu and Jing, "Real Numbers: Asian Women." Only 6.5 percent of Asian American women with PhDs in science or engineering are managers, while 6.7 percent of similarly credentialed white women and 10 percent of black women are.

19. Buck Gee and Denise Peck, *The Illusion of Asian Success: Scant Progress for Minorities in Cracking the Glass Ceiling from 2007–2015*, Ascend Foundation (2017), https://c.ymcdn.com/sites/www.ascendleadership.org/resource/resmgr/research/TheIllusionofAsianSuccess.pdf. All of the following references are from this study, unless otherwise noted, on employment patterns in Silicon Valley.

20. Gee and Peck, *Illusion of Asian Success,* 7–8. While almost half of all professionals in Silicon Valley are Asian Americans, only 25 percent of those Asian Americans professionals are executives. A similar, but not as stark, disparity exists for blacks (1.9 percent of professionals and 1.19 percent of executives) and Hispanics (4.8 percent of professionals and 3.5 percent of executives).

21. Gee and Peck, *Illusion of Asian Success,* 7–8. Whites account for 43.8 percent of professionals and 68.8 percent of tech executives.

22. Gee and Peck, *Illusion of Asian Success,* 3 and 13. Ascend notes that Asian women are 66 percent below parity at the executive level and 31 percent below parity at the manager level. By contrast, white women are 17 percent above parity at the executive level and 45 percent above parity at the manager level.

23. Gee and Peck, *Illusion of Asian Success,* 15. White men are 47 percent more likely to be executives than white women, and Hispanic men are 112 percent more likely to be executives than Hispanic women. The pattern is reversed slightly for blacks, with black women 3 percent more likely to be executives than black men.

24. Ascend Foundation, "Race Trumps Gender in Silicon Valley's Double-Paned Glass Ceiling." *Cision PR Newswire*, October 3, 2017, https://www.prnewswire.com/news-releases/race-trumps-gender-in-silicon-valleys-double-paned-glass-ceiling-300529546.html.

25. Jake Simpson, "2015 Law360 Minority Report," *Law360*, May 19, 2015, https://www.law360.com/articles/657725/2015-law360-minority-report. The ratio of associates to partner for Asian Americans is 3.70 percent, for African-Americans 2.22 percent, for Hispanics 1.92 percent, and for whites 0.6 percent.

26. Eric Chung et al., *A Portrait of Asian Americans in the Law* (New Haven, CT: Yale Law School National Asian Pacific American Bar Association, 2017), 18, http://www.aapa-ca.com/assets/portrait-project---final-report .pdf.

27. Laura Colby, "Asian American Executives Are Missing on Wall Street," *Bloomberg BusinessWeek*, November 22, 2017, https://www.Bloomberg .com/news/articles/2017-11-22/asian-american-executive-are-missing-on -wall-street. For example, at J.P. Morgan Chase, Asian Americans are more than 20 percent of professional employees but substantially less than 10 percent of executives. At Goldman Sachs, Asian Americans comprise over 25 percent of the professional workplace but just over 10 percent of its executives. Indeed, none of Goldman's executive officers is Asian American.

28. Colby, "Asian American Executives."

29. Catalyst, *Advancing Asian Women in the Workplace: What Managers Need to Know*, https://www.catalyst.org/system/files/Advancing_Asian _Women_in_the_Workplace_What_Managers_Need_to_Know.pdf. In 2011, a sample of Fortune 500 executives showed that 1.34 percent of the total number of directors were Asian Americans. In a 2012 study, Asian Americans held only 1.5 percent of the corporate officer positions at all Fortune 500 companies. Richard L. Zweigenhaft and G. William Dom-hoff, *Diversity in the Power Elite: Ironies and Unfulfilled Promises*, 3rd ed. (Lanham, MD: Rowman & Littlefield, 2018), 155–6. In 2012, white men accounted for73.3 percent of Fortune 500 board seats. Catalyst, *Missing Pieces: Women and Minorities on Fortune 500 Boards* (2012 Alliance for Board Diversity (ABD) Census, August 15, 2013), 7, https://www.catalyst .org/system/files/2012_abd_missing_pieces_final_8_15_13.pdf.

30. Stefanie K. Johnson and Thomas Sy, "Why Aren't There More Asian Americans in Leadership Positions?" *Harvard Business Review,* December 19, 2016, https://hbr.org/2016/12/why-arent-there-more-asian-americans-in -leadership-positions.

31. Colin Ho and Jay W. Jackson, "Attitude toward Asian Americans: Theory and Measurement," *Journal of Applied Social Psychology* 31, no. 8 (August 2001), 1553–1581, https://onlinelibrary.wiley.com/doi/abs/10.1111/j.1559 -1816.2001.tb02742.x.

32. Monica H. Lin et al., "Stereotype Content Model Explains Prejudice for an Envied Outgroup: Scale of Anti-Asian American Stereotypes," *Personality and Social Psychology* Bulletin 31, no. 1 (January 2005): 34–47, https://pdfs .semanticscholar.org/3f03/4f7657390b0d44134627605c5cc0d086e871.pdf.

Both the high competence and low social skills ratings negatively correlate with individuals wanting an Asian American roommate.

33. Students for Fair Admissions, Inc. v. President and Fellows of Harvard College, 807 F.3d 472 (1st Cir. 2015).

34. Students for Fair Admissions, Inc., 807 F.3d 472. For example, according to the plaintiff's statistical analysis, 21.3 percent of white applicants received a one or two personal rating, the highest in this category, while only 17.6 percent of Asian Americans did.

35. Alia Wong, "Harvard's Impossible Personality Test," *Atlantic*, June 19, 2018, Education, https://www.theatlantic.com/education/archive/2018/06/harvard-admissions-personality/563198/; Anemona Hartocollis, "Harvard Rated Asian American Applicants Lower Personality Traits," *New York Times*, June 15, 2018, https://www.nytimes.com/2018/06/15/us/harvard-asian-enrollment-applicants.html.

36. Johnson and Sy, "Why Aren't There More;" Stefanie K. Johnson et al., "The Strong, Sensitive Type: Effects of Gender Stereotypes and Leadership Prototypes on the Evaluation of Male and Female Leaders," *Organizational Behavior and Human Decision Processes* 106, no. 1 (May 2008), 39–60.

37. Bourree Lam, "Why We Hate (& Love) the Tiger Mom," *Refinery 29*, May 12, 2018, https://www.refinery29.com/en-us/2018/05/198459/tiger-moms-in-pop-culture.

38. Sabrina Qiao, "Fire Breathing 'Dragon Ladies': Representations of Asian American Women in Media," Penn State, April 19, 2016, http://sites.psu.edu/engl428/2016/04/19/fire-breathing-dragon-ladies-representations-of-asian-american-women-in-media-overview/.

39. "The Uncomfortable Racial Preferences Revealed by Online Dating," *Quartz*, November 20, 2013, https://qz.com/149342/the-uncomfortable-racial-preferences-revealed-by-online-dating/.

40. Tiffany Diane Tso, "The Bamboo Glass Ceiling: Asian American Women Face Particular Challenges in the Workplace. And They're Not Getting the Attention They Need," *Slate*, August 8, 2018, https://slate.com/human-interest/2018/08/Asian-American-women-face-a-glass-ceiling-and-a-bamboo-ceiling@work.html.

41. Amy Schumer, *Mostly Sex Stuff Can't Win*, Comedy Central, August 18, 2012, http://www.cc.com/video-clips/p87njw/stand-up-can-t-win.

42. "About Hispanic Origin," Hispanic Origin, U.S. Census Bureau, accessed December 20, 2018, https://www.census.gov/topics/population/hispanic-origin/about.html. "The U.S. Office of Management and Budget (OMB)

requires federal agencies to use a minimum of two ethnicities in collecting and reporting data: Hispanic or Latino and Not Hispanic or Latino. OMB defines 'Hispanic' or 'Latino' as a person of Cuban, Mexican, Puerto Rican, South or Central American, or other Spanish culture or origin regardless of race."

43. "QuickFacts: United States," U.S. Census Bureau, accessed December 20, 2018, https://www.census.gov/quickfacts/fact/table/US/PST045217. Blacks account for 13.4 percent and Asians account for 5.8 percent of the population.

44. Antonio Flores, *Facts on U.S. Latinos, 2015* (Pew Research Center, September 18, 2017), http://www.pewhispanic.org/2017/09/18/facts-on-u-s-latinos-current-data/.

45. *The Condition of Education: College Enrollment Rates,* National Center for Education Statistics, last updated March 2018, https://nces.ed.gov/programs/coe/indicator_cpb.asp.

46. Anthony P. Carnevale and Jeff Strohl, *Separate and Unequal: How Higher Education Reinforces the Intergenerational Reproduction of White Racial Privilege* (Washington, DC: Georgetown Public Policy Institute and the Center on Education and the Workforce, July 31, 2013), https://cew.georgetown.edu/cew-reports/separate-unequal/.

47. Kurt Bauman, "School Enrollment of the Hispanic Population: Two Decades of Growth," *Census Blogs* (blog), U.S. Census Bureau, August 28, 2017, https://www.census.gov/newsroom/blogs/random-samplings/2017/08/school_enrollmentof.html.

48. Carnevale and Strohl, *Separate and Unequal.*

49. Flores, *Facts on U.S. Latinos.*

50. U.S. Bureau of Labor Statistics, *Labor Force Characteristics by Race and Ethnicity, 2017,* August 2018, https://www.bls.gov/opub/reports/race-and-ethnicity/2017/home.htm.

51. Carnevale and Strohl, *Separate and Unequal.* "Good jobs" are defined as jobs "with annual earnings of $35,000 ($17 per hour for a full-time job) as a floor for those under age 45 and $45,000 ($22 per hour for a full-time job) for workers age 45 and over."

52. Carnevale and Strohl, *Separate and Unequal.*

53. U.S. Department of Labor: Women's Bureau, *Hispanic Women in the Labor Force,* accessed January 8, 2019, https://www.dol.gov/wb/media/Hispanic_Women_Infographic_Final_508.pdf; Catalyst, "Women of Color in the United States," November 7, 2018, https://www.catalyst.org/knowledge/women-color-united-states-0.

54. Anthony P. Carnevale and Megan L. Fasules, *Latino Education and Economic Progress: Running Faster but Still Behind* (Washington, DC: Georgetown Center on Education and the Workforce, November 14, 2017), 55 and 74, https://cew.georgetown.edu/cew-reports/latinosworkforce.

55. Catalyst, "Women of Color"; *2015 Job Patterns for Minorities and Women in Private Industry*, U.S. Equal Employment Opportunity Commission, accessed January 9, 2019, https://www1.eeoc.gov/eeoc/statistics/employment/jobpat-eeo1/2015/index.cfm#select_label; "Employment Projections: Civilian Labor Force by Age, Sex, Race, and Ethnicity," U.S. Department of Labor: Bureau of Labor Statistics, accessed January 9, 2019, https://www.bls.gov/emp/tables/civilian-labor-force-detail.htm. Black women make up 3.6 percent of midlevel managers and 1.6 percent of executives and senior managers. Asian women are 2.4 percent of midlevel managers, and 1.4 percent of senior managers. Combined, Hispanic women account for 7.2 percent of the civilian workforce but only 3 percent of midlevel managers and only 1.6 percent of senior managers. White women, by contrast, are 35.9 percent of the civilian workforce, constituting 29.4 percent of midlevel managers and 24.7 percent of senior managers.

56. Camille L. Ryan and Kurt Bauman Current, *Educational Attainment in the United States: 2015 Population Characteristics*, U.S. Department of Commerce, Economics and Statistics Administration, U.S. Census Bureau, March 16, 2016, https://www.census.gov/content/dam/Census/library/publications/2016/demo/p20-578.pdf. Only 4.7 percent of Hispanics 25 and older have advanced degrees compared with 12.1 percent of whites, 8.2 percent of blacks, and 21.4 percent of Asians.

57. Pew Research Center, *On Views of Race and Inequality, Blacks and Whites Are Worlds Apart* (Pew Research Center, June 27, 2016), http://www.pewsocialtrends.org/2016/06/27/1-demographic-trends-and-economic-well-being/. The median adjusted income for households headed by Hispanics in 2014 was $43,000, which is equivalent to only 61 percent of the household income of whites.

58. Jens Manuel Krogstad, Mark Hugo Lopez, and Molly Rohal, *English Proficiency on the Rise among Latinos* (Pew Research Center, May 12, 2015), http://www.pewhispanic.org/2015/05/12/english-proficiency-on-the-rise-among-latinos/ Only 49 percent of Hispanic women speak English "very well."

59. Patricia Gándara and White House Initiative on Educational Excellence for Hispanics, *Fulfilling America's Future: Latinas in the U.S., 2015*, 14, https://sites.ed.gov/hispanic-initiative/files/2015/09/Fulfilling-Americas-F

uture-Latinas-in-the-U.S.-2015-Final-Report.pdf. 9.7 percent of attorneys are black women and 5.7 percent of attorneys are Asian women.

60. Gándara and White House Initiative on Educational Excellence for Hispanics, *Fulfilling America's Future: Latinas*, 14. 7.8 percent of doctors are black women and 22.5 percent of doctors are Asian women.

61. Gándara and White House Initiative on Educational Excellence for Hispanics, *Fulfilling America's Future: Latinas*.

62. Gándara and White House Initiative on Educational Excellence for Hispanics, *Fulfilling America's Future: Latinas*.

63. Catalyst, *Advancing Latinas in the Workplace: What Managers Need to Know* (New York: Catalyst, 2003), https://www.catalyst.org/system/files/Advancing_Latinas_in_the_Workplace_What_Managers_Need_to_Know.pdf. All of the following statistics about Hispanic professional women, unless otherwise noted, are from this Catalyst study.

64. Catalyst, *Advancing Latinas*. Thirty-three percent of Hispanic women with a sense of low connection reported feeling this way.

65. Joan C. Williams, Katherine W. Phillips, and Erika V. Hall, "Tools for Change: Boosting the Retention of Women in the Stem Pipeline," *Journal of Research in Gender Studies* 6, no. 1 (2016): 11–75. Latina scientists were more likely to be called "angry" or "too emotional" if they behaved assertively.

66. Catalyst, *Advancing Latinas*.

67. Catalyst, *Advancing Latinas*.

68. "Time Inc.'s People en Español Reveals Findings from Exclusive Workplace Study: Latina@Work," *BusinessWire*, August 15, 2016, https://www.businesswire.com/news/home/20160815005797/en/Time-Inc.s-People-en-Español-reveals-findings.

69. Catalyst, *Advancing Latinas*.

70. Maiysha Kai, "Dressing like a Congresswoman: Once Again, Alexandria Ocasio-Cortez Has the Last Laugh," *GlowUp*, January 4, 2019, https://theglowup.theroot.com/dressing-like-a-congresswoman-once-again-alexandria-o-1831500889.

71. Alexa Kissinger, "The Thrill of Watching Alexandria Ocasio-Cortez Bring Her Whole Self to Congress," *Vox*, November 16, 2018, https://www.vox.com/first-person/2018/11/16/18098582/alexandria-ocasio-cortez-congress-first-week.

72. Catalyst, *Advancing Latinas*, 25.

73. Daniel Kahneman, *Thinking: Fast and Slow* (New York: Farrar, Straus and Giroux, 2013).

74. Kahneman, *Thinking: Fast and Slow,* 417.

Chapter 7

1. Catalyst, "Women of Color in the United States," October 12, 2017, http://www.catalyst.org/knowledge/women-color-united-states-0#footnote11_0nwr37l.

2. Fortune Editors, "These Are the Women CEOs Leading Fortune 500 Companies," *Fortune*, June 7, 2017, http://fortune.com/2017/06/07/fortune-500-women-ceos/.

3. Catalyst, "Women in Academia," October 20, 2017, http://www.catalyst.org/ knowledge/women-academia; Tracy Seipel, "Black Female Doctors Represent Only Tiny Fraction of All Doctors Worldwide," *Mercury News*, January 14, 2018, https://www.mercurynews.com/2018/01/15/black-female-doctors-represent-only-tiny-fraction-of-all-doctors-nationwide/; Sarah Ramirez, "Women, Black/African American Associates Lose Ground at Major U.S. Law Firms," *NALP*, November 19, 2015, https://www.nalp.org/lawfirmdiversity_nov2015.

4. Catalyst, "Women in S&P 500 Companies by Race/Ethnicity and Level," October 12, 2017, http://www.catalyst.org/knowledge/women-sp-500-companies-raceethnicity-and-level.

5. Graduate Employees and Students Organization, *The (Un)Changing Face of the Ivy League* (New Haven, CT: Yale University, 2005).

6. Gwendolyn Combs, "The Duality of Race and Gender for Managerial African American Women: Implications of Informal Social Networks on Career Advancement," *Human Resource Development Review* 2, no. 4 (December 2003): 385–405, http://digitalcommons.unl.edu/cgi/viewcontent.cgi?article=1029&context=managementfacpub.

7. Melissa Burkley, "Are Black Women Invisible? Do Black Women Go Unnoticed More Often?" *Psychology Today,* December 8, 2010, https://www.psychologytoday.com/us/blog/the-social-thinker/201012/are-black-women-invisible; Erin Blakemore, "How Women's Studies Erased Black Women," *JSTOR Daily,* February 11, 2017, https://daily.jstor.org/how-womens-studies-erased-black-women/; Laura Smith, "When Feminism Ignored the Needs of Black Women, a Mighty Force Was Born," *Medium,* February 21, 2018, https://timeline.com/feminism-ignored-black-women-44ee502a3c6.

8. Ashleigh Shelby Rosette et al., "Race Matters for Women Leaders: Intersectional Effects on Agentic Deficiencies and Penalties," *The Leadership Quarterly* 27, no. 3 (June 2016): 429–445, https://www.sciencedirect.com/science/article/pii/S1048984316000096; David Pilgrim, "The Sapphire

Caricature," *Ferris State University Jim Crow Museum of Racist Memorabilia,* rev. ed. 2012, https://ferris.edu/HTMLS/news/jimcrow/antiblack/sapphire.htm; Lewis Diuguid, "Study Shows How Media Portrayals Affect Black Girls," *Knoxville News Sentinel,* September 25, 2016, http://archive.knoxnews.com/opinion/columnists/study-shows-how-media-portrayals-affect-black-girls-3d075d91-5e0f-2083-e053-0100007fdc05-394515121.html; Ruchika Tulshyan, "Speaking Up as a Woman of Color at Work," *Forbes,* February 10, 2015, https://www.forbes.com/sites/ruchikatulshyan/2015/02/10/speaking-up-as-a-woman-of-color-at-work/#647244702ea3.

9. Lisa Rosenthal and Marci Lobel, "Stereotypes of Black American Women Related to Sexuality and Motherhood," *Psychology of Women Quarterly* 40, no. 3 (September 2016): 414–427, https://doi.org/10.1177/0361684315627459.

10. David Pilgrim, "The Mammy Caricature," *Ferris State University Jim Crow Museum of Racist Memorabilia,* rev. ed. 2012, https://ferris.edu/jimcrow/mammies/.

11. Layla Eplett, "Not Gone with the Wind—The Perpetuation of the Mammy Stereotype," *Scientific American,* November 30, 2015, https://blogs.scientificamerican.com/food-matters/not-gone-with-the-wind-the-perpetuation-of-the-mammy-stereotype/.

12. Eplett, "Not Gone with the Wind."

13. Ella L. J. Edmondson Bell and Stella M. Nkomo, *Our Separate Ways* (Boston: Harvard Business Review Press, 2003).

14. Tobin Grant, "Poll: Most Whites Say Blacks Are Lazier or Less Intelligent than Whites (3 graphs)," *Religion News Service,* December 8, 2014, https://religionnews.com/2014/12/08/poll-whites-say-blacks-lazier-less-intelligent-whites-3-graphs/.

15. Patricia G. Devine and Andrew J. Elliot, "Are Racial Stereotypes Really Fading? The Princeton Trilogy Revisited," *Personality and Social Psychology Bulletin* 21, no. 11 (November 1995): 1139–50, https://journals.sagepub.com/doi/abs/10.1177/01461672952111002?journalCode=pspc.

16. R.L.G., "Code-Switching: How Black to Be?" *The Economist,* April 10, 2013, https://www.economist.com/johnson/2013/04/10/how-black-to-be.

17. For a discussion of impression management, see Andrea S. Kramer and Alton B. Harris, *Breaking Through Bias: Communication Techniques for Women to Succeed at Work* (New York: Bibliomotion, Inc., 2016), 39–53.

18. Mariese Durr and Adia M. Harvey Wingfield, "Keep Your 'N' in Check: African American Women and the Interactive Effects of Etiquette and Emotional Labor," *Critical Sociology* 37, no. 5 (September 2011): 557–71.

19. Michelle Obama, *Becoming* (New York: Crown Publishing, 2018), x.

20. Obama, *Becoming*, 265.

21. Durr and Harvey Wingfield, "Keep Your 'N' in Check."

22. Siraad Dirshe, "Black Women Speak Up about Their Struggles Wearing Natural Hair in the Workplace," *Essence*, February, 7, 2018, https://www.essence.com/hair/black-women-natural-hair-discrimination-workplace/; Alexia Fernandez Campbell, "A Black Woman Lost a Job Offer Because She Wouldn't Cut Her Dreadlocks. Now She Wants to Go to the Supreme Court," *Vox*, April 18, 2018, https://www.vox.com/2018/4/18/17242788/chastity-jones-dreadlock-job-discrimination.

23. Jena McGregor, "Even among Harvard MBAs, Few Black Women Ever Reach Corporate America's Top Rungs," *Washington Post*, February 20, 2018, https://www.washingtonpost.com/news/on-leadership/wp/2018/02/20/even-among-harvard-mbas-few-black-women-ever-reach-corporate-americans-top-rungs/.

24. Gabriella Gutiérrez y Muhs et al., eds., *Presumed Incompetent: The Intersections of Race and Class for Women in Academia* (Boulder, CO: University Press of Colorado, 2012).

25. Ijeoma Oluo, *So You Want to Talk about Race* (New York: Seal Press, 2018), 3.

26. Edith Cooper, "Why Goldman Sachs Is Encouraging Employees to Talk about Race at Work—and Why as a Black Woman I Think This Is So Important," *Business Insider*, September 23, 2016, https://www.businessinsider.com/edith-cooper-goldman-sachs-on-talking-about-race-at-work-2016-9.

27. Claire Cain Miller, Kevin Quealy, and Margot Sanger-Katz, "The Top Jobs Where Women Are Outnumbered by Men Named John," *New York Times*, April 24, 2018, https://www.nytimes.com/interactive/2018/04/24/upshot/women-and-men-named-john.html.

28. Combs, "The Duality of Race."

29. Janice D. Yoder and Patricia Aniakudo, "'Outsider Within' the Firehouse: Subordination and Difference in the Social Interactions of African American Women Firefighters," *Gender & Society* 11, no. 3 (June 1997): 324–41, https://journals.sagepub.com/doi/10.1177/089124397011003004.

30. Janet E. Gans Epner, "Visible Invisibility: Women of Color in Law Firms," *ABA Commission on Women in the Profession*, 2012, https://www.americanbar.org/content/dam/aba/marketing/women/visibleinvisibility.pdf.

31. Combs, "The Duality of Race."

32. Catalyst, "Women of Color in Corporate Management: Opportunities and Barriers," July 13, 1999, http://www.catalyst.org/knowledge/women-color-corporate-management-opportunities-and-barriers.

33. Joel M. Podolny and James N. Baron, "Resources and Relationships: Social Networks and Mobility in the Workplace," *American Sociological Review* 62, no. 5 (1997): 673–93, http://www.jstor.org/stable/2657354.

34. Ajay Mehra, Martin Kilduff, and Daniel J. Brass, "At the Margins: A Distinctiveness Approach to the Social Identity and Social Networks of Underrepresented Groups," *Academy of Management Journal* 41, no. 4 (1998): 441–452, http://www.jstor.org/stable/257083.

35. Joe R. Feagin and Melvin P. Sikes, *Living with Racism: The Black Middle-Class Experience* (Boston: Beacon Press, 1994).

36. Jasmine Pierce, "It's Not Just a 'Black Thing': Black Women in the Law and Issues of Double Identity and Discrimination" (Washington, DC: American University, 2011), https://www.wcl.american.edu/index.cfm?LinkServID=7384CA99-92E2-8DE0-B7F541AF4F08CE05].

37. Pierce, "It's Not Just a 'Black Thing'"; Mary Hawkesworth, "Congressional Enactments of Race-Gender: Toward a Theory of Raced-Gendered Institutions," *American Political Science Review* 97, no. 4 (2003): 529–50, http://www.jstor.org/stable/3593022.

38. Joan C. Williams and Rachel Dempsey, *What Works for Women at Work: Four Patterns Working Women Need to Know* (New York: New York University Press 2014), 224.

39. Trina Jones and Kimberly Jade Norwood, "Aggressive Encounters & White Fragility: Deconstructing the Trope of the Angry Black Woman," *Iowa Law Review* 102, no. 5 (July 2017), https://ilr.law.uiowa.edu/assets/Uploads/ILR-102-5-Jones.pdf.

40. Phyllis Marynick Palmer, "White Women/Black Women: The Dualism of Female Identity and Experience in the United States," *Feminist Studies* 9, no. 1 (Spring 1983): 151–70, https://www.jstor.org/stable/3177688?seq=1#page_scan_tab_contents.

41. Allan G. Johnson, *Privilege, Power, and Difference* (New York: McGraw-Hill, 2006).

42. Combs, "The Duality of Race."

43. Johnson, *Privilege, Power, and Difference*.

44. Adam Galinsky, "Are Gender Differences Just Power Differences in Disguise?" *Columbia Business School Ideas*, March 13, 2018, https://www8.gsb.columbia.edu/articles/ideas-work/are-gender-differences-just-power-differences-disguise.

45. Ruchika Tulshyan, "Women of Color Get Asked to Do More 'Office Housework.' Here's How They Can Say No," *Harvard Business Review,* April 6,

2018, https://hbr.org/2018/04/women-of-color-get-asked-to-do-more-offic e-housework-heres-how-they-can-say-no.

46. Melissa Burkley, "Are Black Women Invisible? Do Black Women Go Unnoticed More Often?" *Psychology Today,* December 8, 2010. https:// www.psychologytoday.com/us/blog/the-social-thinker/201012/are-black -women-invisible.

47. bell hooks, *Ain't I a Woman: Black Women and Feminism*, 2nd ed. (New York: Routledge, 2014).

48. Burkley, "Are Black Women Invisible?"

49. Burkley, "Are Black Women Invisible?"

50. Mathew Rodriguez, "Here's the Malcolm X Speech about Black Women Beyoncé Sampled in 'Lemonade,'" *MIC,* April 23, 2016, https://mic .com/articles/141642/here-s-the-malcolm-x-speech-about-black-women -beyonce-sampled-in-lemonade#.vhAgDPtX6.

51. Tulshyan, "Speaking Up."

52. Laura Morgan Roberts et al., "Beating the Odds," *Harvard Business Review*, March-April 2018, https://hbr.org/2018/03 beating-the-odds.

53. Roberts et al., "Beating the Odds."

54. Adia Harvery Wingfield, "Being Black—but Not Too Black—in the Work-place," *Atlantic,* October 14, 2015, https://www.theatlantic.com/business/ archive/2015/10/being-black-work/409990/.

55. Gutiérrez y Muhs et al., *Presumed Incompetent*, 403.

56. Alexis Nicole Smith et al., "Interviews with 59 Black Female Executives Explore Intersectional Invisibility and Strategies to Overcome It," *Harvard Business Review*, May 10, 2018, https://hbr.org/2018/05/interviews-with-59 -black-female-executives-explore-intersectional-invisibility-and-strategie s-to-overcome-it.

57. Smith, "Interviews with 59 Black."

58. Sharon Smith, "Black Feminism and Intersectionality," *International Socialist Review* 91 (January 2009), https://isreview.org/issue/91/black -feminism-and-intersectionality]; Benita Roth, *Separate Roads to Femi-nism: Black, Chicana, and White Feminist Movements in America's Second Wave* (Cambridge, UK: Cambridge University Press, 2003).

59. Hilary B. Bergsieker et al., "To Be Liked versus Respected: Divergent Goals in Interracial Interactions," *Journal of Personality and Social Psychology* 99, no. 2 (August 2010): 248–64, http://psycnet.apa.org/record/2010-14719-004.

60. "Do Blacks and Hispanics Get Along?" *Pew Research Center,* January 31, 2008, http://www.pewsocialtrends.org/2008/01/31/do-blacks-and-hispanics-get -along/.

61. Nicolas C. Vaca, *The Presumed Alliance: The Unspoken Conflict between Latinos and Blacks and What It Means for America* (New York: Harper Collins Publishers, 2004).

62. Susy Buchanan, "Tensions Mounting Between Blacks and Latinos Nationwide," *Intelligence Report*, July 27, 2005, https://www.spicenter .org/fighting-hate/intelligence-report/2005/tensions-mounting-between -blacks-and-latinos-nationwide.

63. *Highest Median Household Income on Record*, September 12, 2018. U.S. Census Bureau, https://www.census.gov/library/stories/2018/09/highest -median-household-on-record.html. Fifty-two percent of Asian Americans say their personal financial situation is excellent or good, while only 24 percent of Hispanics and 35 percent of the general public believe that they are in excellent or good shape financially. Pew Research Center, "Life in the United States," chap. 2 in *The Rise of Asian Americans*, June 19, 2012, http://www.pewsocialtrends.org/2012/06/19/chapter-2-life-in-the-united -states/. Ninety-five percent of Asian Americans think that compared with other racial and ethnic minority groups, they have been more or equally successful. Sixty-nine percent of Asian Americans believe people can get ahead if they are willing to work hard, a view shared by just 58 percent of the American public as a whole.

64. Jezzika Chung, "How Asian Immigrants Learn Anti-Blackness from White Culture, and How to Stop It," *Huffington Post*, updated September 7, 2017, https://www.huffingtonpost.com/entry/how-asian-americans-can -stop-contributing-to-anti-blackness_us_599f0757e4b0cb7715bfd3e14.

65. Tiffany Diane Tso, "Nail Salon Brawls & Boycotts: Unpacking the Black-Asian Conflict in America," *Refinery29*, August 21, 2018, https://www.refinery29 .com/en-us/2018/08/207533/red-apple-nails-brawl-block-asian-conflict.

66. Kat Chow, "'Model Minority' Myth Again Used as a Racial Wedge between Asians and Blacks," *NPR*, April 19, 2017, https://www.npr.org/ sections/codeswitch/2017/04/19/524571669/model-minority-myth-again -used-as-a-racial-wedge-between-asians-and-blacks.

67. Leah Fessler, "Gloria Steinem Says Black Women Have Always Been More Feminist than White Women," December 8, 2017, https://qz.com/ 1150028loria-steinem-on-metoo-black-women-have-been-more-feminist -than-white-women/.

68. Cooper, "Why Goldman Sachs."

69. Cooper, "Why Goldman Sachs."

70. Smith, "Interviews with 59 Black."

71. Smith, "Interviews with 59 Black."

Chapter 8

1. Alison Burke, "10 Facts about American Women in the Workforce," *Brookings*, December 5, 2017, Brookings Now, https://www.brookings.edu/blog/brookings-now/2017/12/05/10-facts-about-american-women-in-the-workforce/.

2. Mark DeWolf, "12 Stats about Working Women," *U.S. Department of Labor* (blog), *U.S. Department of Labor*, March 1, 2017, https://blog.dol.gov/2017/03/01/12-stats-about-working-women.

3. Mitra Toossi, "A Century of Change: The U.S. Labor Force, 1950–2050," *Monthly Labor Review* (May 2002): 15–28, https://www.bls.gov/opub/mlr/2002/05/art2full.pdf; "Employment Projections: Median Age of the Labor Force, by Sex, Race and Ethnicity," Bureau of Labor and Statistics, U.S. Department of Labor, last modified October 24, 2017, https://www.bls.gov/emp/tables/median-age-labor-force.htm.

4. Mitra Toossi and Elka Torpey, "Older Workers: Labor Force Trends and Career Options," *Career Outlook*, Bureau of Labor and Statistics, U.S. Department of Labor, May 2017, https://www.bls.gov/careeroutlook/2017/article/older-workers.htm.

5. Richard Fry, "Millennials Are the Largest Generation in the U.S. Labor Force," *Pew Research Center*, April 11, 2018, http://www.pewresearch.org/fact-tank/2018/04/11/millennials-largest-generation-us-labor-force/.

6. Erik Larson, "Future of Work: Research Shows Millennials, Gen Xers and Baby Boomers Make Better Decisions Together," *Forbes*, April 11, 2018, https://www.forbes.com/sites/eriklarson/2018/04/11/future-of-work-research-shows-millennials-gen-xers-and-baby-boomers-make-better-decisions-together/#1e36b1b35b44.

7. Rocío Lorenzo et al., "The Mix that Matters: Innovation through Diversity," *BCG*, April 26, 2017, https://www.bcg.com/en-us/publications/2017/people-organization-leadership-talent-innovation-through-diversity-mix-that-matters.aspx; Katharina Janz et al., "Leveraging Age Diversity in Times of Demographic Change: The Crucial Role of Leadership," in *Handbook of Research on Workforce Diversity in a Global Society: Technologies and Concepts* (Hershey, PA: IGI Global, 2012), 163–184, http://www.igi-global.com/chapter/leveraging-age-diversity-times-demographic/67057.

8. David Koeppel, "Gen Y vs. Boomers: Workplace Conflict Heats Up," *Fiscal Times*, November 11, 2011, http://www.thefiscaltimes.com/Articles/2011/11/11/Gen-Y-vs-Boomers-Workplace-Conflict-Heats-Up; Rob Walker, "How to Approach the Generation Gap in the Workplace," *New*

York Times, August 8, 2015, https://www.nytimes.com/2015/08/09/jobs/how-to-approach-the-generation-gap-in-the-workplace.html; Victor Lipman, "How to Manage Generational Differences in the Workplace," *Forbes*, January 25, 2017, https://www.forbes.com/sites/victorlipman/2017/01/25/how-to-manage-generational-differences-in-the-workplace/#4d691ae64cc4.

9. Haydn Shaw, *Sticking Points: How to Get 4 Generations Working Together in the 12 Places They Come Apart* (Carol Stream, IL: Tyndale House Publishers, Inc., 2013); Lynne C. Lancaster and David Stillman, *When Generations Collide: Who They Are. Why They Clash. How to Solve the Generational Puzzle at Work*, reprinted ed. (New York: HarperCollins, 2009); Jean M. Twenge, *iGen: Why Today's Super-Connected Kids Are Growing Up Less Rebellious, More Tolerant, Less Happy—and Completely Unprepared for Adulthood—and What That Means for the Rest of Us*, reprinted ed. (New York: Atria Books, 2017).

10. John P. Meriac, David J. Woehr, and Christina Banister, "Generational Differences in Work Ethics: An Examination of Measurement Equivalence across Three Cohorts," *Journal of Business Psychology* 25, no. 2 (June 2010): 315–324; Jane Pilcher, "Mannheim's Sociology of Generations: An Undervalued Legacy," *British Journal of Sociology* 45, no. 3 (September 1994): 481–95.

11. "Generations: What Should Employers Consider When Recruiting from Different Generations—Baby Boomers, Generation X, and Generation Y?" *Society for Human Resource Management*, September 20, 2012, https://www.shrm.org/resourcesandtools/tools-and-samples/hr-qa/pages/recruitingdifferentgenerations.aspx; "Recruiting a Multigenerational Workforce," *HR Professionals Magazine*, accessed December 14, 2018, http://hrprofessionalsmagazine.com/recruiting-a-multigenerational-workforce/.

12. Ron Zemke, Claire Raines, and Bob Filipczak, *Generations at Work: Managing the Clash of Boomers, Gen Xers, and Gen Yers in the Workplace*, 2nd ed. (New York: AMACOM, 2013), 12.

13. Tania Lennon, *Managing a Multi-Generational Workforce: The Myths versus the Realities* (Hay Group, 2015), https://focus.kornferry.com/wp-content/uploads/2015/02/HayGroup_Managing_multi-gen_workforce.pdf.

14. Lynda Gratton and Andrew Scott, "Our Assumptions about Old and Young Workers Are Wrong," *Harvard Business Review*, November 14, 2016, https://hbr.org/2016/11/our-assumptions-about-old-and-young-workers-are-wrong; Kelly Pledger Weeks, "Every Generation Wants Meaningful Work—But Thinks Other Age Groups Are in It for the Money," *Harvard Business Review*, July 31, 2017, https://hbr.org/2017/07/every-generation-wants-meaningful-work-but-thinks-other-age-groups-are-in-it-for-the-money.

15. While different commentators assign somewhat different birthdates to each of these generations, those we have set out are sufficiently typical to suggest the rough demarcations of the five age cohorts. Toossi, "*Century of Change.*"

16. Toossi, "*A Century of Change.*"

17. Hans Jaeger, "Generations in History: Reflections on a Controversial Concept," *History and Theory* 24, no. 3 (1985): 273–292.

18. Karl Mannheim, "The Problem of Generations," in *Essays on the Sociology of Knowledge: Collected Works*, ed. Paul Kecskemeti, vol. 5 (New York: Routledge, 1952), 276–322.

19. David M. McCourt, "The 'Problem of Generations' Revisited: Karl Mannheim and the Sociology of Knowledge in International Relations," in *Theory and Application of the "Generation" in International Relations and Politics*, eds. Brent J. Steele and Jonathan M. Acuff (New York: Palgrave Macmillan, 2012), 47–70.

20. Karen Wey Smola and Charlotte D. Sutton, "Generational Differences: Revisiting Generational Work Values for the New Millennium," *Journal of Organizational Behavior* 23, no. 4 (June 2002): 363–382, https://onlineli brary.wiley.com/doi/abs/10.1002/job.147.

21. Jean M. Twenge, *Generation Me: Why Today's Young Americans Are More Confident, Assertive, Entitled—and More Miserable than Ever Before* (New York: Atria, 2014), 4.

22. Twenge, *Generation Me*, 266.

23. Jean M. Twenge et al., "Generational Differences in Work Values: Leisure and Extrinsic Values Increasing, Social and Intrinsic Values Decreasing," *Journal of Management* 36, no. 5 (September 2010): 1117–42, https://jour nals.sagepub.com/doi/abs/10.1177/0149206309352246.

24. Twenge, *Generation Me*, 68.

25. Twenge, *Generation Me*, 277–8.

26. Smola and Sutton, "Generational Differences," is an example.

27. Bernard M. Bass and Bruce J. Avolio, eds., *Improving Organizational Effectiveness through Transformational Leadership* (Thousand Oaks, CA: Sage Publications, 1994).

28. David P. Costanza et al., "Generational Differences in Work-Related Attitudes: A Meta-Analysis," *Journal of Business and Psychology* 27, no. 4 (2012): 375–94.

29. Constanza et al., "Generational Differences in Work-Related Attitudes." Citizenship behaviors are activities women engage in over and above core task requirements, while minimum performance behaviors are

counterproductive work behaviors, including on-the-job aggressiveness, substance use, tardiness, and absence.

30. Brian A. Nosek, Mahzarin R. Banaji, and Anthony G. Greenwald, "Harvesting Implicit Group Attitudes and Beliefs from a Demonstration Web Site," *Group Dynamics: Theory, Research, and Practice* 6, no. 1 (2002), 101–115. http://projectimplicit.net/nosek/papers/harvesting.GroupDynamics.pdf.

31. Mary E. Kite and Blair T. Johnson, "Attitudes toward Older and Younger Adults: A Meta-Analysis," *Psychology and Aging* 3, no. 3 (1988): 233–44, http://psycnet.apa.org/record/1989-04767-001.

32. Chris Blauth et al., *Age-Based Stereotypes: Silent Killer of Collaboration and Productivity* (*Achieveglobal*, 2011), https://www.rpi.edu/dept/hr/docs/ Age-Based%20Stereotypes.pdf; See also B. Evan Blaine and Kimberly J. McClure Brenchley, "Understanding Age Stereotypes and Ageism," in *Understanding the Psychology of Diversity*, 3rd ed. (Los Angeles: SAGE Publications, Inc., 2017).

33. Bruce W. Hayward et al., *Evaluation of the Campaign for Older Workers* (London: Her Majesty's Stationery Office, 1997).

34. Lynn M. Shore, Jeanette N. Cleveland, and Caren B. Goldberg, "Work Attitudes and Decisions as a Function of Manager Age and Employee Age," *Journal of Applied Psychology* 88, no. 3 (2003): 529–37.

35. Warren C.K. Chiu et al., "Age Stereotypes and Discriminatory Attitudes Towards Older Workers: An East-West Comparison," *Human Relations* 54, no. 5 (2001): 629–61, https://journals.sagepub.com/doi/10.1177/0018 726701545004#articleCitationDownloadContainer; Elizabeth M. Weiss and Todd J. Maurer, "Age Discrimination in Personnel Decisions: A Reexamination," *Journal of Applied Social Psychology* 34, no. 8 (August 2004): 1551–62, https://onlinelibrary.wiley.com/doi/abs/10.1111/j.1559-1816.2004. tb02786.x.

36. Lisa M. Finkelstein and Michael J. Burke, "Age Stereotypes at Work: The Role of Rater and Contextual Factors on Evaluations of Job Applicants," *Journal of General Psychology* 125, no. 4 (October 1998): 317–45.

37. Esther J. Dedrick and Gregory H. Dobbins, "The Influence of Subordinate Age on Managerial Actions: An Attributional Analysis," *Journal of Organizational Behavior* 12, no. 5 (1991): 367–77, http://psycnet.apa.org/record/ 1992-11003-001; Kimberly A. Wrenn and Todd J. Maurer, "Beliefs About Older Workers' Learning and Development Behavior in Relation to Beliefs about Malleability of Skills, Age-Related Decline, and Control," *Journal of Applied Social Psychology* 34, no. 2 (February 2004): 223–42.

38. Peter J. Naus, "Some Correlates of Attitude Towards Old People," *International Journal of Aging and Human Development* 4, no. 3 (1973): 229–43; Nancy C. Sherman and Joel A. Gold, "Perceptions of Ideal and Typical Middle and Old Age," *International Journal of Aging and Human Development* 9, no. 1 (1979): 67–73.

39. Richard A. Posthuman and Michael A. Campion, "Age Stereotypes in the Workplace: Common Stereotypes, Moderators, and Future Research Directions," *Journal of Management* 35, no. 1 (February 2009): 158–88.

40. Lynda Gratton and Andrew Scott, "How Work Will Change When Most of Us Live to 100," *Harvard Business* Review, June 27, 2016, https://hbr.org/2016/06/how-work-will-change-when-most-of-us-live-to-100.

41. Gratton and Scott, "Our Assumptions About Old and Young Workers Are Wrong."

42. María Triana, *Managing Diversity in Organizations: A Global Perspective* (New York: Routledge, 2017); Michéle C. Kaufmann et al., "Age Bias in Selection Decisions: The Role of Facial Appearance and Fitness Impressions," *Frontiers in Psychology*, 8 (2017).

43. Deborah Auerbach, "Generational Differences in the Workplace," CareerBuilder, August 27, 2014, https://www.careerbuilder.com/advice/generational-differences-in-the-workplace.

44. Triana, *Managing Diversity*, 26.

45. Jessica Holland, "Why the Millennial Stereotype Is Wrong," *BBC*, July 16, 2017, Capital, www.bbc.com/capital/story/20170713-why-the-millennial-stereotype-is-wrong.

46. Holland, "Why the Millennial Stereotype Is Wrong."

47. Holland, "Why the Millennial Stereotype Is Wrong."

48. Bruce J. Avolio and Gerald V. Barrett, "Effects of Age Stereotyping in a Simulated Interview," *Psychology and Aging* 2, no. 1 (1987): 56–63, http://psycnet.apa.org/record/1987-15538-001; Randall A. Gordon, Richard M. Rozelle, and James C. Baxter, "The Effect of Applicant Age, Job Level, and Accountability on the Evaluation of Job Applicants," *Organizational Behavior and Human Decision Processes* 41, no. 1 (1988): 20–33, http://psycnet.apa.org/record/1988-18676-001.

49. Kim Cassady, "3 Ways Technology Influences Generational Divides at Work," *Entrepreneur*, March 29, 2017, https:/www.entrepreneur.com/article/290763.

50. Cassady, "3 Ways"

51. Jodie Eckleberry-Hunt and Jennifer Tucciarone, "The Challenges and Opportunities of Teaching 'Generation Y,'" *Journal of Graduate Medical*

Education 3, no. 4 (December 2011): 458–61, https://www.ncbi.nlm.nih
.gov/pmc/articles/PMC3244307/.

52. Sarah DeArmond et al., "Age and Gender Stereotypes: New Challenges in
     a Changing Workplace and Workforce," *Journal of Applied Social Psychol-
     ogy* 36, no. 9 (September 2006): 2184–2214."

53. Scott W. Lester et al., "Actual versus Perceived Generational Differences at
     Work: An Empirical Examination," *Journal of Leadership and Organiza-
     tional Studies* 19, no. 3 (August 2012): 341–54.

54. DeArmond, "Age and Gender Stereotypes."

55. Auerbach, "Generational Differences."

56. Florian Kunze and Jochen I. Menges, "Younger Supervisors, Older Subor-
     dinates: An Organizational-Level of Age Differences, Emotions, and Per-
     formance," *Journal of Organizational Behavior*, 38 (2017): 461–86.

57. Kunze and Menges, "Younger Supervisors, Older Subordinates."

58. Auerbach, "Generational Differences."

59. Anne S. Tsui and Charles A. O'Reilly, "Beyond Simple Demographic Effects:
     The Importance of Relational Demographics in Superior-Subordinate
     Dyads," *Academy of Management Journal* 32, no. 2 (June 1989): 402–23.

60. Mary Hair Collins, Joseph F. Hair Jr., and Tonette S. Rocco, "The Older
     -Worker–Younger-Supervisor Dyad: A Test of the Reverse Pygmalion
     Effect," *Human Resource Development Quarterly* 20, no. 1 (1989): 21–41,
     http://psycnet.apa.org/record/2009-05466-006.

61. Lisa M. Finkelstein, Katherine M. Ryan, and Eden B. King, "What Do the
     Young (Old) People Think of Me? Content and Accuracy of Age-Based
     Meta-Stereotypes," *European Journal of Work and Organizational Psychol-
     ogy* 22, no. 6 (2013): 633–57, https://www.tandfonline.com/doi/abs/10.1080
     /1359432X.2012.673279.

Chapter 9

1. A recent large scale national study found that when other factors were
    comparable, "race/ethnicity did not significantly predict work-to-fam-
    ily or family-to-work conflict among women." Samantha K. Ammons et
    al., "Work-Family Conflict among Black, White, and Hispanic Men and
    Women," *Community, Work and Family* 20, no. 4 (2017): 1–26.

2. Anne-Marie Slaughter, "Why Women Still Can't Have It All," *Atlantic*,
    July/August 2012, https://www.theatlantic.com/magazine/archive/2012/07/
    why-women-still-cant-have-it-all/309020/.

3. Gail Collins, *When Everything Changed: The Amazing Journey of American Women from the 1960s to the Present* (New York: Little Brown and Company, 2009), 393.

4. Betty Friedan, *The Feminine Mystique* (New York: W.W. Norton & Company, 2001), 472.

5. Family and Medical Leave Act of 1993, 29 U.S.C. §§ 2601 et seq.

6. Sarah Fass, *Paid Leave in the States: A Critical Support for Low-Wage Workers and Their Families* (National Center for Children in Poverty, March 2009).

7. Center for Economic and Policy Research, *United States Lags World in Paid Sick Days for Workers and Families*, accessed December 11, 2018, http://cepr.net/documents/publications/psd-summary.pdf; Jody Heymann et al., *Contagion Nation: A Comparison of Paid Sick Day Policies in 22 Countries (Center for Economic and Policy Research)* (May 2009), http://cepr.net/documents/publications/paid-sick-days-2009-05.pdf.

8. Sarah Jane Glynn, "Fact Sheet: Childcare," Center for American Progress, August 16, 2012, https://cdn.americanprogress.org/wp-content/uploads/2012/10/ChildCareFactsheet.pdf.

9. Lynda Laughlin, *Who's Minding the Kids? Child Care Arrangements: Spring 2011* (Washington, DC: U.S. Census Bureau, April 2013), https://www.census.gov/prod/2013pubs/p70-135.pdf.

10. Rasheed Malik et al., *Child Care Deserts: An Analysis of Child Care Centers by ZIP Code in 8 States* (Center for American Progress, October 27, 2016), https://www.americanprogress.org/issues/early-childhood/reports/2016/10/27/225703/child-care-deserts/.

11. Malik et al., *Child Care Deserts*.

12. Kristen Bahler, "It Costs More to Send Your Kid to Day Care than to College," *Time*, September 29, 2016, Money, time.com/money/4512858/daycare-college-cost-comparison/.

13. Brigid Schulte and Alieza Durana, *The New America Care Report* (New America, September 2016), 6, https://www.newamerica.org/better-life-lab/policy-papers/new-america-care-report/.

14. Child Care and Development Block Grant Act of 2014, 42 U.S.C. § 618.

15. "Paying for Childcare," Childcare Aware of America, accessed December 11, 2018, http://childcareaware.org/help-paying-child-care-federal-and-state-child-care-programs/.

16. "Tax Credit for Child and Dependent Care Expenses," efile.com, accessed December 11, 2018, https://www.efile.com/tax-credit/dependent-care-tax-credit/; Schulte and Durana, *The New America Care Report*, 6.

17. Louise Stoney, "The Iron Triangle: A Simple Formula for ECE Finance" (PowerPoint presentation, Opportunities Exchange and BUILD Early Childhood, June 13, 2014), http://opportunities-exchange.org/wp-content/uploads/Iron-Triangle-Webinar-FINAL-6.13.14.pdf.

18. Schulte and Durana, *The New America Care Report*, 6.

19. Jessica Deahl, "Child Care Scarcity Has Very Real Consequences for Working Families," January 3, 2017, in *All Things Considered, NPR*, podcast, https://www.npr.org/sections/health-shots/2017/01/03/506448993/child-care-scarcity-has-very-real-consequences-for-working-families.

20. For a clear-eyed analysis of what it would take for the US to have a truly comprehensive, high-quality childcare system, see Madeline M. Kunin, *The New Feminist Agenda: Determining the Next Revolution for Women, Work, and Family* (White River Junction, VT: Chelsea Green Publishing, 2012).

21. Susan Douglas and Meredith Michaels, *The Mommy Myth: The Idealization of Motherhood and How It Has Undermined All Women* (New York: Free Press, 2005), introduction, Kindle.

22. Jill K. Walls, Heather M. Helms, and Joseph G. Grzywacz, "Intensive Mothering Beliefs among Full-Time Employed Mothers of Infants," *Journal of Family Issues* 37, no. 2 (January 2016): 245–69, http://dx.doi.org/10.1177/0192513X13519254.

23. Sharon Hays, *The Cultural Contradictions of Motherhood* (New Haven, CT: Yale University Press, 1996).

24. Walls, Heims, and Grzywacz, "Intensive Mothering Beliefs."

25. Linda Rose Ennis, ed., *Intensive Mothering: The Cultural Contradictions of Modern Motherhood* (Ontario: Demeter Press, 2014); Claire Cain Miller, "The Relentlessness of Modern Parenting," *New York Times*, December 25, 2018, https://www.nytimes.com/2018/12/25/upshot/the-relentlessness-of-modern-parenting.html.

26. Pamela Druckerman, *Bringing Up Bébé: One American Mother Discovers the Wisdom of French Parenting* (New York: Penguin Books, 2014).

27. Lenore Skenazy, *Free-Range Kids: How to Raise Safe, Self-Reliant Children (Without Going Nuts with Worry)* (San Francisco: Jossey-Bass, 2009).

28. Fatherly, "Bringing Up Bebe Review: Why French Parenting Helps Kids Eat Normal Foods, Behave Themselves, and Sleep All Night," *Fatherly*, May 1, 2015, https://www.fatherly.com/health-science/why-french-kids-eat-normal-foods-behave-them.

29. Skenazy, *Free-Range Kids*, 4–5.

30. Wednesday Martin, *Primates of Park Avenue: A Memoir* (New York: Simon & Schuster, 2015), 164–194.

31. Deirdre D. Johnston and Debra H. Swanson, "Constructing the 'Good Mother': The Experience of Mothering Ideologies by Work Status," *Sex Roles* 54, no. 7–8 (April 2006): 509–519, https://link.springer.com/article/10.1007%2Fs11199-006-90251-3.

32. Tania Lombrozo, "Privileged Primates and the Mothers Who Mock Them," quoting Gwen Dewar, *NPR*, June 15, 2015, https://www.npr.org/sections/13.7/2015/06/15/414563780/privileged-primates-and-the-mothers-that-mock-them.

33. Gretchen Livingston and Kristen Bialik, "7 Facts about U.S. Moms," *Pew Center Research*, May 10, 2018, http://www.pewresearch.org/fact-tank/2018/05/10/facts-about-u-s-mothers/.

34. Livingston and Bialik, "7 Facts."

35. Kristen Fischer, "Are You a Lawnmower Parent? Here's How It Can Harm Your Kids," *Sheknows*, December 21, 2018, Parenting, https://www.sheknows.com/parenting/articles/1975800/lawnmower-parenting-harms-kids/?utm_medium=email&utm_source=exacttarget&utm_campa.

36. Sonja Haller, "Meet the 'Lawnmower Parent,' the New Helicopter Parents of 2018," *USA Today*, September 19, 2018, https://www.usatoday.com/story/life/allthemoms/2018/09/meet-lawnmower-parent-new-helicopter-parents-types-parents-tiger-attachment/13473580.

37. Vivia Chen, "Can We Stop the Mommy Anxiety Nonsense?" *American Lawyer*, May 18, 2016, https://www.law.com/americanlawyer/almID/1202758039166/.

38. Walls, Heims, and Grzywacz, "Intensive Mothering Beliefs."

39. Andrea S. Kramer and Alton B. Harris, *Breaking Through Bias: Communication Techniques for Women to Succeed at Work* (New York: Bibliomotion, 2016), 169–171.

40. Kramer and Harris, *Breaking Through Bias*, 171.

41. Stephanie Coontz, "Progress at Work, but Mothers Still Pay a Price," *New York Times*, June 8, 2013, https://hbr.org/2013/09/New York Times.

42. "Women in the Workplace: A Research Roundup," *Harvard Business Review*, September 2013, http://hbr.org/2013/09/women-in-the-workplace-a-research-roundup; Joan Williams, "Pay Gap Deniers," *Huff Post*, August 6, 2013, https://huffingtonpost.com/joan-williams/pay-gap-deniers_b_3391524.html.

43. Jennifer Thorpe-Moscon, "Minority Women Report Downsizing Their Ambitions Because of Bias," *Harvard Business Review*, January 16, 2014, https://hbr.org/2014/01/minority-women-report-downsizing-their-ambitions-because-of-bias; Ammons et al., "Work-Family Conflict."

44. Alice H. Eagly and Steven J. Karau, "Role Congruity Theory of Prejudice toward Female Leaders," *Psychological Review* 109, no. 3 (July 2002): 573–98, https://www.rci.rutgers.edu/~search1/pdf/Eagley_Role_Congruity _Theory.pdf; Madeline E. Heilman, "Description and Prescription: How Gender and Prescription Prevent Women's Ascent up the Organizational Ladder," *Journal of Social Issues* 57, no. 4 (2001): 657–74, https://spssi. onlinelibrary.wiley.com/doi/abs/10.1111/0022-4537.00234; Madeline E. Heilman and Alice H. Eagly, "Gender Stereotypes Are Alive, Well, and Busy Producing Workplace Discrimination," *Industrial and Organizational Psychology* 1, no. 4 (December 2008): 393–98.

45. Amy J. C. Cuddy, Susan T. Fiske, and Peter Glick, "When Professionals Become Mothers, Warmth Doesn't Cut the Ice," *Journal of Social Issues* 60, no. 4 (2004): 701–18, http://www.people.hbs.edu/acuddy/2004,%20 cuddy,%20fiske,%20&%20glick,%20JSI.pdf.

46. Shelley J. Correll, Stephen Benard, and In Paik, "Getting a Job: Is There a Motherhood Penalty?" *American Journal of Sociology* 112, no. 5 (March 2007): 1297–1339, https://sociology.stanford.edu/sites/default/files/publi cations/getting_a_job-_is_there_a_motherhood_penalty.pdf.

47. Jane A. Halpert, Midge L. Wilson, and Julia L. Hickman, "Pregnancy as a Source of Bias in Performance Appraisals," *Journal of Organizational Behavior* 14, no. 7 (December 1993): 649–63.

48. Pamela Stone, "The Rhetoric and Reality of 'Opting Out,' " *American Sociological Association Journal* 6, no. 4 (Fall 2007): 14–19.

49. Stephen Benard and Shelley J. Correll, "Normative Discrimination and the Motherhood Penalty," *Gender and Society* 24, no. 5 (October 2010): 616–646.

50. Ellen Galinsky et al., *Leaders in a Global Economy: A Study of Executive Women and Men* (Families and Work Institute, 2003), https://familiesand-work.org/site/research/summary/globalsumm.pdf.

51. Emma Cahusac and Shireen Kanji, "Giving Up: How Gendered Organizational Cultures Push Mothers Out," *Gender, Work & Organization* 21, no. 1 (January 2014): 57–70.

52. Kramer and Harris, *Breaking Through Bias*, 169–71.

53. Cahusac and Kanji, "Giving Up."

54. Elissa Strauss, "The Judgmental Mom Is Little More than a Stereotype," *CNN*, December 20, 2018, https://www.cnn.com/2018/12/13/health/ judgmental-mom-parenting-strauss/index.html.

55. Lilia M. Cortina, "Unseen Injustice: Incivility as Modern Discrimination in Organizations," *Academy of Management Review* 33, no. 1 (January 2008): 55–75.

56. KPMG, YSC, and 30% Club, *Cracking the Code* (2014), 10, https://home .kpmg/content/dam/kpmg/pdf/2015/04/Cracking-the-code.pdf.

57. KPMG, *Cracking the Code*, 10.

58. KPMG, 9.

Chapter 10

1. "Project Implicit," Harvard University, accessed February 16, 2019, https:// implicit.harvard.edu/implicit/selecta test.html.

2. Ijeoma Oluo, *So You Want to Talk about Race* (New York: Seal Press, 2018), 45.

3. Catalyst, "Flip the Script," https://www.catalyst.org/knowledge/flip-script.

Chapter 11

1. Claudia Goldin and Cecilia Rouse, "Orchestrating Impartiality: The Impact of "Blind" Auditions on Female Musicians," *American Economic Review* 90, no. 4 (September 2000): 715–41.

2. Daniel Kahneman, *Thinking, Fast and Slow* (New York: Farrar, Straus, and Giroux, 2011), 19–25.

3. Kahneman, *Thinking: Fast and Slow*, 417.

4. Mahzarin R. Banaji and Anthony G. Greenwald, *Blindspot: Hidden Biases of Good People* (New York: Delacorte Press, 2013), 4–20.

5. Banaji and Greenwald, *Blindspot*, 146.

6. Charlotte Carroll, "What Is the Rooney Rule? Explaining the NFL's Diversity Policy for Hiring Coaches," *Sports Illustrated*, December 21, 2018, NFL, https://www.si.com/nfl/2018/12/31/rooney-rule-explained-nfl-diver sity-policy.

7. Kenneth Johnson, "What Corporations Can Learn about Diversity from the Rooney Rule," *Forbes*, February 1, 2018, https://www.forbes.com/sites/ forbescoachescouncil/2018/02/01/what-corporations-can-learn-about -diversity-from-the-nfls-rooney-rule/#5782077c47de.

8. Ellen McGirt, "How Lawyers Are Working to Change Their Industry's Diversity Problem," *Fortune*, August 30, 2017, fortune.com/go/careers/ the-mansfield-rule-lawyers-diversity.

9. Keith O'Brien, *Fly Girls: How Five Daring Women Defied All Odds and Made Aviation History* (New York: Houghton Mifflin Harcourt, 2018), chapter 19, Kindle.

10. Sylvia Ann Hewlett, "Executive Women and the Myth of Having It All," *Harvard Business Review*, April 2002, http://hbr.org/2002/04/executive-women-and-the-myth-of-having-it-all.

11. Rachel Thomas, "Corporate America Is Not on the Path to Gender Equality," LeanIn, September 30, 2015, http://leanin.org/news-inspiration/corporate-america-is-not-on-the-path-to-gender-equality/; McKinsey & Company, *Women in the Workplace* (McKinsey & Company Insights & Publications, September 2015), http://www.mckinsey.com/insights/organization/women_in_the_workplace.

12. Joan C. Williams and Marina Multhaup, "How Managers Can Be Fair about Flexibility for Parents and Non-Parents Alike," *Harvard Business Review*, April 27, 2018, https://hbr.org/2018/04/how-managers-can-be-fair-about-flexibility-for-parents-and-non-parents-alike.

13. Williams and Multhaup, "How Managers Can Be Fair."

14. AICPA, "Women's Initiatives Executive Committee: 2017 CPA Firm Gender Survey," accessed February 17, 2019 https://www.aicpa.org/content/dam/aicpa/career/womenintheprofession/downloadabledocuments/wiec-2017-cpa-firm-gender-survey-brochure.pdf.

15. National Partnership for Women and Families, "Flexibility for Success: How Workplace Flexibility Policies Benefit All Workers and Employers," accessed February 16, 2019, www.nationalpartnership.org/our-work/resources/workplace/flexibility-for-success.pdf.

16. Anne Donovan, "What PwC Learned from Its Policy of Flexible Work for Everyone," *Harvard Business Review*, January 28, 2019, https://hbr.org/2019/01/what-pwc-learned-from-its-policy-of-flexible-work-for-everyone.

17. Shelly J. Correll, "Sociologists for Women in Society 2016 Feminist Lecture: Reducing Gender Biases in Modern Workplaces: A Small Wins Approach to Organizational Change," *Gender and Society* 31, no. 6 (December 1, 2017): 725-50.

18. Correll, "Sociologists for Women in Society."

19. Correll, "Sociologists for Women in Society."

20. Katie Abouzahr et al., "Dispelling the Myths of the Gender 'Ambition Gap,'" Boston Consulting Group, April 5, 2017, https://www.bcg.com/en-cz/publications/2017/people-organization-leadership-change-disspelling-the-myths-of-the-gender-ambition-gap.aspx.

21. Matt Krentz et al., "Fixing the Flawed Approach to Diversity," Boston Consulting Group, January 17, 2019, https://www.bcg.com/en-us/publications/2019/fixing-the-flawed-approach-to-diversity.aspx.

22. Stephan Turban, Dan Wu, and Letian (LT) Zhang, "Research: When Gender Diversity Makes Firms More Productive," *Harvard Business Review*, February 11, 2019, https://hbr.org/2019/research-when-gender-diversity-makes-firms-more-productive.

23. Anne Fischer, "Women: Want a Promotion? Find the Boss Whose Wife Has a Career," *Fortune*, August 1, 2012, fortune.com/2012/08/01/women-want-a-promotion-find-a-boss-whose-wife-has-a-career/.

24. Sreedhari D. Desai, Dolly Chugh, and Arthur Brief, "The Organizational Implications of a Traditional Marriage: Can a Domestic Traditionalist by Night Be an Organizational Egalitarian by Day?" (research paper no. 2013–19, UNC Kenan-Flagier Research Paper, March 2012).

25. Ellen Galinsky et al., *Leaders in a Global Economy: A Study of Executive Women and Men* (Families and Work Institute, 2003), https://familiesand work.org/site/research/summary/globalsumm.pdf.

26. Joan Acker, "Hierarchies, Jobs, Bodies: A Theory of Gendered Organizations," *Gender and Society* 4, no. 2 (June 1990): 139–58.

27. Patricia Yancey Martin, "'Said and Done' versus 'Saying and Doing': Gendering Practices, Practicing Gender at Work," *Gender and Society* 17, no. 3 (June 2003): 342–66.

28. Martin, "'Said and Done.'"

29. Joan Acker, "Inequality Regimes: Gender, Class and Race in Organizations," *Gender & Society* 20, no. 4 (2006): 441–64.

30. Kevin Stainback, Sibyl Kleiner, and Sheryl Skaggs, "Women in Power: Undoing or Redoing the Gendered Organization?" *Gender and Society* 30, no. 1 (February 2016): 109–35.

31. Colleen Chesterman, Anne Ross-Smith, and Margaret Peters, "The Gendered Impact on Organizations of a Critical Mass of Women in Senior Management," *Policy and Society* 24, no. 4 (2005): 69–91.

32. Chesterman, Ross-Smith, and Peters, "The Gendered Impact."

33. Chesterman, Ross-Smith, and Peters, "The Gendered Impact."

Glossary

1. *Merriam-Webster*, s.v. "tension," accessed January 10, 2019, https://www.Merriam-Webster.com/dictionary/tension.

2. *Merriam-Webster*, s.v. "conflict," accessed January 10, 2019, https://www.Merriam-Webster.com/dictionary/conflict.

3. "Gender, Equity, and Human Rights," World Health Organization, accessed January 17, 2019, https://www.who.int/gender-equity-rights/en/.

4. "Gender, Equity, and Human Rights: Gender," World Health Organization, accessed January 17, 2019, https://www.who.int/gender-equity-rights/understanding/gender-definition/en/.

5. Angeline Goh, "An Attributional Analysis of Counterproductive Work Behavior (CWB) in Response to Occupational Stress" (dissertation, University of South Florida, November 21, 2006), http://digital.lib.usf.edu/content/SF/S0/02/62/13/00001/E14-SFE0001895.pdf.

6. Lilia M. Cortina, "Unseen Injustice: Incivility as Modern Discrimination in Organizations," *Academy of Management Review* 33, no. 1 (January 2008), 55–75.

7. *Merriam-Webster*, s.v. "microaggression," accessed December 27, 2018, https://www.Merriam-Webster.com/dictionary/microaggression.

8. "Sexual and Reproducutive Health: Defining Sexual Health," World Health Organization, accessed December 28, 2018, https://www.who.int/reproductivehealth/topics/sexual_health/sh_definitions/en/.

ACKNOWLEDGMENTS

We could not have written this book without the comments, criticisms, suggestions, and support of a great many people. In fact, we're almost embarrassed by the number of people we turned to for help, every one of whom agreed to roll up their sleeves and give us a hand. Many of our reviewers and commentators were old friends, but we met many others in writing this book, and many of them have become friends. In alphabetical order and without suggesting the nature and extent of the help they provided us, here they are. Katie A. Ahern, Dahlia Ali, Irma Alvarado, Monique Austin, Abigail Baker, Deborah Baker, Vicki Banks, Felice Batlan, Peter B. Bensinger Jr., Kate Benson, Jessica Berardi, Jennifer A. Berman, Barbara J. Best, Kay Bowers, Wileen Chick, Shruti Costales, Judy and Adrian Coté, Charlie and Rochelle Curtis, the Dancing Queens, Ariana Danquah, Jennifer Dawson, Katelin Drass, Julie Fenton, Lynne Flater, Carol Frohlinger, Susan G. Gallagher, Sandy A. Goldberg, Ruth Goran, Sadie Grunewald, Claire Haffner, Christopher Haigh, Margaret Hanson, Saman Haque, Bethany Whittles Harris, Cynthia K. Harris, Les Harris, Erika Heilman, Kristine Johnson, Molly Keelan, Cecilia Kim, Frances H. Krasnow, Haley Laird, Ursula Laskowski, Leslie Lambert, Lisa A. Linsky, Bendita Cynthia Malakia, Margaret and Louis Manetti, Wendy A. Manning, Lori McCarthy, Jennifer Mikulina, Nicholas C. Mowbray, Orion Mowbray, Michael M. Mullaney, Maria Ojeda, Karen Pinkney, Colleen M. Redden, Roseanne Rega, Leslie Richards-Yellen, Nancy Rizzuto, Tracy Rosen, Madison C. Schmid, Jay Schreiber, Jayne Schreiber, April Sedall, Elizabeth J. Shampnoi, Nancy Shilepsky, Jodi Silberman, Pamela Simon, Alicia Simons, Akshita Singh, Chester Singleteary, Delena D. Spann, Janet Tasigianis, Mary Tidwell, Ellen Rozelle

Turner, Angela Vasandani, Regina Vasilopoulos, Tara Venditte, Anthony Warren, Wendy K. White Eagle, Sally Wildman, Tess Woods, Darla Zink, and Jennifer Zordani.

We would also like to thank Alison Hankey and everyone at our publisher, Nicholas Brealey, for their first-rate professionalism and advice. Their support made it a pleasure having our book published.

And we would like to end with a huge thanks to the hundreds of women (and men) who shared their stories and situations with us. Some of you will see yourselves and your experiences in our anecdotes. As we promised, we have changed your names and other identifying characteristics to protect your confidentiality.

REFERENCES

"About Hispanic Origin." U.S. Census Bureau: Hispanic Origin, accessed December 20, 2018. https://www.census.gov/topics/population/hispanic -origin/about.html.

Abouzahr, Katie, Matt Krentz, Frances Brooks Taplett, Claire Tracey, and Miki Tsusaka. "Dispelling the Myths of the Gender 'Ambition Gap.'" Boston Consulting Group, April 5, 2017. https://www.bcg.com/en-us/publications/ 2017/people-organization-leadership-change-dispelling-the-myths-of -the-gender-ambition-gap.aspx.

Achor, Shawn. *Big Potential: How Transforming the Pursuit of Success Raises Our Achievement, Happiness, and Well-Being.* New York: Currency, 2018.

Achor, Shawn. "Do Women's Networking Events Move the Needle on Equality?" *Harvard Business Review.* February 13, 2018. https://hbr.org/2018/02/do -womens-networking-events-move-the-needle-on-equality.

Acker, Joan. "Hierarchies, Jobs, Bodies: A Theory of Gendered Organizations." *Gender and Society* 4, no. 2 (June 1990): 139-58.

Acker, Joan. "Inequality Regimes: Gender, Class, and Race in Organizations." *Gender and Society* 20, no. 4 (2006): 441-64.

AICPA. "Women's Initiatives Executive Committee: 2017 CPA Firm Gender Survey." Accessed February 17, 2019. https://www.aicpa.org/content/dam/ aicpa/career/womenintheprofession/downloadabledocuments/wiec-2017 -cpa-firm-gender-survey-brochure.pdf.

Albright, Madeleine. "Speech at New Hampshire Campaign Rally for Hillary Clinton." Filmed February 6, 2016. https://www.washingtonpost.com/ video/politics/madeleine-albright-stumps-for-clinton/2016/02/06/f42095 dc-cd1e-11e5-b9ab-26591104bb19_video.html?utm_term=.3ea70248c6aa.

Allen, Samantha. "Just How Many LGBT Americans Are There?" *Daily Beast,* January 14, 2017. https://www.thedailybeast.com/just-how-many-lgbt-americans -are-there.

American Psychological Association. "Political Talk Plagues Workers Months After U.S. Election." Press release, May 3, 2017. https://www.apa.org/news/press/releases/2017/05/political-talk.aspx.

American Psychological Association. "1 in 4 Employees Negatively Affected by Political Talk at Work This Election Season, Finds New Survey." Press release, September 14, 2016. https://www.apa.org/news/press/releases/2016/09/employees-political-talk.aspx.

Ammons, Samantha K., Eric C. Dahlin, Penny Edgell, and Jonathan Bruce Santo. "Work-Family Conflict among Black, White, and Hispanic Men and Women." *Community, Work, and Family* (2017): 1–26.

Andersen, Steve. "How Men Can Be a Great Ally for Women by Breaking Patterns." *Good Men Project,* April 22, 2017. https://goodmenproject.com/ethics-values/how-men-can-be-a-great-ally-for-women-by-br.

Andrews, Shawn. *The Power of Perception: Leadership, Emotional Intelligence, and the Gender Divide.* New York: Morgan James, 2018. Kindle.

Ascend Foundation. "Race Trumps Gender in Silicon Valley's Double-Paned Glass Ceiling." *Cision PR Newswire,* October 3, 2017. https://www.prnewswire.com/news-releases/race-trumps-gender-in-silicon-valleys-double-paned-glass-ceiling-300529546.html.

Auerbach, Deborah. "Generational Differences in the Workplace." *CareerBuilder,* August 27, 2014. https://www.careerbuilder.com/advice/generational-differences-in-the-workplace.

Avolio, Bruce J., and Gerald V. Barrett. "Effects of Age Stereotyping in a Simulated Interview." *Psychology and Aging* 2, no. 1 (1987): 56–63. http://psycnet.apa.org/record/1987-15538-001.

Bahler, Kristen. "It Costs More to Send Your Kid to Day Care than to College." *Time.* September 29, 2016. Money. time.com/money/4512858/daycare-college-cost-comparison/.

Baim, Tracy. "The Battle Within, Cis and Trans Women, Can We Get Along." *Windy City Times,* August 1, 2018. http://www.windycitymediagroup.com/lgbt/ESSAY-The-Battle_Within_Cis-and_Trans-Wo.

Ball, Molly. "Donald Trump Didn't Really Win 52% of White Women in 2016." *Time,* October 18, 2018. Politics. http://time.com/5422644/trump-white-women-2016/.

Banaji, Mahzarin R., and Anthony G. Greenwald. *Blindspot: Hidden Biases of Good People.* New York: Delacorte Press, 2013.

Barash, Susan Shapiro. *Tripping the Prom Queen: The Truth about Women and Rivalry.* New York: St. Martin's Griffin, 2006.

Bass, Bernard M., and Bruce J. Avolio, eds. *Improving Organizational Effectiveness through Transformational Leadership.* Thousand Oaks, CA: Sage Publications, 1994.

Bauman, Kurt. "School Enrollment of the Hispanic Population: Two Decades of Growth," *Census Blogs,* U.S. Census Bureau. August 28, 2017. https://www.census.gov/newsroom/blogs/random-samplings/2017/08/school_enrollmentof.html.

Belkin, Lisa. "The Opt-Out Revolution." *New York Times Magazine,* October 26, 2003. http://www.nytimes.com/2003/10/26/magazine/the-opt-out-revolution.html.

Bell, Ella L. J. Edmondson, and Stella M. Nkomo. *Our Separate Ways.* Boston: Harvard Business Review Press, 2003.

Benard, Stephen, and Shelley J. Correll. "Normative Discrimination and the Motherhood Penalty." *Gender and Society* 24, no. 5 (October 2010): 616–646.

Bennet, Jessica. "Do Women-Only Networking Groups Help or Hurt Female Entrepreneurs?" *Inc.,* September 21, 2017. https://www.inc.com/magazine/201710/jessica-bennett/women-coworking-spaces.html.

Bergland, Christopher. "The Male and Female Brain Are More Similar than Once Assumed." *Psychology Today,* November 2, 2015. https://www.psychologytoday.com/us/blog/the-athletes-way/201511/the-male-and-female-brain-are-more-similar-once-assumed.

Bird, Caroline. *What Women Want: From the Official Report to the President, the Congress and the People of the United States.* New York: Simon and Schuster, 1977.

Blaine, B. Evan, and Kimberly J. McClure Brenchley. "Understanding Age Stereotypes and Ageism." In *Understanding the Psychology of Diversity.* 3rd ed. Los Angeles: SAGE Publications, Inc., 2017.

Blakemore, Erin. "How Women's Studies Erased Black Women." *JSTOR Daily,* February 11, 2017. https://daily.jstor.org/how-womens-studies-erased-black-women/.

Blauth, Chris, Jack McDaniel, Craig Perrin, and Paul B. Perrin. *Age-Based Stereotypes: Silent Killer of Collaboration and Productivity.* Tampa: Achieveglobal, 2011. https://www.rpi.edu/dept/hr/docs/Age-Based%20Stereotypes.pdf.

Boissoneault, Lorraine. "The 1977 Conference on Women's Rights that Split America in Two." *Smithsonian,* last modified February 15, 2017. https://www.smithsonianmag.com/history/1977-conference-womens-rights-split-america-two-180962174/.

Bonney, Grace. *In the Company of Women: Inspiration and Advice from over 100 Makers, Artists, and Entrepreneurs.* New York: Artisan, 2016.

Bowman, Emma. "Female Breakout 'Captain Marvel' Screenwriter Is Disrupting the Superheroine Trope." *NPR,* September 9, 2018. Movie Interviews. https://www.npr.org/2018/09/09/645703206/female-breakout-captain-marvel -screenwriter-is-disrupting-the-superheroine-trope.

Brandon, Emily. "Why Older Workers Can't Get Hired." *U.S. News and World Report.* May 18, 2012. https://money.usnews.com/money/blogs/planning -to-retire/2012/05/18/why-older-workers-cant-get-hired.

Brickman, Philip, and Ronnie Janoff-Bulman. "Pleasure and Pain in Social Comparison." In *Social Comparison Processes: Theoretical and Empirical Perspectives,* edited by Jerry M. Suls and Richard L. Miller. Washington, DC: Hemisphere Press, 1977.

Burke, Alison. "10 Facts about American Women in the Workforce." *Brookings,* December 5, 2017. Brookings Now. https://www.brookings.edu/ blog/brookings-now/2017/12/05/10-facts-about-american-women-in-the -workforce/.

Burkley, Melissa. "Are Black Women Invisible? Do Black Women Go Unnoticed More Often?" *Psychology Today,* December 8, 2010. https://www.psychology today.com/us/blog/the-social-thinker/201012/are-black-women-invisible.

Byker, Tanya. "The Opt Out Continuation: Education, Work, and Motherhood from 1984 to 2012." *RSF: The Russell Sage Foundation Journal of the Social Sciences* 2, no. 4 (August 2016): 34–70.

Cahusac, Emma, and Shireen Kanji. "Giving Up: How Gendered Organizational Cultures Push Mothers Out." *Gender, Work & Organization* 21, no. 1 (January 2014): 57–70.

Campbell, Alexia Fernandez. "A Black Woman Lost a Job Offer Because She Wouldn't Cut Her Dreadlocks. Now She Wants to Go to the Supreme Court." *Vox,* April 18, 2018. https://www.vox.com/2018/4/18/17242788/ chastity-jones-dreadlock-job-discrimination.

Carnevale, Anthony P., and Megan L. Fasules. *Latino Education and Economic Progress: Running Faster but Still Behind.* Washington, DC: Georgetown Center on Education and the Workforce, November 14, 2017. https://cew .georgetown.edu/cew-reports/latinosworkforce.

Carnevale, Anthony P., and Jeff Strohl. *Separate and Unequal: How Higher Education Reinforces the Intergenerational Reproduction of White Racial Privilege.* Washington, DC: Georgetown Public Policy Institute and the Center on Education and the Workforce, July 31, 2013. https://cew.georgetown .edu/cew-reports/separate-unequal/.

Carroll, Charlotte. "What Is the Rooney Rule? Explaining the NFL's Diversity Policy for Hiring Coaches." *Sports Illustrated,* December 21, 2018. NFL. https://www.si.com/nfl/2018/12/31/rooney-rule-explained-nfl-diversity-policy.

Carter, Nancy M., and Christine Silva. *The Myth of the Ideal Worker: Does Doing All the Right Things Really Get Women Ahead?* New York: Catalyst, 2011. https://www.catalyst.org/system/files/The_Myth_of_the_Ideal_Worker_Does_Doing_All_the_Right_Things_Really_Get_Women_Ahead.pdf.

Cassady, Kim. "3 Ways Technology Influences Generational Divides at Work." *Entrepreneur,* March 29, 2017. https:/www.entrepreneur.com/article/290763.

Castilla, Emilio J., and Stephan Benard. "The Paradox of Meritocracy in Organizations." *Administrative Science Quarterly* 55, no. 4 (December 1, 2010): 543–676.

Catalyst. *Advancing Asian Women in the Workplace: What Managers Need to Know.* https://www.catalyst.org/system/files/Advancing_Asian_Women_in_the_Workplace_What_Managers_Need_to_Know.pdf.

Catalyst. *Advancing Latinas in the Workplace: What Managers Need to Know.* New York: Catalyst, 2003. https://www.catalyst.org/system/files/Advancing_Latinas_in_the_Workplace_What_Managers_Need_to_Know.pdf.

Catalyst. "Catalyst Study Explodes Myths about Why Women's Careers Lag Men's." Press release. https://www.catalyst.org/media/catalyst-study-explodes-myths-about-why-womens-careers-lag-mens.

Catalyst. "Flip the Script." https://www.catalyst.org/knowledge/flip-script.

Catalyst. *Missing Pieces: Women and Minorities on Fortune 500 Boards.* 2012 Alliance for Board Diversity (ABD) Census, August 15, 2013. https://www.catalyst.org/system/files/2012_abd_missing_pieces_final_8_15_13.pdf.

Catalyst. "Paying It Forward Pays Back for Business Leaders." 2012. https://www.catalyst.org/media/paying-it-forward-pays-back-business-leaders.

Catalyst. "Women in Academia." October 20, 2017. http://www.catalyst.org/knowledge/women-academia.

Catalyst. "Women in S&P 500 Companies by Race/Ethnicity and Level." October 12, 2017. http://www.catalyst.org/knowledge/women-sp-500-companies-raceethnicity-and-level.

Catalyst. "Women of Color in Corporate Management: Opportunities and Barriers." July 13, 1999. http://www.catalyst.org/knowledge/women-color-corporate-management-opportunities-and-barriers.

Catalyst. "Women of Color in the United States." November 7, 2018. https://www.catalyst.org/knowledge/women-color-united-states-0.

Catalyst. *2009 Catalyst Census: Fortune 500 Women Executive Officers and Top Earners.* December 9, 2009. https://www.catalyst.org/system/files/2009 fortune 500 census women executive officers and top earners.pdf.

Center for Economic and Policy Research. *United States Lags World in Paid Sick Days for Workers and Families.* Accessed December 11, 2018. http://cepr.net/documents/publications/psd-summary.pdf.

Center for Women and Business at Bentley University. "Taking Employee Resource Groups to the Next Level," Fall 2016. https://www.bentley.edu/files/2017/03/17/Bentley%20CWB%20ERG%20Research%20Report%20Fall%202016.pdf.

"Changes in Women's Labor Force Participation in the 20th Century." United States Department of Labor: Bureau of Labor Statistics, February 16, 2000. https://www.bls.gov/opub/ted/2000/feb/wk3/art03.htm?view_full.

Chen, Vivia. "Can We Stop the Mommy Anxiety Nonsense?" *American Lawyer,* May 18, 2016. https://www.law.com/americanlawyer/almID/1202758039166/.

Chesler, Phyllis. *Woman's Inhumanity to Woman.* Chicago: Lawrence Hill Books, 2009.

Chesterman, Colleen, Anne Ross-Smith, and Margaret Peters. "The Gendered Impact on Organisations of Critical Mass of Women in Senior Management." *Policy and Society* 24, no. 4 (2005): 69-91.

Child Care and Development Block Grant Act of 2014. 42 U.S.C. § 618.

Chiu, Warren C.K., Andy W. Chan, Ed Snape, and Tom Redman. "Age Stereotypes and Discriminatory Attitudes towards Older Workers: An East-West Comparison." *Human Relations* 54, no. 5 (2001): 629–61. https://journals.sagepub.com/doi/10.1177/0018726701545004#articleCitationDownloadContainer.

Chodorow, Nancy J. *The Reproduction of Mothering.* Berkeley, CA: University of California Press, 1978.

Chung, Eric, Samuel Dong, Xiaonan April Hu, Christine Kwon, and Goodwin Liu. *A Portrait of Asian Americans in the Law.* New Haven, CT: Yale Law School National Asian Pacific American Bar Association, 2017. http://www.aapa-ca.com/assets/portrait-project---final-report.pdf.

Chung, Jezzika. "How Asian Immigrants Learn Anti-Blackness from White Culture, and How to Stop It." *Huffington Post,* updated September 7, 2017. https://www.huffingtonpost.com/entry/how-asian-americans-can-stop-contributing-to-anti-blackness_us_599f0757e4b0cb7715bfd3e14.

Civil Rights Act of 1964 (Title VII). 42 U.S.C. § 2000e et seq.

CNN. "Woman Fired After Coming Out Transgender Could Take Case to the Supreme Court." *NBC26 Green Bay,* August 29, 2018. https://www.nbc26.com/news/national/woman-fired-after-coming-out-transgender-could-take-case-to-the-supreme-court.

Coates, G. "Integration or Separation: Women and the Appliance of Organizational Culture." *Women in Management Review* 13, no. 3 (1998): 114–24.

Cochran, Susan D., and Letitia Anne Peplau. "Value Orientations in Heterosexual Relationships." *Psychology of Women Quarterly* 9, no. 4 (December 1985): 477–88, 483. https://journals.sagepub.com/doi/10.1111/j.1471-6402 .1985.tb00897.x.

Coffman, Julie, and Bill Neuenfeldt. *Everyday Moments of Truth: Frontline Managers Are Key to Women's Career Aspirations.* Bain & Company, June 17, 2014. https://www.bain.com/insights/everyday-moments-of-truth.

Colby, Laura. "Asian American Executives Are Missing on Wall Street." *Bloomberg BusinessWeek.* November 22, 2017. https://www.Bloomberg.com/ news/articles/2017-11-22/asian-american-executive-are-missing-on-the -wall-the-street.

Collins, Gail. *When Everything Changed: The Amazing Journey of American Women from the 1960s to the Present.* New York: Little Brown and Company, 2009.

Collins, Mary Hair, Joseph F. Hair Jr., and Tonette S. Rocco. "The Older-Worker–Younger-Supervisor Dyad: A Test of the Reverse Pygmalion Effect." *Human Resource Development Quarterly* 20, no. 1 (1989): 21–41. http://psycnet.apa.org/record/2009-05466-006.

Combs, Gwendolyn. "The Duality of Race and Gender for Managerial African American Women: Implications of Informal Social Networks on Career Advancement." *Human Resource Development Review* 2, no. 4 (December 2003): 385–405. http://digitalcommons.unl.edu/cgi/viewcontent.cgi?articl e=1029&context=managementfacpub.

"The Condition of Education: College Enrollment Rates." National Center for Education Statistics, last updated March 2018. https://nces.ed.gov/ programs/coe/indicator_cpb.asp.

Coontz, Stephanie. "Progress at Work, but Mothers Still Pay a Price." *New York Times,* June 8, 2013. https://hbr.org/2013/09/New York Times.

Cooper, Edith. "Why Goldman Sachs Is Encouraging Employees to Talk about Race at Work—and Why as a Black Woman I Think This Is So Important." *Business Insider,* September 23, 2016. https://www.businessinsider .com/edith-cooper-goldman-sachs-on-talking-about-race-at-work-2016-9.

Cooper, Marianne. "For Women Leaders, Likability and Success Hardly Go Hand-in-Hand." *Harvard Business Review,* April 30, 2013. https://hbr .org/2013/04/for-women-leaders-likeability-a.

Correll, Shelly J. "Sociologists for Women in Society 2016 Feminist Lecture: Reducing Gender Biases in Modern Workplaces; A Small Wins Approach to Organizational Change." *Gender and Society* 31, no. 6 (December 1, 2017): 725–50.

Correll, Shelley J., Stephen Benard, and In Paik. "Getting a Job: Is There a Motherhood Penalty?" *American Journal of Sociology* 112, no. 5 (March 2007): 1297–1339. https://sociology.stanford.edu/sites/default/files/publications/getting_a_job-_is_there_a_motherhood_penalty.pdf.

Cortina, Lilia M. "Unseen Injustice: Incivility as Modern Discrimination in Organizations." *Academy of Management Review* 33, no. 1 (January 2008): 55–75.

Cortina, Lilia M., Vicki J. Magley, Jill Hunter Williams, and Regina Day Langhout. "Incivility in the Workplace: Incidence and Impact." *Journal of Occupational Health Psychology* 6, no. 1 (January 2001): 64–80.

Costanza David P., Jessica M. Badger, Rebecca L. Fraser, Jamie B. Severt, and Paul A. Gade. "Generational Differences in Work-Related Attitudes: A Meta-Analysis." *Journal of Business and Psychology* 27, no. 4 (2012): 375–94.

Crenshaw, Kimberle. "Mapping the Margins: Intersectionality, Identity Politics, and Violence against Women of Color." *Stanford Law Review* 43, no. 6 (July 1991): 1241-99.

Crites, S. N., Kevin E. Dickson, and A. Lorenz. "Nurturing Gender Stereotypes in the Face of Experience: A Study of Leader Gender, Leadership Style, and Satisfaction." *Journal of Organizational Culture, Communications and Conflicts* 19, no. 1 (January 2015): 1–23.

Crocker, Lizzie. "Why Do Women Say They Don't Like Working for Female Bosses?" *Daily Beast,* November, 13, 2013. https://www.thedailybeast.com/why-do-women-say-they-dont-like-working-for-female-bosses.

Crowley, Katherine, and Kathi Elster. *Mean Girls at Work: How to Stay Professional When Things Get Personal.* New York: McGraw Hill, 2013.

Cuddy, Amy J. C., Susan T. Fiske, and Peter Glick. "When Professionals Become Mothers, Warmth Doesn't Cut the Ice." *Journal of Social Issues* 60, no. 4 (2004): 701–18. http://www.people.hbs.edu/acuddy/2004,%20cuddy,%20fiske,%20&%20glick,%20JSI.pdf.

Davey, Melissa. "Workplaces that Consider Themselves Meritocracies 'Often Hide Gender Biases.'" *Guardian,* August 24, 2016. https://www.theguardian.com/australia-news/2016/aug/24/workplaces-that-consider-themselves-meritocracies-often-hide-gender-biases

Deahl, Jessica. "Child Care Scarcity Has Very Real Consequences for Working Families." NPR, January 3, 2017, *All Things Considered,* podcast. https://www.npr.org/sections/health-shots/2017/01/03/506448993/child-care-scarcity-has-very-real-consequences-for-working-families.

DeArmond, Sarah, Mary Tye, Peter Y. Chen, Autumn Krauss, D. Apryl Rogers, and Emily Sintek. "Age and Gender Stereotypes: New Challenges in a Changing Workplace and Workforce." *Journal of Applied Social Psychology* 36, no. 9 (September 2006): 2184–2214.

Dedrick, Esther J., and Gregory H. Dobbins. "The Influence of Subordinate Age on Managerial Actions: An Attributional Analysis." *Journal of Organizational Behavior* 12, no. 5 (1991): 367–77. http://psycnet.apa.org/record/1992-11003-001.

Dellasega, Cheryl. *Mean Girls Grown Up: Adult Women Who Are Still Queen Bees, Middle Bees, and Afraid-to-Bees.* Hoboken, NJ: John Wiley & Sons, 2005.

Derks, Belle, Naomi Ellemers, Colette Van Laar, and Kim de Groot. "Do Sexist Organizational Cultures Create the Queen Bee?" *British Journal of Social Psychology* 50, no. 3 (March 2011): 519–35.

Derks, Belle, Colette Van Laar, Naomi Ellemers, and Kim de Groot. "Gender-Bias Primes Elicit Queen-Bee Responses among Senior Policewomen." *Psychological Science* 22, no. 10 (2011): 1243–49.

Desai, Sreedhari D., Dolly Chugh, and Arthur Brief. "The Organizational Implications of a Traditional Marriage: Can a Domestic Traditionalist by Night Be an Organizational Egalitarian by Day?" Research paper no. 2013-19, UNC Kenan-Flagier Research Paper, March 2012.

Devine, Patricia G., and Andrew J. Elliot. "Are Racial Stereotypes Really Fading? The Princeton Trilogy Revisited." *Personality and Social Psychology Bulletin* 21, no. 11 (November 1995): 1139–50. https://journals.sagepub.com/doi/abs/10.1177/01461672952111002?journalCode=pspc.

DeWolf, Mark. "12 Stats about Working Women." *U.S. Department of Labor Blog,* March 1, 2017. https://blog.dol.gov/2017/03/01/12-stats-about-working-women.

Dirshe, Siraad. "Black Women Speak Up about Their Struggles Wearing Natural Hair in the Workplace." *Essence,* February, 7, 2018. https://www.essence.com/hair/black-women-natural-hair-discrimination-workplace/.

Diuguid, Lewis. "Study Shows How Media Portrayals Affect Black Girls." *Knoxville News Sentinel,* September 25, 2016. http://archive.knoxnews.com/opinion/columnists/study-shows-how-media-portrayals-affect-black-girls-3d075d91-5e0f-2083-e053-0100007fdc05-394515121.html.

Donovan, Anne. "What PwC Learned from Its Policy of Flexible Work for Everyone." *Harvard Business Review,* January 28, 2019. https://hbr.org/2019/01-what-pwc-learned-from-its-policy-of-flexible-work-for-everyone.

Douglas, Susan, and Meredith Michaels. *The Mommy Myth: The Idealization of Motherhood and How It Has Undermined All Women.* New York: Free Press, 2005. Kindle.

Drexler, Peggy. "Americans Prefer Their Bosses Male." *Psychology Today*, August 14, 2014. https://www.psychologytoday.com/us/blog/our-gender -ourselves/201408/americans-prefer-their-bosses-male.

Druckerman, Pamela. *Bringing Up Bébé: One American Mother Discovers the Wisdom of French Parenting.* New York: Penguin Books, 2014.

Durr, Mariese, and Adia M. Harvey Wingfield. "Keep Your 'N' in Check: African American Women and the Interactive Effects of Etiquette and Emotional Labor." *Critical Sociology* 37, no. 5 (September 2011): 557–71.

Eagly, Alice H., and Maureen Crowley. "Gender and Helping Behavior: A Meta-Analytic Review of the Social Psychological Literature." *Psychological Bulletin* 100, no. 3 (1986): 283–308.

Eagly, Alice H., and Blair T. Johnson. "Gender and Leadership Style: A Meta-Analysis." *Psychological Bulletin* 108, no. 2 (1990): 233–56. https:// opencommons.uconn.edu/cgi/viewcontent.cgi?referer=https://www .google.com/&httpsredir=1&article=1010&context=chip_docs.

Eagly, Alice H., and Steven J. Karau. "Role Congruity Theory of Prejudice Toward Female Leaders." *Psychological Review* 109, no. 3 (July 2002): 573–98. https:// www.rci.rutgers.edu/~search1/pdf/Eagley_Role_Congruity_Theory.pdf.

Eckleberry-Hunt, Jodie, and Jennifer Tucciarone. "The Challenges and Opportunities of Teaching 'Generation Y.'" *Journal of Graduate Medical Education* 3, no. 4 (December 2011): 458–61. https://www.ncbi.nlm.nih.gov/pmc/ articles/PMC3244307/.

EEOC and Woodward v. A&E Tire. 325 F. Supp. 3d 1129 (D. Colo. 2018).

Egan, Matt. "Still Missing: Female Business Leaders." *CNN,* March 24, 2015. Business. https://money.cnn.com/2015/03/24/investing/female-ceo-pipeline -leadership/index.html.

Ely, Robin J. "The Effects of Organizational Demographics and Social Identity on Relationships among Professional Women." *Administrative Science Quarterly* 39, no. 2 (June 1994): 203–238.

Ely, Robin J., Herminia Ibarra, and Deborah M. Kolb. "Taking Gender into Account: Theory and Design for Women's Leadership Development Programs." *Academy of Management Learning & Education* 10, no. 3 (September 2011): 474–93.

Ely, Robin J., Pamela Stone, and Colleen Ammerman. "Rethink What You 'Know' about High-Achieving Women." *Harvard Business Review.* December 2014. https://hbr.org/2014/12/rethink-what-you-know-about-high -achieving-women.

"Employment Projections: Civilian Labor Force by Age, Sex, Race, and Ethnicity." United States Department of Labor: Bureau of Labor Statistics, accessed January 9, 2019. https://www.bls.gov/emp/tables/civilian-labor-force-detail.htm.

"Employment Projections: Median Age of the Labor Force, by Sex, Race and Ethnicity." U.S. Department of Labor: Bureau of Labor and Statistics, last modified October 24, 2017. https://www.bls.gov/emp/tables/median-age-labor-force.htm.

Ending Secrecy about Workplace Sexual Harassment Act, H.R. 4729, § 1(b), 15th Cong. (2017).

Ennis, Linda Rose, ed. *Intensive Mothering: The Cultural Contradictions of Modern Motherhood.* Ontario: Demeter Press, 2014.

Eplett, Layla. "Not Gone with the Wind—The Perpetuation of the Mammy Stereotype." *Scientific American,* November 30, 2015. https://blogs.scientificamerican.com/food-matters/not-gone-with-the-wind-the-perpetuation-of-the-mammy-stereotype/.

Epner, Janet E. Gans. "Visible Invisibility: Women of Color in Law Firms." ABA Commission on Women in the Profession, 2012. https://www.americanbar.org/content/dam/aba/marketing/women/visibleinvisibility.pdf.

"Facts on U.S. Immigrants, 2016: Statistical Portrait of the Foreign-Born Population in the United States." Pew Research Center Hispanic Trends. September 14, 2018. http://www.pewhispanic.org/2018/09/14/facts-on-u-s-immigrants/.

Family and Medical Leave Act of 1993. 29 U.S.C. §§ 2601 et seq.

Fass, Sarah. *Paid Leave in the States: A Critical Support for Low-Wage Workers and Their Families.* National Center for Children in Poverty, March 2009.

Fatherly. "Bringing Up Bebe Review: Why French Parenting Helps Kids Eat Normal Foods, Behave Themselves, and Sleep All Night." *Fatherly,* May 01, 2015. https://www.fatherly.com/health-science/why-french-kids-eat-normal-foods-behave-them.

Feagin, Joe R., and Melvin P. Sikes. *Living with Racism: The Black Middle-Class Experience.* Boston: Beacon Press, 1994.

Feldblum, Chai R., and Victoria A. Lipnic. *Select Task Force on the Study of Harassment in the Workplace.* United States Equal Employment Opportunity Commission, June 2016.

Fessler, Leah. "Gloria Steinem Says Black Women Have Always Been More Feminist than White Women." December 8, 2017. https://qz.com/1150028loria-steinem-on-metoo-black-women-have-been-more-feminist-than-white-women/.

Filipovic, Jill. "Our President Has Always Degraded Women—And We've Always Let Him." *Time,* December 5, 2017. time.com/5047771/donald-trump-comments-billy-bush/.

Finkelstein, Lisa M., and Michael J. Burke. "Age Stereotypes at Work: The Role of Rater and Contextual Factors on Evaluations of Job Applicants." *Journal of General Psychology* 125, no. 4 (October 1998): 317–45.

Finkelstein, Lisa M., Katherine M. Ryan, and Eden B. King. "What Do the Young (Old) People Think of Me? Content and Accuracy of Age-Based Meta-Stereotypes." *European Journal of Work and Organizational Psychology* 22, no. 6 (2013): 633–57. https://www.tandfonline.com/doi/abs/10.1080/1359432X.2012.673279.

Fischer, Anne. "Women: Want a Promotion? Find a Boss Whose Wife Has a Career." *Fortune*, August 1, 2012. Fortune.com/2012/08/01/women-want-a-promotion-find-a-boss-whose-wife-has-a-career.

Fischer, Kristen. "Are You a Lawnmower Parent? Here's How It Can Harm Your Kids." *Sheknows,* December 21, 2018. Parenting. https://www.sheknows.com/parenting/articles/1975800/lawnmower-parenting-harms-kids/?utm_medium=email&utm_source=exacttarget&utm_campa.

Fiske, Susan T. "Stereotyping, Prejudice and Discrimination." In *The Handbook of Social Psychology,* edited by D.T. Gilbert, S.T. Fiske, and G. Lindzey. 4th ed. New York: McGraw-Hill, 1998.

"Flip the Script." Catalyst. https://www.catalyst.org/knowledge/flip-script.

Flores, Antonio. *Facts on U.S. Latinos, 2015.* Pew Research Center, September 18, 2017. http://www.pewhispanic.org/2017/09/18/facts-on-u-s-latinos-current-data/.

Fortune Editors. "These Are the Women CEOs Leading Fortune 500 Companies." *Fortune,* June 7, 2017. http://fortune.com/2017/06/07/fortune-500-women-ceos/.

"FORTUNE 500 Non-Discrimination Project." Equality Forum, accessed December 20, 2018. https://equalityforum.com/fortune500.

Foster, Mindi D., and E. Micha Tsarfati. "The Effects of Meritocracy Beliefs on Women's Well-Being After First-Time Gender Discrimination." *Personality and Social Psychology Bulletin* 31, no. 12 (December 2005): 1730–1738.

Friedan, Betty. *The Feminine Mystique.* New York: W.W. Norton & Company, 2001.

Fry, Richard. "Millennials Are the Largest Generation in the U.S. Labor Force." Pew Research Center, April 11, 2018. http://www.pewresearch.org/fact-tank/2018/04/11/millennials-largest-generation-us-labor-force/.

Fuller, Meredith. "Why Are Women Nasty to Other Women?" *Psychology Today.* August 4, 2013. https://www.psychologytoday.com/U.S./blog/working-btches/201308/why-are-some-women-nasty-other-women.

Fuller, Meredith. *Working with Bitches: Identify the Eight Types of Office Mean Girls and Rise Above Workplace Nastiness.* Boston: Da Capo Press, 2013.

Gabriel, Allison S., Marcus M. Butts, and Michael T. Sliter. "Women Experience More Incivility at Work—Especially from Other Women." *Harvard Business Review,* March 28, 2018. https://hbr.org/2018/03/women-experience-more-incivility-at-work-especially-from-other-women.

Gabriel, Allison S., Marcus M. Butts, Zhenyu Yuan, Rebecca L. Rosen, and Michael T. Sliter. "Further Understanding Incivility in the Workplace: The Effects of Gender, Agency, and Communion." *Journal of Applied Psychology* 103, no. 4 (2018): 362–82.

Galinsky, Adam. "Are Gender Differences Just Power Differences in Disguise?" Columbia Business School Ideas, March 13, 2018. https://www8.gsb.columbia.edu/articles/ideas-work/are-gender-differences-just-power-differences-disguise.

Galinsky, Ellen, Kimberlee Salmond, James T. Bond, Marcia Brumit Kropf, Meredith Moore, and Brad Harrington. *Leaders in a Global Economy: A Study of Executive Women and Men,* Families and Work Institute, 2003. http://familiesandwork.org/downloads/LeadersinaGlobalEconomy.pdf.

Galuppo, Mia. "3 Female Screenwriters on Crashing the Blockbuster Boys Club: I Want to See a Female Darth Vader." *Hollywood Reporter,* December 11, 2017. Movies. https://www.hollywoodreporter.com/news/3-female-screenwriters-crashing-blockbuster-boys-club-i-want-to-see-a-female-darth-vader-1063482.

Gándara, Patricia, and White House Initiative on Educational Excellence for Hispanics. *Fulfilling America's Future: Latinas in the U.S., 2015.* https://sites.ed.gov/hispanic-initiative/files/2015/09/Fulfilling-Americas-Future-Latinas-in-the-U.S.-2015-Final-Report.pdf.

Gee, Buck, and Denise Peck. "Asian Americans Are the Least Likely Group in the U.S. to Be Promoted to Management." *Harvard Business Review,* May 31, 2018. https://hbr.org/2018/05/asian-americans-are-the-least-likely-group-in-the-u-s-to-be-promoted-to-management.

Gee, Buck, and Denise Peck. *The Illusion of Asian Success: Scant Progress for Minorities in Cracking the Glass Ceiling from 2007-2015.* Ascend Foundation, 2017. https://c.ymcdn.com/sites/www.ascendleadership.org/resource/resmgr/research/TheIllusionofAsianSuccess.pdf.

"Gender, Equity, and Human Rights." World Health Organization, accessed January 17, 2019. https://www.who.int/gender-equity-rights/en/.

"Gender, Equity, and Human Rights: Gender." World Health Organization, accessed January 17, 2019. https://www.who.int/gender-equity-rights/understanding/gender-definition/en/.

"Gender Identity (Female, Male, or Non-Binary)." California Department of Motor Vehicles, accessed January 1, 2019. https://www.dmv.ca.gov/portal/dmv/detail/dl/gender_id.

"Generations: What Should Employers Consider When Recruiting from Different Generations—Baby Boomers, Generation X, and Generation Y?" Society for Human Resource Management, September 20, 2012. https://www.shrm.org/resourcesandtools/tools-and-samples/hr-qa/pages/recruitingdifferentgenerations.aspx.

Gilligan, Carol. In a Different Voice: Psychological Theory and Women's Development. Boston: Harvard University Press, 1982.

Gilman, Charlotte Perkins. Herland: A Lost Feminist Utopian Novel. New York: Pantheon, 1979.

Glynn, Sarah Jane. "Fact Sheet: Childcare." Center for American Progress, August 16, 2012. https://cdn.americanprogress.org/wp-content/uploads/2012/10/ChildCareFactsheet.pdf.

Goh, Angeline. "An Attributional Analysis of Counterproductive Work Behavior (CWB) in Response to Occupational Stress." Dissertation, University of South Florida, November 21, 2006. http://digital.lib.usf.edu/content/SF/S0/02/62/13/00001/E14-SFE0001895.pdf.

Goldin, Claudia, and Cecilia Rouse. "Orchestrating Impartiality: The Impact of 'Blind' Auditions on Female Musicians." American Economic Review 90, no. 4 (September 2000): 715–41.

Goleman, Daniel. "Sexual Harassment: It's about Power, Not Lust." New York Times, October 22, 1991. Archives.

Gordon, Randall A., Richard M. Rozelle, and James C. Baxter. "The Effect of Applicant Age, Job Level, and Accountability on the Evaluation of Job Applicants." Organizational Behavior and Human Decision Processes 41, no. 1 (1988): 20–33. http://psycnet.apa.org/record/1988-18676-001.

Graduate Employees and Students Organization. The (Un)Changing Face of the Ivy League. New Haven, CT: Yale University, 2005.

Grant, Tobin. "Poll: Most Whites Say Blacks Are Lazier or Less Intelligent than Whites (3 graphs)." Religion News Service, December 8, 2014. https://religionnews.com/2014/12/08/poll-whites-say-blacks-lazier-less-intelligent-whites-3-graphs/.

Gray, Emma. "Women at Work: Jealousy and Envy Impact Women Differently than Men." Huffington Post (blog), May 6, 2012. The Blog. https://

www.huffingtonpost.com/emma-gray/women-at-work-jealousy-envy
-men_b_1480030.html.

Gratton, Lynda, and Andrew Scott. "How Work Will Change When Most of Us Live to 100." *Harvard Business Review,* June 27, 2016. https://hbr
.org/2016/06/how-work-will-change-when-most-of-us-live-to-100.

Gratton, Lynda, and Andrew Scott. "Our Assumptions about Old and Young Workers Are Wrong." *Harvard Business Review,*November 14, 2016. https://hbr
.org/2016/11/our-assumptions-about-old-and-young-workers-are-wrong.

Green, Jeff, and Jordyn Holman. "Men Are Replacing Women as CEOs in a Step Backward on Diversity." *Bloomberg,* August 5, 2017. https://www.bloom
berg.com/news/articles/2017-08-03/men-replacing-women-as-ceos-marks
-big-step-backward-on-diversity?eminfo=%7b%22EMAIL.

Grier, Sam. "Survey Finds Workplace Technology Etiquette Blurred Between Generations." IT Managers Toolbox: Resources for IT Managers, accessed December 15, 2018. http://itmanagersinbox.com/1265/survey-finds-workplace
-technology-etiquette-blurred-between-generations/.

Guilder, George. "Women in the Work Force." *Atlantic,* September 1986. https://www.theatlantic.com/magazine/archive/1986/09/women-in-the
-work-force/304924/.

Gutiérrez y Muhs, Gabriella, Yolanda Flores Niemann, Carmen G. Gonzalez, Angela P. Harris, eds. *Presumed Incompetent: The Intersections of Race and Class for Women in Academia.* Boulder, CO: University Press of Colorado, 2012.

Haller, Sonja. "Meet the 'Lawnmower Parent,' the New Helicopter Parents of 2018." *USA Today,* September 19, 2018. https://www.usatoday.com/story/
life/allthemoms/2018/09/meet-lawnmower-parent-new-helicopter-parents
-types-parents-tiger-attachment/13473580.

Halpert, Jane A., Midge L. Wilson, and Julia L. Hickman. "Pregnancy as a Source of Bias in Performance Appraisals." *Journal of Organizational Behavior* 14, no. 7 (December 1993): 649–63.

Hanauer, Cathi. *The Bitch in the House: 26 Women Tell the Truth about Sex, Solitude, Work, Motherhood, and Marriage.* New York: William Morrow Paperbacks, 2003.

Hartocollis, Anemona. "Harvard Rated Asian American Applicants Lower Personality Traits." *New York Times,* June 15, 2018. https://www.nytimes
.com/2018/06/15/us/harvard-asian-enrollment-applicants.html.

Hawkesworth, Mary. "Congressional Enactments of Race-Gender: Toward a Theory of Raced-Gendered Institutions." *American Political Science Review* 97, no. 4 (2003): 529–50. http://www.jstor.org/stable/3593022.

Hays, Sharon. *The Cultural Contradictions of Motherhood.* New Haven, CT: Yale University Press, 1996.

Hayward, Bruce W., S. Taylor, N. Smith, and G. Davies. *Evaluation of the Campaign for Older Workers.* London: Her Majesty's Stationery Office, 1997.

Heilman, Madeline E. "Description and Prescription: How Gender and Prescription Prevent Women's Ascent up the Organizational Ladder." *Journal of Social Issues* 57, no. 4 (2001): 657–74. https://spssi.onlinelibrary.wiley.com/doi/abs/10.1111/0022-4537.00234.

Heilman, Madeline E. "Sex Stereotypes and Their Effects in the Workplace: What We Know and What We Don't Know." *Journal of Social Behavior and Personality* 10, no. 6 (1995): 2–26.

Heilman, Madeline E., Caryn J. Block, and Richard F. Martell. "Sex Stereotypes: Do They Influence Perceptions of Managers?" *Journal of Social Behavior & Personality* 10, no. 6 (1995): 237–52.

Heilman, Madeline E., and Alice H. Eagly. "Gender Stereotypes Are Alive, Well, and Busy Producing Workplace Discrimination." *Industrial and Organizational Psychology* 1, no. 4 (December 2008): 393–98.

Heilman, Madeline E., and Tyler G. Okimoto. "Why Are Women Penalized for Success at Male Tasks? The Implied Communality Deficit." *Journal of Applied Psychology* 92, no. 1 (January 2007): 81–92.

Heilman Madeline E., Aaron S. Wallen, Daniella Fuchs, and Melinda M. Tamkins. "Penalties for Success: Reactions to Women Who Succeed at Male-Gender-Typed Tasks." *Journal of Applied Psychology* 89, no. 3 (2004): 416–27.

Heim, Pat, Susan Murphy, and Susan K. Golant. *In the Company of Women: Indirect Aggression among Women: Why We Hurt Each Other and How to Stop.* New York: Jeremy P. Tarcher/Putnam, 2001.

Hekman, David R., Stephanie K. Johnson, Maw-Der Foo, and Wei Yang. "Does Diversity-Valuing Behavior Result in Diminished Performance Ratings for Non-White and Female Leaders?" *Academy of Management Journal* 60, no. 2 (2017): 771–97.

Hewlett, Sylvia Ann. "Executive Women and the Myth of Having It All." *Harvard Business Review,* April 2012. http://hbr.org/2002/04/executive-women-and-the-myth-of-having-it-all.

Heymann, Jody, Hye Jin Rho, John Schmitt, and Alison Earle. *Contagion Nation: A Comparison of Paid Sick Day Policies in 22 Countries.* Center for Economic and Policy Research, May 2009. http://cepr.net/documents/publications/paid-sick-days-2009-05.pdf.

Highest Median Household Income on Record. U.S. Census Bureau, September 12, 2018. https://www.census.gov/library/stories/2018/09/highest-median -household-on-record.html.

"Hillary's Vision for America." Office of Hillary Rodham Clinton, accessed December 17, 2018. https://www.hillaryclinton.com/issues/.

Ho, Colin, and Jay W. Jackson. "Attitude toward Asian Americans: Theory and Measurement." *Journal of Applied Social Psychology* 31, no. 8 (August 2001), 1553–1581. https://onlinelibrary.wiley.com/doi/abs/10.1111/j.1559 -1816.2001.tb02742.x.

Holiday, Erika, and Joan I. Rosenberg. *Mean Girls, Meaner Women: Understanding Why Women Backstab, Betray and Trash-Talk Each Other and How to Heal.* California: Orchid Press, 2009.

Holland, Jessica. "Why the Millennial Stereotype Is Wrong." *BBC,* July 16, 2017. Capital. www.bbc.com/capital/story/20170713-why-the-millennial -stereotype-is-wrong.

hooks, bell. *Ain't I a Woman: Black Women and Feminism.* 2nd ed. New York: Routledge, 2014.

Horowitz, Juliana Menasce, Kim Parker, and Renee Stepler. "Wide Partisan Gaps in U.S. over How Far the Country Has Come on Gender Equality." *Pew Research Center.* October 18, 2017. http://www.pewsocialtrends. org/2017/10/18/wide-partisan-gaps-in-u-s-over-how-far-the-country-has -come-on-gender-equality/.

Hurst, Jane Ann. "It's All about Relationships: Women Managing Women and the Impact on Their Careers." Dissertation, Massey University, Albany, New Zealand, 2017.

Ibarra, Herminia. "Women Are Over-Mentored (But Under-Sponsored)." Interview by Julia Kirby. *Harvard Business Review.* 2010. https://hbr .org/2010/08/women-are-over-mentored-but-un.

Ibarra, Herminia, Nancy M. Carter, and Christine Silva. "Why Men Still Get More Promotions than Women." *Harvard Business Review,* September 2010.

Ibarra, Herminia, Robin J. Ely, and Deborah M. Kolb. "Women Rising: The Unseen Barriers." *Harvard Business Review,* September 2013. https://hbr .org/2013/09/women-rising-the-unseen-barriers.

Jaeger, Hans. "Generations in History: Reflections on a Controversial Concept." *History and Theory* 24, no. 3 (1985): 273-92.

Janz, Katharina, Claudia Buengeler, Robert A. Eckhoff, Astrid C. Homan, Sven C. Voelpel. "Leveraging Age Diversity in Times of Demographic Change:

The Crucial Role of Leadership." In *Handbook of Research on Workforce Diversity in a Global Society: Technologies and Concepts.* Hershey, PA: IGI Global, 2012. http://www.igi-global.com/chapter/leveraging-age-diversity -times-demographic/67057.

Johnson, Allan G. *Privilege, Power, and Difference.* New York: McGraw-Hill, 2006.

Johnson, Kenneth. "What Corporations Can Learn About Diversity from the Rooney Rule." *Forbes,* February 1, 2018. https://www.forbes.com/sites/ forbescoachescouncil/2018/02/01/what-corporations-can-learn-about -diversity-from-the-nfls-rooney-rule/#5782077c47de.

Johnson, Stefanie K., and David R. Hekman. "Women and Minorities Are Penalized for Promoting Diversity." *Harvard Business Review,* March 23, 2016. https://hbr.org/2016/03/women-and-minorities-are-penalized-for -promoting-diversity.

Johnson, Stefanie K., Susan Elaine Murphy, Selamawit Zewdie, Rebecca J. Reichard. "The Strong, Sensitive Type: Effects of Gender Stereotypes and Leadership Prototypes on the Evaluation of Male and Female Leaders." *Organizational Behavior and Human Decision Processes* 106, no. 1 (May 2008): 39–60.

Johnson, Stefanie K., and Thomas Sy. "Why Aren't There More Asian Americans in Leadership Positions?" *Harvard Business Review,* December 19, 2016. https://hbr.org/2016/12/why-arent-there-more-asian-americans-in -leadership-positions.

Johnston, Deirdre D., and Debra H. Swanson. "Constructing the 'Good Mother': The Experience of Mothering Ideologies by Work Status." *Sex Roles* 54, no. 7–8 (April 2006): 509–519. https://link.springer.com/ article/10.1007%2Fs11199-006-90251-3.

Jones, Trina, and Kimberly Jade Norwood. "Aggressive Encounters & White Fragility: Deconstructing the Trope of the Angry Black Woman." *Iowa Law Review* 102, no. 5 (July 2017). https://ilr.law.uiowa.edu/assets/Uploads/ ILR-102-5-Jones.pdf.

Joy, Alison. "Queen Bees Sting: How Good Are Female Leaders at Mentoring the Next Generation?" *Comstock's,* May 2, 2016. https://www.comstocks mag.com/commentary/queen-bees-sting.

Kahneman, Daniel. *Thinking: Fast and Slow.* New York: Farrar, Straus and Giroux, 2013.

Kai, Maiysha. "Dressing Like a Congresswoman: Once Again, Alexandria Ocasio-Cortez Has the Last Laugh." *GlowUp,* January 4, 2019. https:// theglowup.theroot.com/dressing-like-a-congresswoman-once-again -alexandria-o-1831500889.

Kanter, Rosabeth Moss. *Men and Women of the Corporation*. New York: Basic-Books, 1977.

Khan, Saera R., and Alan J. Lambert. "Ingroup Favoritism versus Black Sheep Effects in Observations of Informal Conversations." *Basic and Applied Social Psychology* 20, no. 4 (1998): 263–69.

Khazan, Olga. "Why Do Women Bully Each Other at Work?" *Atlantic*, September 2017. https://www.theatlantic.com/magazine/archive/2017/09/the-queen-bee-in-the-corner-office/534213.

Khazan, Olga. "Why Don't More Women Want to Work with Other Women?" *Atlantic*, January 21, 2014. Business. https://www.theatlantic.com/business/archive/2014/01/why-don't-more-women-want-to-work-with-other-women/283216.

Kissinger, Alexa. "The Thrill of Watching Alexandria Ocasio-Cortez Bring Her Whole Self to Congress." *Vox*, November 16, 2018. https://www.vox.com/first-person/2018/11/16/18098582/alexandria-ocasio-cortez-congress-first-week.

Kite, Mary E., and Blair T. Johnson. "Attitudes toward Older and Younger Adults: A Meta-Analysis." *Psychology and Aging* 3, no. 3 (1988): 233–44. http://psycnet.apa.org/record/1989-04767-001.

Koeppel, David. "Gen Y vs. Boomers: Workplace Conflict Heats Up." *Fiscal Times*, November 11, 2011. http://www.thefiscaltimes.com/Articles/2011/11/11/Gen-Y-vs-Boomers-Workplace-Conflict-Heats-Up.

KPMG. *Leadership Study: Moving Women Forward into Leadership Roles.* 2015. https://home.kpmg/content/dam/kpmg/ph/pdf/ThoughtLeadershipPublication/KPMGWomensLeadershipStudy.pdf.

KPMG, YSC, and 30% Club. *Cracking the Code.* 2014. https://home.kpmg/content/dam/kpmg/pdf/2015/04/Cracking-the-code.pdf.

Kramer, Andrea S., and Alton B. Harris. *Breaking Through Bias: Communication Techniques for Women to Succeed at Work*. New York: Bibliomotion, Inc., 2016.

Kramer, Andrea S., and Alton B. Harris. "How Do Your Workers Feel about Harassment? Ask Them." *Harvard Business Review*, January 29, 2018. https://hbr.org/2018/01/how-do-your-workers-feel-about-harassment-ask-them. Reprinted in *HBR's 10 Must Reads, On Women and Leadership*. Boston: Harvard Business Review, 2018.

Kramer, Andrea S., and Alton B. Harris. "The Impropriety Bias." *Andie&Al* (blog), August 30, 2017. https://andieandal.com/the-impropriety-bias/.

Krentz, Matt, Justin Dean, Jennifer Garcia-Alonso, Frances Brooks Taplett, Miki Tsusaka, and Elliot Vaughn. "Fixing the Flawed Approach to

Diversity." Boston Consulting Group, January 17, 2019. https://www.bcg .com/en-us/publications/2019/fixing-the-flawed-approach-to-diversity .aspx.

Krogstad, Jens Manuel, Mark Hugo Lopez, and Molly Rohal. *English Proficiency on the Rise among Latinos.* Pew Research Center, May 12, 2015. http://www.pewhispanic.org/2015/05/12/english-proficiency-on-the-rise -among-latinos/.

Kruger, Pam. "The Myth of the Office Bitch." *CBS News,* April 14, 2011. Money Watch. https://www.cbsnews.com/news/the-myth-of-the-office-bitch.

Kulik, Carol T., and Mara Olekalns. "Negotiating the Gender Divide: Lessons from the Negotiation and Organizational Behavior Literatures." *Journal of Management* 38, no. 4 (July 2012): 1387–1415.

Kunin, Madeline M. *The New Feminist Agenda: Determining the Next Revolution for Women, Work, and Family.* White River Junction, VT: Chelsea Green Publishing, 2012.

Kunze, Florian, and Jochen I. Menges. "Younger Supervisors, Older Subordinates: An Organizational-Level of Age Differences, Emotions, and Performance." *Journal of Organizational Behavior,* 38 (2017): 461–86.

"Labor Force, Female (% of Total Labor Force)." World Bank. September 2018. https://data.worldbank.org/indicator/SL.TLF.TOTL.FE.ZS.

Lam, Bourree. "Why We Hate (& Love) the Tiger Mom." *Refinery 29,* May 12, 2018. https://www.refinery29.com/en-us/2018/05/198459/tiger-moms-in -pop-culture.

Lancaster, Lynne C., and David Stillman. *When Generations Collide: Who They Are. Why They Clash. How to Solve the Generational Puzzle at Work.* Reprinted ed. New York: HarperCollins, 2009.

Larkin-Wong, Katherine. "Ms. JD and Levo League Partnership—The DQs Show Us Why Women Helping Women Works!" *Ms. JD* (blog), January 23, 2012. https://ms-jd.org/blog/article/ms-jd-and-levo-league-partnership -dqs-show-us-why-women-helping-women-works.

Larson, Erik. "Future of Work: Research Shows Millennials, Gen Xers and Baby Boomers Make Better Decisions Together." *Forbes,* April 11, 2018. https:// www.forbes.com/sites/eriklarson/2018/04/11/future-of-work-research -shows-millennials-gen-xers-and-baby-boomers-make-better-decisions -together/#1e36b1b35b44.

Laughlin, Lynda. *Who's Minding the Kids? Child Care Arrangements: Spring 2011.* Washington, DC: U.S. Census Bureau, April 2013. https://www.cen sus.gov/prod/2013pubs/p70-135.pdf.

Leader, Shelah Gilbert, and Patricia Rusch Hyatt. *American Women on the Move: The Inside Story of the National Women's Conference, 1977.* Lanham, MD: Lexington Books, 2016.

Leicht, Carola, Malgorzata A. Goclowska, Jolien A. van Breen, Soledad de Lemus, and Georgina Randsley de Moura. "Counter-Stereotypes and Feminism Promote Leadership Aspirations in Highly Identified Women." *Frontiers in Psychology* 8: 883 (June 2, 2017).

Lennon, Tania. *Managing a Multi-Generational Workforce: The Myths versus the Realities.* Hay Group, 2015. https://focus.kornferry.com/wp-content/uploads/2015/02/HayGroup_Managing_multi-gen_workforce.pdf.

Lester, Scott W., Rhetta L. Standifer, Nicole J. Schultz, and James M. Windsor. "Actual versus Perceived Generational Differences at Work: An Empirical Examination." *Journal of Leadership and Organizational Studies* 19, no. 3 (August 2012): 341–54.

Lin, Monica H., Virginia S.Y. Kwan, Anna Cheung, Susan T. Fiske. "Stereotype Content Model Explains Prejudice for an Envied Outgroup: Scale of Anti–Asian American Stereotypes." *Personality and Social Psychology* Bulletin 31, no. 1 (January 2005): 34–47. https://pdfs.semanticscholar.org/3f03/4f7657390b0d44134627605c5cc0d086e871.pdf.

Linshi, Jack. "The Real Problem When It Comes to Diversity and Asian-Americans." *Time,* October 14, 2014. http://time.com/3475962/asian-american-diversity/.

Lipman, Victor. "How to Manage Generational Differences in the Workplace." *Forbes,* January 25, 2017. https://www.forbes.com/sites/victorlipman/2017/01/25/how-to-manage-generational-differences-in-the-workplace/#4d691ae64cc4.

Livingston, Gretchen, and Kristen Bialik. "7 Facts about U.S. Moms." Pew Center Research, May 10, 2018. http://www.pewresearch.org/fact-tank/2018/05/10/facts-about-u-s-mothers/.

Lombrozo, Tania. "Privileged Primates and the Mothers Who Mock Them." Quoting Gwen Dewar. *NPR.* June 15, 2015. https://www.npr.org/sections/13.7/2015/06/15/414563780/privileged-primates-and-the-mothers-that-mock-them.

López, Gustavo, Neil G. Ruiz, and Eileen Patten. "Key Facts about Asian Americans, a Diverse and Growing Population." Pew Research Center, September 8, 2017. http://www.pewresearch.org/fact-tank/2017/09/08/key-facts-about-asian-americans/.

Lorenzo, Rocío, Nicole Voigt, Karin Schetelig, Annika Zawadzki, Isabel Welpe, Prisca Brosi. "The Mix that Matters: Innovation through Diversity." BCG,

April 26, 2017. https://www.bcg.com/en-us/publications/2017/people-orga nization-leadership-talent-innovation-through-diversity-mix-that-matte rs.aspx.

Lowbrow, Yeoman. "You've Come a Long Way, Baby: Virginia Slims Advertising Year-by-Year." *Flashbak,* October 3, 2016. https://flashbak.com/youve -come-a-long-way-baby-virginia-slims-advertising-year-by-year-365664/.

Macoukji, Fred George. "Gay, Straight, or Slightly Bent? The Interaction of Leader Sexual Orientation and Gender on Leadership Evaluations." Dissertation, University of South Florida Scholar Commons, January 2014. https://scholarcommons.usf.edu/cgi/viewcontent.cgi?referer=https://www .google.com/&httpsredir=1&article=6458&context=etd.

Madsen, Susan R. *On Becoming a Woman Leader: Learning from the Experiences of University Presidents.* San Francisco: Jossey-Bass, 2008.

Mainiero, Lisa A., and Sherry E. Sullivan. "Kaleidoscope Careers: An Alternate Explanation for the 'Opt-Out' Revolution." *Academy of Management Executive* 19, no. 1 (February 2005): 106–23.

Mainiero, Lisa A., and Sherry E. Sullivan. *The Opt-Out Revolt: Why People Are Leaving Companies to Create Kaleidoscope Careers.* Mountain View, CA: Davies-Black Publishing, 2006.

"Making America Great Again." Accessed December 17, 2018. https://www .DonaldTrump.com/.

Malacoff, Julia. "Why Women Are Becoming Increasingly Dissatisfied with Their Workplace Over Time." kununu US, March 6, 2017. https:// www.kununu.com/us/kununu-us/news/why-women-are-becoming-increasingly-dissatisfied-with-their-workplace-over-time.

Malik, Rasheed, Katie Hamm, Maryam Adamu, and Taryn Morrissey. *Child Care Deserts: An Analysis of Child Care Centers by ZIP Code in 8 States.* Center for American Progress, October 27, 2016. https://www.americanprogress. org/issues/early-childhood/reports/2016/10/27/225703/child-care-deserts/.

Manheim, Karl. "The Problem of Generations." In *Essays on the Sociology of Knowledge: Collected Works,* edited by Paul Kecskemeti. New York: Routledge, 1952.

Marcus, Bonnie. "It's Obstacles Women Face in the Workplace–Not a Lack of Ambition–that Causes Them to Opt Out." *Forbes,* August 15, 2016. https:// www.forbes.com/sites/bonniemarcus/2016/08/15/its-the-obstacles-women -face-in-the-workplace-not-a-lack-of-ambition-that-causes-them-to-opt -out/#7d9601e12667.

Martin, Patricia Yancey. "'Said and Done' versus 'Saying and Doing': Gendering Practices, Practicing Gender at Work." *Gender and Society* 17, no. 3 (June 2003): 342-66.

Martin, Wednesday. *Primates of Park Avenue: A Memoir*. New York: Simon & Schuster, 2015.

"The 'Masculine' and 'Feminine' Sides of Leadership and Culture: Perception vs Reality." *Knowledge@Wharton*, October 5, 2005. http://knowledge.wharton.upenn.edu/article/the-masculine-and-feminine-sides-of-leadership-and-culture-perception-vs-reality/.

Mavin, Sharon. "Venus Envy: Problematizing Solidarity Behaviour and Queen Bees." *Women in Management Review* 21, no. 4 (June 2006): 264–76.

McCourt, David M. "The 'Problem of Generations' Revisited: Karl Mannheim and the Sociology of Knowledge in International Relations." In *Theory and Application of the "Generation" in International Relations and Politics*, edited by Brent J. Steele and Jonathan M. Acuff. New York: Palgrave Macmillan, 2012.

McGirt, Ellen. "How Lawyers Are Working to Change Their Industry's Diversity Problem." *Fortune*, August 30, 2017. Fortune.com/go/careers/the-mansfield-rule-lawyers-diversity.

McGlone, Jeannette. "Sex Differences in Human Brain Organization." *Behavioral and Brain Sciences* 3, no. 2 (June 1980): 217–27. https://www.cambridge.org/core/journals/behavioral-and-brain-sciences/article/sex-differences-in-human-brain-asymmetry-a-critical-survey/93B49551A4D139B20E39C7F2019CC57D.

McGregor, Jena. "Even among Harvard MBAs, Few Black Women Ever Reach Corporate America's Top Rungs." *Washington Post*, February 20, 2018. https://www.washingtonpost.com/news/on-leadership/wp/2018/02/20/even-among-harvard-mbas-few-black-women-ever-reach-corporate-americans-top-rungs/.

McKinsey&Company. *Women in the Workplace*. McKinsey&Company Insights and Publications, September 2015. http://www.mckinsey.com/insights/organization/women_in_the_workplace.

McNulty, Anne Welsh. "Don't Underestimate the Power of Women Supporting Each Other at Work." *Harvard Business Review*, September 3, 2018. https://hbr.org/2018/09/dont-underestimate-the-power-of-women-supporting-each-other-at-work.

Mehra, Ajay, Martin Kilduff, and Daniel J. Brass. "At the Margins: A Distinctiveness Approach to the Social Identity and Social Networks of Underrepresented Groups." *The Academy of Management Journal* 41, no. 4 (1998): 441–452. http://www.jstor.org/stable/257083.

Melich, Tanya. *The Republican War against Women: An Insider's Report from Behind the Lines*. Updated ed. New York: Bantam Books, 1998.

"Men and Women: No Big Difference." American Psychological Association, October 20, 2005. https://www.apa.org/research/action/difference.aspx.

Meriac, John P., David J. Woehr, and Christina Banister. "Generational Differences in Work Ethics: An Examination of Measurement Equivalence across Three Cohorts." *Journal of Business Psychology* 25, no. 2 (June 2010): 315–324.

Merriam-Webster. s.v. "conflict." Accessed January 10, 2019. https://www.Merriam-Webster.com/dictionary/conflict.

Merriam-Webster, s.v. "microaggression." Accessed December 27, 2018. https://www.Merriam-Webster.com/dictionary/microaggression.

Merriam-Webster. s.v. "tension." Accessed January 10, 2019. https://www.Merriam-Webster.com/dictionary/tension.

Milam, Alex C., Christiane Spitzmueller, and Lisa M. Penney. "Investigating Individual Differences among Targets of Workplace Incivility." *Journal of Occupational Health Psychology* 14, no. 1 (2009): 58–69.

Miller, Claire Cain. "The Relentlessness of Modern Parenting." *New York Times,* December 25, 2018. https://www.nytimes.com/2018/12/25/upshot/the-relentlessness-of-modern-parenting.html.

Miller, Claire Cain, Kevin Quealy, and Margot Sanger-Katz. "The Top Jobs Where Women Are Outnumbered by Men Named John." *New York Times,* April 24, 2018. https://www.nytimes.com/interactive/2018/04/24/upshot/women-and-men-named-john.html.

Miller, Jean Baker. *Toward a New Psychology of Women.* 2nd ed. Boston: Beacon Press, 1986.

Mills-Scofield, Deborah. "It's Not Just Semantics: Managing Outcomes vs. Outputs." *Harvard Business Review,* November 26, 2012. https://hbr.org/2012/11/its-not-just-semantics-managing-outcomes.

Morgan, Robin. *Sisterhood Is Powerful: An Anthology of Writings from the Women's Liberation Movement.* New York: Vintage Books, 1970.

Myers, Michelle. "Women Wanted—Building a Strong Network for Women in Your Workplace." *Progressive Women's Leadership,* November 23, 2015. https://www.progressivewomensleadership.com/women-wanted-building-a-strong-network-for-women-in-your-workplace/.

NALP. "LGBT Representation among Lawyers in 2017." *NALP Bulletin,* January 2018. https://www.nalp.org/0118Research.

National Partnership for Women and Families. "Flexibility for Success: How Workplace Flexibility Policies Benefit All Workers and Employers." Accessed February 16, 2019. www.nationalpartnership.org/our-work/resources/workplace/flexibility-for-success.pdf.

Naus, Peter J. "Some Correlates of Attitude towards Old People." *International Journal of Aging and Human Development* 4, no. 3 (1973): 229–43.

Nelson, Sophia A. "Time to Put the 'Sister' Back in 'Sisterhood.'" *Huffpost,* updated February 10, 2014. https://www.huffingtonpost.com/sophia-a -nelson/what-is-sisterhood-really_b_4410051.html.

Newport, Frank. "In U.S., Estimate of LGBT Population Rises to 4.5%." *Gallup,* May 22, 2018. Politics. https://news.gallup.com/poll/234863/estimate-lgbt -population-rises.aspx.

Nosek, Brian A., Mahzarin R. Banaji, and Anthony G. Greenwald. "Harvest-ing Implicit Group Attitudes and Beliefs from a Demonstration Web Site." *Group Dynamics: Theory, Research, and Practice* 6, no. 1 (2002), 101–115. http://projectimplicit.net/nosek/papers/harvesting.GroupDynamics.pdf.

Obama, Michelle. *Becoming.* New York: Crown Publishing, 2018.

Obergefell v. Hodges. 135 S. Ct. 2584 (2015).

O'Brien, Keith. *Fly Girls: How Five Daring Women Defied All Odds and Made Aviation History.* New York: Houghton Mifflin Harcourt, 2018.

Oluo, Ijeoma. *So You Want to Talk about Race.* New York: Seal Press, 2018.

O'Neill, Olivia A., and Charles A. O'Reilly III. "Reducing the Backlash Effect: Self-Monitoring and Women's Promotions." *Journal of Occupational and Organizational Psychology* 84, no. 4 (2010): 825–32.

Ortiz-Ospina, Esteban, and Sandra Tzvetkova. "Working Women: Key Facts and Trends in Female Labor Force Participation." *Our World in Data* (blog). October 16, 2017. https://ourworldindata.org/female-labor-force -participation-key-facts.

Palmer, Phyllis Marynick. "White Women/Black Women: The Dualism of Female Identity and Experience in the United States." *Feminist Studies* 9, no. 1 (Spring 1983): 151–70. https://www.jstor.org/stable/3177688?seq= 1#page_scan_tab_contents.

Pao, Ellen. *Reset: My Fight for Inclusion and Everlasting Change.* New York: Spiegel & Grau, 2017.

Parker, Kim, Juliana Menasce Horowitz, and Renee Shepler. "How Do Your Views on Gender Compare with Those of Other Americans?" *Pew Research Center,* December 5, 2017. http://www.pewresearch.org/fact -tank/2017/12/05/how-do-your-views-on-gender-compare-with-those-of -other-americans/.

Parks-Stamm, Elizabeth J., Madeline E. Heilman, and Krystle A. Hearns. "Moti-vated to Penalize: Women's Strategic Rejection of Successful Women." *Personality and Social Psychology Bulletin* 34, no. 2 (December 4, 2007): 237–47. https://journals.sagepub.com/doi/10.1177/0146167207310027.

"Paying for Childcare." Childcare Aware of America, accessed December 11, 2018. http://childcareaware.org/help-paying-child-care-federal-and-state -child-care-programs/.

Pew Research Center. *A Survey of LGBTQ Americans: Attitudes, Experiences and Values in Changing Times*. June 13, 2013. http://www.pewsocialtrends .org/2013/06/13/a-survey-of-lgbt-americans/.

Pew Research Center. *On Views of Race and Inequality, Blacks and Whites Are Worlds Apart*. June 27, 2016. http://www.pewsocialtrends.org/2016/06/27/1 -demographic-trends-and-economic-well-being/.

Pew Research Center. *The Rise of Asian Americans*. Updated ed. April 4, 2013. http://www.pewsocialtrends.org/2012/06/19/the-rise-of-asian-americans/.

Pierce, Jasmine. "It's Not Just a 'Black Thing': Black Women in the Law and Issues of Double Identity and Discrimination." Washington, DC: American University, 2011. https://www.wcl.american.edu/index.cfm?LinkServID= 7384CA99-92E2-8DE0-B7F541AF4F08CE05.

Pilcher, Jane. "Mannheim's Sociology of Generations: An Undervalued Legacy." *British Journal of Sociology* 45, no. 3 (September 1994): 481–95.

Pilgrim, David. "The Mammy Caricature." *Ferris State University Jim Crow Museum of Racist Memorabilia*, rev. ed., 2012. https://ferris.edu/jimcrow/ mammies/.

Pilgrim, David. "The Sapphire Caricature." *Ferris State University Jim Crow Museum of Racist Memorabilia,* rev. ed., 2012. https://ferris.edu/HTMLS/ news/jimcrow/antiblack/sapphire.htm.

Podolny, Joel M., and James N. Baron. "Resources and Relationships: Social Net-works and Mobility in the Workplace." *American Sociological Review* 62, no. 5 (1997): 673–93. http://www.jstor.org/stable/2657354.

Pogrebin, Letty Cottin. "Competing with Women." *Ms.*, July 1972. In *Competition: A Feminist Taboo? edited by* Valerie Miner and Helen E. Longino. New York: The Feminist Press, 1987.

Posthuman, Richard A., and Michael A. Campion. "Age Stereotypes in the Workplace: Common Stereotypes, Moderators, and Future Research Directions." *Journal of Management* 35, no. 1 (February 2009): 158–88.

Pratto, Felicia, Jim Sidanius, and Shana Levin. "Social Dominance Theory and the Dynamics of Intergroup Relations: Taking Stock and Looking Forward." *European Review of Social Psychology* 17, no. 1 (January 2006): 271–320.

Pratto, Felicia, Jim Sidanius, Lisa M. Stallworth, Bertram F. Malle. "Social Dominance Orientation: A Personality Variable Predicting Social and Political Attitudes." *Journal of Personality and Social Psychology* 67, no. 4 (1994): 741–63.

PriceWaterhouseCoopers. *Time to Talk: What Has to Change for Women at Work*. 2018. https://www.pwc.com/gx/en/about/diversity/iwd/international-womens-day-pwc-time-to-talk-report.pdf.

"Project Implicit." Harvard University, accessed February 16, 2019. https://implicit.harvard.edu/implicit/selectatest.html.

Qiao, Sabrina. "Fire Breathing 'Dragon Ladies': Representations of Asian American Women in Media." Penn State, April 19, 2016. http://sites.psu.edu/engl428/2016/04/19/fire-breathing-dragon-ladies-representations-of-asian-american-women-in-media-overview/.

"Quick Facts." U.S. Census Bureau, accessed January 8, 2018. https://www.census.gov/quickfacts/fact/table/US/RHI425217.

"Quick Facts: United States." U.S. Census Bureau, accessed December 20, 2018. https://www.census.gov/quickfacts/fact/table/US/PST045217.

Quora. "Why Women Leave the Tech Industry at a 45% Higher Rate than Men." *Forbes,* February 28, 2017. https://www.forbes.com/sites/quora/2017/02/28/why-women-leave-the-tech-industry-at-a-45-higher-rate-than-men/#1b38ef0b4216.

Radish, Christina. "'Tomb Raider' Screenwriter Geneva Robertson-Dworet on Rethinking Lara Croft and 'Captain Marvel.'" *Collider,* March 19, 2018. http://collider.com/tomb-raider-geneva-robertson-dworet-interview/.

Rajesh, Saundarya. "How Networking Benefits Women in Their Career." *People Matters* (blog), July 12, 2016. https://www.peoplematters.in/blog/diversity/how-networking-benefits-women-in-their-career-13649?utm_source=peoplematters&utm_medium=interstitial&utm_campaign=learnings-of-the-day.

Ramirez, Sarah. "Women, Black/African American Associates Lose Ground at Major U.S. Law Firms." NALP, November 19, 2015. https://www.nalp.org/lawfirmdiversity _nov2015.

Rapoport, Rhona, Lotte Bailyn, Joyce K. Fletcher, and Betty H. Pruitt. *Beyond Work-Family Balance: Advancing Gender Equity and Workplace Performance*. San Francisco: Jossey-Bass, 2001.

"Recruiting a Multigenerational Workforce." *HR Professionals Magazine,* accessed December 14, 2018. http://hrprofessionalsmagazine.com/recruiting-a-multigenerational-workforce/.

Ridgeway, Cecilia L. *Framed by Gender: How Gender Inequality Persists in the Modern World*. New York: Oxford University Press, 2011.

Risman, Barbara J. "Intimate Relationships from a Microstructural Perspective: Men Who Mother." *Gender and Society* 1, no. 1 (March 1987): 6–32. https://journals.sagepub.com/doi/10.1177/089124387001001002.

R.L.G. "Code-Switching: How Black to Be?" *The Economist,* April 10, 2013. https://www.economist.com/johnson/2013/04/10/how-black-to-be.

Roberts, Laura Morgan, Anthony J. Mayo, Robin J. Ely, and David A. Thomas. "Beating the Odds." *Harvard Business Review,* March-April 2018. https://hbr.org/2018/03 beating-the-odds.

Rodriguez, Mathew. "Here's the Malcolm X Speech about Black Women Beyoncé Sampled in 'Lemonade.'" *MIC,* April 23, 2016. https://mic.com/articles/141642/here-s-the-malcolm-x-speech-about-black-women-beyonce-sampled-in-lemonade#.vhAgDPtX6.

Rosenthal, Lisa, and Marci Lobel. "Stereotypes of Black American Women Related to Sexuality and Motherhood." *Psychology of Women Quarterly* 40, no. 3 (September 2016): 414–427. https://doi.org/10.1177/0361684315627459.

Rosette, Ashleigh Shelby, Christy Zhou Koval, Anyi Ma, and Robert Livingston. "Race Matters for Women Leaders: Intersectional Effects on Agentic Deficiencies and Penalties." *The Leadership Quarterly* 27, no. 3 (June 2016): 429-445. https://www.sciencedirect.com/science/article/pii/S1048984316000096.

Rosin, Hanna. "Why Doesn't Marissa Mayer Care about Sexism?" *XXfactor* (blog). *Slate,* July 16, 2012. https://slate.com/human-interest/2012/07/new-yahoo-ceo-marissa-mayer-does-she-care-about-sexism.html.

Rowatt, Wade C., Jordan LaBouff, Megan Johnson, Paul Froese, and Jo-Ann Tang. "Associations among Religiousness, Social Attitudes, and Prejudice in a National Random Sample of American Adults." *Psychology of Religion and Spirituality* 1, no. 1 (2009): 14–24.

Ruckwardt, M. L. Sam. "Opting Out of Law Practice and Opting Back In." *GPSolo Magazine,* September 26, 2018. https://www.americanbar.org/groups/gpsolo/publications/gp_solo/2012/september_october/opting_out_law_practice_back_in/.

Ryan, Camille L., and Kurt Bauman Current. *Educational Attainment in the United States: 2015 Population Characteristics.* U.S. Census Bureau: U.S. Department of Commerce, March 16, 2016. https://www.census.gov/content/dam/Census/library/publications/2016/demo/p20-578.pdf.

Sandberg, Sheryl, and Adam Grant. "Sheryl Sandberg on the Myth of the Catty Woman." *New York Times,* June 23, 2016. Opinion. https://www.nytimes.com/2016/06/23/opinion/sunday/sheryl-sandberg-on-the-myth-of-the-catty-woman.html.

Schlafly, Phyllis. *Feminist Fantasies.* Dallas: Spence Publishing Company, 2003.

Schlafly, Phyllis, Ed Martin, and Brett M. Decker. *The Conservative Case for Trump.* Washington, DC: Regnery Publishing, 2016.

Schulte, Brigid, and Alieza Durana. *The New America Care Report*. New America, September 2016. https://www.newamerica.org/better-life-lab/policy-papers/new-america-care-report/.

Schumer, Amy. *Mostly Sex Stuff—Can't Win*. Comedy Central. August 18, 2012. http://www.cc.com/video-clips/p87njw/stand-up-can-t-win.

Seipel, Tracy. "Black Female Doctors Represent Only Tiny Fraction of All Doctors Worldwide." *Mercury News*, January 14, 2018. https://www.mercurynews.com/2018/01/15/black-female-doctors-represent-only-tiny-fraction-of-all-doctors-nationwide/.

"Sexual and Reproductive Health: Defining Sexual Health." World Health Organization, accessed December 28, 2018. https://www.who.int/reproductivehealth/topics/sexual_health/sh_definitions/en/.

Sharrow, Elizabeth A., Dara Z. Strolovitch, Michael T. Heaney, Seth E. Masket, and Joanne M. Miller. "Gender Attitudes, Gendered Partisanship: Feminism and Support for Sarah Palin and Hillary Clinton among Party Activists." *Journal of Women, Politics & Policy* 37, no. 4 (2016): 394–416.

Shaw, Haydn. *Sticking Points: How to Get 4 Generations Working Together in the 12 Places They Come Apart*. Carol Stream, IL: Tyndale House Publishers, Inc., 2013.

Sheppard, Leah D., and Karl Aquino. "Sisters at Arms: A Theory of Female Same-Sex Conflict and Its Problematization in Organizations." *Journal of Management* 43, no. 3 (March 1, 2017): 691–715.

Sherman, Nancy C., and Joel A. Gold. "Perceptions of Ideal and Typical Middle and Old Age." *International Journal of Aging and Human Development* 9, no. 1 (1979): 67–73.

Shook, Ellyn, and Julie Sweet. "When She Rises, We All Rise." Accenture, 2018. https://www.accenture.com/es-es/_acnmedia/PDF-73/Accenture-when-she-rises-we-all-rise.pdf.

Shore, Lynn M., Jeanette N. Cleveland, and Caren B. Goldberg. "Work Attitudes and Decisions as a Function of Manager Age and Employee Age." *Journal of Applied Psychology* 88, no. 3 (2003): 529–37.

Simpson, Jake. "2015 Law360 Minority Report." *Law360*, May 19, 2015. https://www.law360.com/articles/657725/2015-law360-minority-report.

Skenazy, Lenore. *Free-Range Kids: How to Raise Safe, Self-Reliant Children (without Going Nuts with Worry)*. San Francisco: Jossey-Bass, 2009.

Slaughter, Anne-Marie. "Why Women Still Can't Have It All." *Atlantic*, July/August 2012. U.S. https://www.theatlantic.com/magazine/archive/2012/07/why-women-still-cant-have-it-all/309020/.

Smith, Laura. "When Feminism Ignored the Needs of Black Women, a Mighty Force Was Born." *Medium,* February 21, 2018. https://timeline.com/feminism-ignored-black-women-44ee502a3c6.

Smola, Karen Wey, and Charlotte D. Sutton. "Generational Differences: Revisiting Generational Work Values for the New Millennium." *Journal of Organizational Behavior* 23, no. 4 (June 2002): 363–382. https://onlinelibrary.wiley.com/doi/abs/10.1002/job.147.

Sorkin, Andrew Ross. "When a Female C.E.O. Leaves, the Glass Ceiling Is Restored." *New York Times,* August 6, 2018. https://www.nytimes.com/2018/08/06/business/dealbook/indra-nooyi-women-ceo.html.

Spruill, Marjorie J. *Divided We Stand: The Battle over Women's Rights and Family Values that Polarized American Politics.* New York: Bloomsbury, 2017.

Stainback, Kevin, Sibyl Kleiner, and Sheryl Skaggs. "Women in Power: Undoing or Redoing Gendered Organization?" *Gender and Society* 30, no. 1 (February 2016): 109-35.

"State Maps of Laws & Policies." Human Rights Campaign, updated January 11, 2019. https://www.hrc.org/state-maps/employment.

Steinem, Gloria. "Address to the Women of America." Speech, National Women's Political Caucus, July 10, 1971.

Stone, Pamela. "The Rhetoric and Reality of 'Opting Out.'" *American Sociological Association Journal* 6, no. 4 (Fall 2007): 14–19.

Stoney, Louise. "The Iron Triangle: A Simple Formula for ECE Finance." PowerPoint presentation, Opportunities Exchange and BUILD Early Childhood, June 13, 2014. http://opportunities-exchange.org/wp-content/uploads/Iron-Triangle-Webinar-FINAL-6.13.14.pdf.

Strauss, Elissa. "The Judgmental Mom Is Little More than a Stereotype." *CNN,* December 20, 2018. https://www.cnn.com/2018/12/13/health/judgmental-mom-parenting-strauss/index.html.

Students for Fair Admissions, Inc. v. President and Fellows of Harvard College. 807 F.3d 472 (1st Cir. 2015).

Sue, Derald Wing. *Microaggressions in Everyday Life: Race, Gender, and Sexual Orientation.* Hoboken, NJ: John Wiley & Sons, Inc., 2010.

Tan, Anh, Wenli Ma, Amit Vira, Dhruv Marwha, and Lise Eliot. "The Human Hippocampus Is Not Sexually-Dimorphic: Meta-Analysis of Structural MRI Volumes." *NeuroImage* 124, Part A (January 2016): 350–366.

Tanenbaum, Leora. *Catfight: Women and Competition.* New York: Seven Stories Press, 2011.

Tariyal, Ridhi. "To Succeed in Silicon Valley, You Still Have to Act Like a Man." *Washington Post,* July 24, 2018. https://www.washingtonpost.com/news/

posteverything/wp/2018/07/24/to-succeed-in-silicon-valley-you-still
-have-to-act-like-a-man/?utm_term=.386045c03507.

Tavris, Carol. *Mismeasure of Woman: Why Women Are Not the Better Sex, the Inferior Sex, or the Opposite Sex*. New York: Touchstone, 1992.

"Tax Credit for Child and Dependent Care Expenses." efile.com, accessed December 11, 2018. https://www.efile.com/tax-credit/dependent-care-tax-credit/.

Thomas, Rachel. "Corporate America Is Not on the Path to Gender Equality." LeanIn, September 30, 2015. http://leanin.org/news-inspiration/corporate-america-is-not-on-the-path-to-gender-equality.

Thorpe-Moscon, Jennifer. "Minority Women Report Downsizing Their Ambitions because of Bias." *Harvard Business Review,* January 16, 2014. https://hbr.org/2014/01/minority-women-report-downsizing-their-ambitions-because-of-bias.

"Time Inc.'s People en Español Reveals Findings from Exclusive Workplace Study: Latina@Work." *BusinessWire,* August 15, 2016. https://www.businesswire.com/news/home/20160815005797/en/Time-Inc.s-People-en-Español-reveals-findings.

Toossi, Mitra. "A Century of Change: The U.S. Labor Force, 1950–2050." *Monthly Labor Review* (May 2002): 15–28. https://www.bls.gov/opub/mlr/2002/05/art2full.pdf.

Toossi, Mitra, and Elka Torpey. "Older Workers: Labor Force Trends and Career Options." *Career Outlook.* U.S. Department of Labor: Bureau of Labor and Statistics, May 2017. https://www.bls.gov/careeroutlook/2017/article/older-workers.htm.

Torres, Nicole. "Women Can Benefit When They Downplay Gender." *Harvard Business Review,* July-August 2018. https://hbr.org/2018/07/women-benefit-when-they-downplay-gender.

"Tracking the 2018 Governors Race Results." *Governing: The States and Localities,* last updated November 7, 2018. http://www.governing.com/governor-races-2018.

"Trading Action for Access: The Myth of Meritocracy and the Failure to Remedy Structural Discrimination." *Harvard Law Review* 121, no. 8 (June 2008): 2157.

Travis, Elizabeth. "Academic Medicine Needs More Women Leaders." *AAMC News,* January 16, 2018. https://news.aamc.org/diversity/article/academic-medicine-needs-more-women-leaders/.

Triana, María. *Managing Diversity in Organizations: A Global Perspective*. New York: Routledge, 2017.

Tso, Tiffany Diane. "The Bamboo Glass Ceiling: Asian American Women Face Particular Challenges in the Workplace. And They're Not Getting the

Attention They Need." *Slate,* August 8, 2018. https://slate.com/human-inte rest/2018/08/Asian-American-women-face-a-glass-ceiling-and-a-bamboo -ceiling@work.html.

Tso, Tiffany Diane. "Nail Salon Brawls & Boycotts: Unpacking the Black Asian Conflict in America." *Refinery29,* August 21, 2018. https://www.refinery29 .com/en-us/2018/08/207533/red-apple-nails-brawl-black-asian-conflict.

Tsui, Anne S., and Charles A. O'Reilly. "Beyond Simple Demographic Effects: The Importance of Relational Demographics in Superior-Subordinate Dyads." *Academy of Management Journal* 32, no. 2 (June 1989): 402–23.

Tulshyan, Ruchika. "Speaking Up as a Woman of Color at Work." *Forbes,* February 10, 2015. https://www.forbes.com/sites/ruchikatulshyan/2015/02/10/ speaking-up-as-a-woman-of-color-at-work/#647244702ea3.

Tulshyan, Ruchika. "Women of Color Get Asked to Do More 'Office Housework.' Here's How They Can Say No." *Harvard Business Review,* April 6, 2018. https://hbr.org/2018/04/women-of-color-get-asked-to-do-more-office -housework-heres-how-they-can-say-no.

Turban, Stephan, Dan Wu, and Letian (LT) Zhang. "Research: When Gender Diversity Makes Firms More Productive." *Harvard Business Review,* February 11, 2019. https://hbr.org/2019/02/research-when-gender-diversity -makes-firms-more-productive.

Twenge, Jean M. *Generation Me: Why Today's Young Americans Are More Confident, Assertive, Entitled—and More Miserable than Ever Before.* New York: Atria, 2014.

Twenge, Jean M. *iGen: Why Today's Super-Connected Kids Are Growing Up Less Rebellious, More Tolerant, Less Happy—and Completely Unprepared for Adulthood—and What That Means for the Rest of Us.* Reprinted ed. New York: Atria Books, 2017.

Twenge, Jean M., Stacy M. Campbell, Brian J. Hoffman, and Charles E. Lance. "Generational Differences in Work Values: Leisure and Extrinsic Values Increasing, Social and Intrinsic Values Decreasing." *Journal of Management* 36, no. 5 (September 2010): 1117–42. https://journals.sagepub.com/ doi/abs/10.1177/0149206309352246.

"The Uncomfortable Racial Preferences Revealed by Online Dating." *Quartz,* November 20, 2013. https://qz.com/149342/the-uncomfortable-racial -preferences-revealed-by-online-dating/.

U.S. Bureau of Labor Statistics. *Labor Force Characteristics by Race and Ethnicity, 2017.* August 2018. https://www.bls.gov/opub/reports/race-and -ethnicity/2017/home.htm.

U.S. Census Bureau. *Highest Median Household Income on Record*. September 12, 2018. https://www.census.gov/library/stories/2018/09/highest-median -household-income-on-record.html.

U.S. Commission on Civil Rights. *Working for Inclusion: Time for Congress to Enact Federal Legislation to Address Workplace Discrimination against Lesbian, Gay, Bisexual, and Transgender Americans*. Washington, DC: November 2017. http://www.washingtonblade.com/content/files/2017/11/Report-Final.pdf.

U.S. Department of Labor: Bureau of Labor Statistics. *Women in the Labor Force: A Databook*. BLS Report, November 2017. https://www.bls.gov/ opub/reports/womens-databook/2017/home.htm.

U.S. Department of Labor: Women's Bureau. *Hispanic Women in the Labor Force*. Accessed January 8, 2019. https://www.dol.gov/wb/media/Hispanic_ Women_Infographic_Final_508.pdf.

U.S. Equal Employment Opportunity Commission. "EEOC Release Preliminary FY2018 Sexual Harassment Data." Press release, October 4, 2018. https://www.eeoc.gov/eeoc/newsroom/release/10-4-18.cfm.

U.S. Equal Employment Opportunity Commission. *2015 Job Patterns for Minorities and Women in Private Industry*. Accessed December 19, 2018. https://www.eeoc.gov/eeoc/statistics/employment/jobpat-eeo1/.

University of Notre Dame. "Women, Your Inner Circle May Be Key to Gaining Leadership Roles." *ScienceDaily*, January 22, 2019. https://www.science daily.com/releases/2019/01/190122133334.htm.

Urquhart, Evan, and Parker Marie Molloy. "Can Cis Lesbians and Trans Women Learn to Get Along?" *Slate,* February 16, 2015. https://slate.com/ human-interest/2015/02/cisgender-lesbians-and-trans-women-how-to -mend-the-rift.html.

Valen, Kelly. *The Twisted Sisterhood: Unraveling the Fallout of Aggression among Girls and Women, Pushing for a More Mindful Civility*. New York: Ballantine Books, 2010. Kindle.

van Breen, Jolien A., Russell Spears, T. Kuppens, and Soledad de Lemus. "A Multiple Identity Approach to Gender: Identification with Women, Identification with Feminists, and Their Interaction." *Frontiers in Psychology* 8:1019 (June 30, 2017).

Villalobos, Michelle. *The Stiletto in Your Back: The Good Girl's Guide to Backstabbers, Bullies, Gossips & Queen Bees at Work (the Good Girl's Guide to Getting Ahead)*. 2013. Kindle.

Vuillemot, Kelsey. "These Nine Women Lawyers Love Two Things: Dancing, and Makin' It Rain." *National Association of Women Laywers* (blog), January 29, 2016. https://www.nawl.org/p/bl/et/blogaid=405.

Wajcman, Judy. *Managing like a Man: Women and Men in Corporate Management.* Cambridge, UK: Blackwell Publishers, 1998.

Walker, Rob. "How to Approach the Generation Gap in the Workplace." *New York Times,* August 8, 2015. https://www.nytimes.com/2015/08/09/jobs/how-to-approach-the-generation-gap-in-the-workplace.html.

Walls, Jill K., Heather M. Helms, and Joseph G. Grzywacz. "Intensive Mothering Beliefs among Full-Time Employed Mothers of Infants." *Journal of Family Issues* 37, no. 2 (January 2016): 245–69. http://dx.doi.org/10.1177/0192513X13519254.

Wamsley, Laurel. "Oregon Adds a New Gender Option to Its Driver's Licenses: X." *NPR,* June 16, 2017. https://www.NPR.org/sections/thetwoway/2017/06/16/533207483/Oregon-adopt _December 18, 2018.

Warner, Judith, Nora Ellmann, and Diana Boesch. *The Women's Leadership Gap.* Center for American Progress, November 20, 2018. https://www.americanprogress.org/issues/women/reports/2018/11/20/461273/womens-leadership-gap-2/.

Weeks, Kelly Pledger. "Every Generation Wants Meaningful Work—but Thinks Other Age Groups Are in It for the Money." *Harvard Business Review,* July 31, 2017. https://hbr.org/2017/07/every-generation-wants-meaningful-work-but-thinks-other-age-groups-are-in-it-for-the-money.

Weiss, Elizabeth M., and Todd J. Maurer. "Age Discrimination in Personnel Decisions: A Reexamination." *Journal of Applied Social Psychology* 34, no. 8 (August 2004): 1551–62. https://onlinelibrary.wiley.com/doi/abs/10.1111/j.1559-1816.2004.tb02786.x.

Wensil, Brenda F, and Kathryn Heath. "4 Ways Women Can Build Relationships When They Feel Excluded at Work." *Harvard Business Review,* July 27, 2018. https://hbr.org/2018/07/4-ways-women-can-build-relationships-when-they-feel-excluded-at-work.

"What You Should Know about EEOC and the Enforcement Protections for LGBT Workers." U.S. Equal Employment Opportunity Commission, accessed January 9, 2019. https://www.eeoc.gov/eeoc/newsroom/wysk/enforcement_protections_lgbt_workers.cfm.

Wich, Scott M. "Federal Law Protects Stereotyped Transgender Employees." *Society for Human Resource Management,* December 18, 2018. https://www.shrm.org/resourcesandtools/legal-and-compliance/employment-law/pages/court-report-protection-stereotyped-transgender-employees.aspx.

Williams, Joan. "Pay Gap Deniers." *HuffPost.* August 6, 2013. https://huffingtonpost.com/joan-williams/pay-gap-deniers_b_3391524.html.

Williams, Joan C., Rachel Dempsey, and Anne-Marie Slaughter. *What Works for Women at Work: Four Patterns Working Women Need to Know.* New York: New York University Press, 2014.

Williams, Joan C., and Marina Multhaup. "How Managers Can Be Fair about Flexibility for Parents and Non-Parents Alike." *Harvard Business Review,* April 27, 2018. https://hbr.org/2018/04/how-managers-can-be-fair-about-flexibility-for -parents-and-non-parents-alike.

Williams, Joan C., Katherine W. Phillips, and Erika V. Hall. "Tools for Change: Boosting the Retention of Women in the Stem Pipeline." *Journal of Research in Gender Studies* 6, no. 1 (2016): 11–75.

"Women in the Workplace: A Research Roundup." *Harvard Business Review,* September 2013. http://hbr.org/2013/09/women-in-the-workplace-a-research -roundup.

Wong, Alia. "Harvard's Impossible Personality Test." *Atlantic,* June 19, 2018. Education. https://www.theatlantic.com/education/archive/2018/06/harvard -admissions-personality/563198/.

Wong, Kristen. "Are Women Afraid to Compete with Each Other at Work?" *Glamour,* July 5, 2018. Culture. https://www.glamour.com/story/are -women-afraid-to-compete-with-each-other-at-work.

Wrenn, Kimberly A., and Todd J. Maurer. "Beliefs about Older Workers' Learning and Development Behavior in Relation to Beliefs about Malleability of Skills, Age-Related Decline, and Control." *Journal of Applied Social Psychology* 34, no. 2 (February 2004): 223–42.

Wu, Lilian, and Wei Jing. "Real Numbers: Asian Women in STEM Careers: Invisible Minority in a Double Bind." *Issues in Science and Technology* 28, no. 1 (Fall 2011).

Yang Yang, Nitesh V. Chawla, and Brian Uzzi. "A Network's Gender Compassion and Communication Pattern Predict Women's Leadership Success." *Proceedings of the National Academy of Sciences of the United States of America* 116, no. 6 (February 2019): 2033-38.

Yoder, Janice D., and Patricia Aniakudo. "'Outsider Within' the Firehouse: Subordination and Difference in the Social Interactions of African American Women Firefighters." *Gender & Society* 11, no. 3 (June 1997): 324–41. https://journals.sagepub.com/doi/10.1177/089124397011003004.

Zemke, Ron, Claire Raines, and Bob Filipczak. *Generations at Work: Managing the Clash of Boomers, Gen Xers, and Gen Yers in the Workplace.* 2nd ed. New York: AMACOM, 2013.

Zurbrügg, Lauren, and Kathi N. Miner. "Gender, Sexual Orientation, and Workplace Incivility: Who Is Most Targeted and Who Is Most Harmed?"

Frontiers in Psychology 7 (May 2016). https://www.ncbi.nlm.nih.gov/pmc/articles/PMC4851979/pdf/fpsyg-07-00565.pdf.

Zweigenhaft, Richard L., and G. William Domhoff. *Diversity in the Power Elite: Ironies and Unfulfilled Promises.* 3rd ed. Lanham, MD: Rowman & Littlefield, 2018.

"#MentorHer: Key Findings." LeanIn, accessed February 8, 2019. https://leanin.org/sexual-harassment-backlash-survey-results#key-finding-1.

INDEX

About the Authors

ANDREA S. KRAMER

is a partner in an international law firm. Her work helping women achieve career success is nationally recognized. Andie is coauthor, with Al, of the book *Breaking Through Bias: Communication Techniques for Women to Succeed at Work.*

ALTON B. HARRIS

was a founding partner of a successful law firm. He speaks broadly about promoting diversity, inclusion, and overcoming stereotypes and biases. Al is coauthor, with Andie, of the book *Breaking Through Bias: Communication Techniques for Women to Succeed at Work.*

We'd love to hear from you!

Please visit us at AndieandAl.com and sign up
for our newsletter, send us a note,
or follow us on Twitter!

✉ Info@AndieandAl.com

🐦 @AndieandAl